Kindreds of the Earth

Kindreds of the Earth

Badaga Household Structure and Demography

•

Paul Hockings

with a Foreword by

John C. Caldwell

SAGE PUBLICATIONS
New Delhi • Thousand Oaks • London

First published in 1999 by

Sage Publications India Pvt Ltd
M–32 Market, Greater Kailash–I
New Delhi — 110 048

Sage Publications Inc.
2455 Teller Road
Thousand Oaks, California 91320

Sage Publications Ltd
6 Bonhill Street
London EC2A 4PU

Published by Tejeshwar Singh for Sage Publications India Pvt Ltd, laser typeset by the author, and printed at Chaman Enterprises, Delhi.

Library of Congress Cataloging-in-Publication Data

Hockings, Paul.
Kindreds of the earth: Badaga household structure and demography / Paul Hockings with a foreword by John C. Caldwell.
p. cm. (cloth : alk. paper; pbk. : alk. paper).
Includes bibliographical references and index.
1. Badaga (Indic people)—Kinship. 2. Badaga (Indic people)—Population. 3. Badaga (Indic people)—Social life and customs. 4. Fertility, Human—India—Nilgiri Hills. 5. Demographic anthropology—India—Nilgiri Hills. 6. Nilgiri Hills (India)—Social life and customs.
I. Title.
DS432.B25H62. 306′.089′94814—dc21 1999 98–39262

ISBN: 0-7619-9292-8 (US-HB) 81-7036-753-0 (India-HB)
0-7619-9299-5 (US-PB) 81-7036-763-8 (India-PB)

Sage Production Team: Gaurav Ghose, N.K. Negi and Santosh Rawat

CONTENTS

LIST OF TABLES

LIST OF MAPS AND FIGURES

Figures

LIST OF PLATES

(between pages 127 and 129)

1. The Ke:ti Valley viewed from near Hulla:ḍa, ca. 1949. (Photo: David G. Mandelbaum)
2. The Ke:ti Valley viewed from near Ke:ti Toreke:ri, 1963. (Photo: William A. Noble)
3. Ke:ti Toreke:ri as seen from Hulla:ḍa
4. Arched doorway inside a Ke:ti house. (Photo: W. A. Noble)
5. Hulla:ḍa village, 1963
6. Fields and eucalyptus plantations near O:rana:yi, 1963
7. Threshing grain on the yard, O:rana:yi
8. Grain and vegetables drying on the yard, Ka:ṭe:ri
9. Winnowing grain, O:rana:yi
10. K. Sithamma, mother of M.N. Thesingh
11. M.N. Thesingh with two of his daughters, 1963
12. Second and fourth generation members of Gunḍa Jogi's lineage, Hulla:ḍa, 1990 (see Figure 7.6)
13. An entrance to Ki:y Oḍeyaraṭṭi village, 1990
14. Modern and traditional houses, Ki:y Oḍeyaraṭṭi
15. Ka:ṭe:ri, the only village in the area with a dam
16. Village water source in Ka:ṭe:ri, 1963
17. Ke:ti's headman (behind fire) conducts a discussion, 1963
18. Sunday afternoon on the village green, Eḍappaḷḷi, 1994
19. *Ganga pūja,* worshipping the stream in Ke:ti, 1963
20. Woḍeya priest from Ki:y Oḍeyaraṭṭi being venerated in Ke:ti during the Hiriodea festival, 1963
21. *Linga* and *pūja* materials: a temple ornament in O:rana:yi
22. A Ha:ruva bride from Ha:la:ḍa reaches her new house, 1963
23. The bride's first task, to fetch water, in Kundesappe, 1963
24. Ha:ruva bride and Gauḍa groom garland each other
25. Wedding couple, Kundesappe. (Photo: William A. Noble)
26. Bride and groom bow down to his parents
27. A wedding feast is prepared for the village
28. Ke:ti headman (left, without hat) and council of elders, 1963
29. Badagas create a dance drama at a Coonoor hotel, to promote

Foreword

It is rare to come across a manuscript which satisfies the needs of so many of one's interests. The exception was this book. For many years I have been interested in cross-fertilization between the disciplines of demography and anthropology (see, for instance, Caldwell, Hill and Hull 1988). I have also focused much of my work on demographic transition and on social change over time. With regard to the last, my most common reaction has been how few good studies exist. Finally, Dr P. H. Reddy, Director of the Population Centre, Bangalore, Pat Caldwell and I were involved between 1979 and 1984 in a study of a series of neighbouring villages in southern Karnataka less than 150 miles from where the Badaga live and Paul Hockings worked (Caldwell *et al.* 1988). P.H. Reddy has now followed up on our earlier study 15 years after it commenced. But Paul Hockings, almost uniquely in the field of anthropological demography, is reporting a longitudinal study covering 26 years of measurement and cultural change. He brought to the work a knowledge of anthropology, demography and linguistics and focused on the transition in kinship, household structure, marriage and fertility and recorded those changes often decribed as *modernization.*

The central importance for many of us is his evidence of how fertility transmission actually gets underway. That there has been such a transition over the last 30 years is shown both by his censuses and by the age structure recorded in the latest age pyramid. In the four villages, the average age at first birth has crept up to around 21 years and that of the last birth has fallen dramatically to under 34 years. These processes have gone so far that in two of the villages, women's average reproductive span halved over the last two decades and consequently fertility has also halved. By the beginning of the 1990s the Badaga were competing with, and even surpassing, the demographic achievements in the Indian state of Kerala and India's neighbour, Sri Lanka. The birth rate was under 14, the death rate under 6, and infant mortality below 22 per 1,000. These are levels only recently passed by the industrial countries.

As in the rest of India, the main mechanism for achieving small family size was female sterilization. But Hockings went further and probed the underlying reasons for these changes. Child death rates had plummeted. The children were going to school and staying there, thereby putting great pressure on family finances. In conflict with the arguments of many theorists, the Badaga wanted their gratification now, and saw no alternative to fertility control. Daughters threatened to become even more expensive as the dowry system began to take over.

The Badaga took up potato growing and later switched to small tea plantations. They are better off than most Indians and their demographic transition is further ahead. Nevertheless, there is a reassuring similarity between Hockings' major findings and ours in Karnataka. The study is almost certainly a reliable guide to an explanation of what will eventually happen over much of the sub-continent.

John C. Caldwell
Australian National University, Canberra

Acknowledgements

A research project which has gone on for more than three decades is of necessity much more than a one-man endeavour. It began when I arrived in India as a graduate student in 1962, just two weeks before the Chinese Army (Peoples' Liberation, indeed!) also entered the country. Now that the project is drawing to a close, I can look back over a whole generation of people, some of them no longer living, who have helped me in my anthropological investigations. Perhaps a thousand Badagas have submitted to my data-gathering procedures, many of them several times over, and always with good grace.

On this page I can only name a handful of good friends and associates who helped this project to its fruition. First and foremost have been my Badaga colleagues and field assistants, K. Lakshmanan of Ke:ti, and the late M.N. Thesingh of O:rana:yi. I cannot calculate how many months of their time I have absorbed. Recently the Coonoor manager of the Family Planning Association of India, Mrs Sudha Christopher, provided me with much valuable information about their programme. In addition, a number of young Nilgiri people have helped me in the field for shorter periods in 1963 and 1990, namely S. Ananthanarayan, T. Deveraj, E. R. Francis, N. Gangadharan, Meera Gopalan, L. Kannapiran, A. Krishnan, M. Pathan, B. Ramalingam, Ahmed Sait, Premala Sukumaran, C.K. Sundaram, and Mathew Varghese. It is a pleasure also to remember here the Rev. Philip Mulley, a Badaga from Kotagiri, who not only helped me in villages on quite a few occasions but—like K. Lakshmanan too—read through the entire manuscript of this book and supplied many useful comments. Other kind readers who have gone through it include John C. Caldwell of the Australian National University, who was also gracious enough to supply the Foreword, and Jack Prost of the University of Illinois at Chicago. George Rosen, of the same university, gave me some useful advice on the economic sections.

I should also acknowledge the technical help I received from several quarters. Robert W. Gage assisted me with the complexities of statistical analysis and an early IBM 7090 computer, while I was at the Institute for Communication Research at Stanford University in 1964–1965; my father, the late Arthur Hockings, drafted Figure 1.4; while much more recently Raymond M. Brod, of the Cartography Laboratory in my own department, and William A. Noble, formerly of the Department of Geography, University of Missouri, Columbia, have been good enough to provide several other diagrams which do so much to clarify my discussion of the funeral, population growth, and the household; and Hans von Lengerke of the Volkswagenstiftung, Hannover, drew the district map (Map 1.1). To all of these friends I express my warm thanks.

Another kind of debt must be acknowledged here as well, to the American Institute of Indian Studies, which gave me the finances for fieldwork in its very first year of operation. (I was not only one of the first grantees but, to their great credit, the first non-U.S. citizen to receive an award.) I also thank the National Museum of Ethnology, at Osaka, which gave me many facilities during a Visiting Professorship in 1993 that were to make possible the final data analysis and drafting of this book. The Office of Social Science Research at the University of Illinois made several useful small grants to advance my work. Funds for reproducing the plates were provided by the Institute for the Humanities at the University of Illinois, Chicago, which has always provided me with unlimited access to computer facilities when my own department was unable to give me any.

Paul Hockings
Chicago, December 1998

Introduction

The Buddagurs, so called from their having settled on the mountains from the northward, speak the Cannady language, and are the principal inhabitants as well as cultivators of the land. The Lingbund and Thorayers likewise speak the same language and cultivate the land.

— William Keys

The Badagas

The Badagas are the largest indigenous community among over a dozen tribal groups on the Nilgiri hills in the far northwest of Tamil Nadu state, in southern India. Their name (meaning 'northerner') came after migrating here from the plains just to the north, in the decades following the end of the Vijayanagar empire in 1565.

Their villages consist of several rows of houses lying along the slope of a hill, surrounded by fields (Plate 16). A few Hindu temples or shrines are also included, and modern villages have piped water, often some shops, perhaps a school and a bus service. One other feature is a village green. Villagers rely on the rainfall of two regular monsoons. After establishing farms on the hills, the men, using fixed fields and some swidden cultivation, grew millets, barley, wheat, and many European vegetables.

Traditionally Badaga society was a chiefdom, and they still have a hereditary paramount chief, below whom are four divisional headmen. Every village also has its own headman, and several neighbouring villages together constitute a commune or circle of villages. At each of these levels councils still exist, but their authority has been greatly undermined by modern lawcourts. The headmen, who could once dictate severe punishments, today are mainly involved with petty disputes or ceremonial duties.

The community is divided into a number of phratries, large social groups made up of two or more exogamous clans, and culturally distinct from or differently ranked from each other. There are two clans each in the case of the Toreyas, Be:ḍas and Kumba:ras, three in the case of Woḍeyas, and rather more in the other cases. Some might prefer to call the phratries subcastes, for, though they have no economic specialization, they like Indian subcastes do form a social hierarchy; with the conservative Lingayat group, the Woḍeyas, somewhat isolated culturally at the top, and the commune headman's erstwhile servants, the Toreyas, at the bottom. Between these two extremes there are one phratry of vegetarians and four others of meat-eaters, including the numerically dominant Gauḍa one. The Christian Badagas, started as a small minority by the first Protestant conversion, now form a separate meat-eating phratry ranked below the Toreyas but still respected.

Most villages belong to just one particular clan, and at marriage a bride normally moves from her natal village to her husband's. Polygyny is acceptable, though rare. Divorce and remarriage are easy, and widows can remarry. Although a dowry, a financial settlement on the groom, has become required during the past two decades, it is not a traditional part of Badaga marriage arrangements. Instead a bridewealth of up to Rs 200 or so was paid by the groom's family. People prefer to marry a cross-cousin, a father's sister's daughter (FZD) or mother's brother's daughter (MBD). But other more distant relations are acceptable, if in the appropriate clan.

Except for nearly 4,000 Christians, all Badagas are Saivite Hindus. A sizeable minority are however Lingayats, a sect almost confined to Karnataka state. They take Siva as their prime deity, and worship him through a phallic emblem, the *linga.* Among the Badaga Lingayats are the Woḍeyas, a culturally distinct phratry of conservative Viraśaivas.

The Hindu Badagas, including even the Lingayat clans, worship quite a number of gods, all viewable as 'aspects' of Siva. During the year each village has several festivals, and several life-cycle rituals are practised.

Badaga farmers continued some swidden cultivation until the 1870s. By then they grew millets, barley, wheat, and European crops. They have since continued to adopt certain alien customs and techniques. Thus crops of foreign origin are grown on machine-made terraces with the help of chemical fertilizers, lorry transport, improved seed, and even crop insurance; and their small, newly developed tea plantations must maintain standards necessary for the world markets.

Such progressive attitudes mark the Badagas as unusually successful farmers, and population figures reflect this: they rose from a reported

2,207 people in 1812 to about 150,000 in 1995. By developing cash-crop cultivation they have managed to accommodate this greatly increased labour force and also improve their standard of living. There is now a sizeable middle class living in the four British-built towns on the plateau (Ootacamund, Kotagiri, Coonoor and Wellington), and the community has several thousand college graduates. For nearly a century, fathers have been willing to invest in college education for their sons; so that today Badaga doctors, lawyers, engineers, teachers and government officials are numerous, and there are also professors, agronomists, military and judicial personnel, and politicians.

The Research

The Badaga study started as a piece of exploratory research. Day after day and month after month, in 1962–63 and again in 1969–70 and 1976–77 (as well as at several other shorter periods, most recently in 1994), I went out into innumerable villages not knowing what I would record, even though I always had a general plan of procedure in mind. There was no way that I could tell where my first two censuses, in 1963 and 1972, would eventually lead; and explanatory hypotheses were only slowly formulated. (The following outline is basically a synopsis of Chapter 2.)

Beginning in 1963 I did four nine-yearly censuses of four villages, chosen to represent hierarchically differentiated strata of Badaga society. The resultant longitudinal database reflects structural changes occurring in the households, and covers virtually all persons living during the study period in these villages. This amounts to one generation of about 26 years of cultural change. For comparative purposes it also proved possible to use data on Christian Badagas in the same immediate area during the period 1860–1914.

For all the fluidity of social life, there are some areas of any culture which show much more rigid patterning than others. The language and the kinship system are two such areas: both mediate thought and action, and both are extremely regularized in any society. For the Badaga community I have already made a study of their language and its relationship with the society (Hockings 1988; Hockings and Pilot–Raichoor 1992), and have also published a theoretical study of their kinship system (Hockings 1982, revised here in Chapter 3). The present volume now completes the longitudinal study of the Badaga household which I have been working on intermittently since 1963. It also brings up to date an earlier book, *Ancient Hindu Refugees: Badaga Social History 1550–1975* (Hockings 1980a).

The household, rather than the family, was chosen as the unit of analysis throughout because it can be directly observed in the field. The Badaga household is clearly definable as in every instance it is in one village house with one front door and one hearth. Emphasis on the household in no way obscures the structure of the Badaga family, however. Indeed, that structure emerges from a comparison of the sets of data from the successive censuses of each particular household. Household types, according to these censuses, are quite varied, although the nuclear family is the numerically dominant type and the extended family the ideal.

Other demographic characteristics emerge from a comparative analysis too, and so this volume will include a discussion of nuptiality, fertility, migration patterns, morbidity and mortality. The data on morbidity and mortality are only partly my own field observations, for by good fortune it was possible to discover baptismal and burial registers dealing with the entire Christian population of the immediate study area, namely Ketti Pastorate. The entries covered every baptism and death between 1860 and 1914, and indeed went on beyond that date down to the present. These early observations record considerable detail on social status, family, whether the Christian was a Badaga, place of residence, probable cause of death, etc.; and they thus allow me to extend my own observations backwards in time for a sample of the population quite comparable to my own, but who were living there a century ago.[1]

The guiding hypotheses which this book now attempts to support can be succinctly phrased as follows:

(1) modernization for this community has entailed a move away from subsistence farming towards tea plantations, from ascribed status towards the educated professions, and from peasant self-sufficiency towards urbanizing 'middle-class' tastes, needs, attitudes and professions;
(2) Badaga modernization has occurred without significant industrialization (beyond the commercialization of agriculture);
(3) population trends have reacted to this modernization;
(4) fertility has declined significantly during one generation, a rapid growth earlier in the century having now stabilized;

(5) changing attitudes towards children's inherent worth have resulted in the fertility decline;
(6) the easy availability of education in these villages since the 19th century has underpinned modernizing tendencies.

In the latter half of the 20th century, more and more male Badagas from these villages have been able to acquire the educational qualifications and local political connections necessary to move into urban professions. This change has, however, resulted in a loss to villages of the most qualified, influential and affluent, as some have tended to move their residences to a nearby town. The high costs of educating their children, and of providing dowries for adult daughters, have however placed severe strains on these urbanizing Badagas, one prominent effect of which has been the reduction in the size of the family and a concomitant change in the value of children.

One expected conclusion was that, while the extended or joint family remains a residential ideal, it has become rather impractical for most Badagas to live in anything other than a type of nuclear family unit. Yet no such change was clearly documented over the sequence of my censuses: in a total sample of 263 households, 20 had changed from joint to nuclear during the course of my study, but 32 had changed from nuclear to joint, mainly joint-stem. The extended family has not withered away but has adapted to modern living conditions, especially to the small size of village homes. Even when a group of adult, married brothers can no longer live under the same roof, they usually live in neighbouring houses and continue to think of themselves as an extended family, as their neighbours do.

There is a big excess of young women of marriageable age, as compared with available young men: hence the willingness or perceived duty on the part of girls' fathers to pay hefty dowries to get them married off. The high monetary demands, something quite new in Badaga society, combined with this excess of marriageable young females, have led to large numbers of never-married women (plus divorcées) in their 20s and even 30s living at home with their parents. Traditionally girls were married at 13–15 years, but no more, and so this is a new departure.

Another finding of interest that is also unusual for South Asian societies is that the sex ratio has been right around 100:100 at all censuses in this community, even as far back as 1812. There are no indications of female infanticide, as has long been noted among the neighbouring

Toda tribe, nor even of neglect of infant girls.

A final noteworthy finding is that the combination of late age for marriage of women and their subsequent decision to have a tubectomy after two or three births has brought the fertility rate down to about 1.6 children per couple in some sectors of the Badaga society. This is not sufficient to reproduce the current population of those sectors. While the official family planning programme cannot claim all the credit for this result, it is the most intriguing finding of the study. It may be compared with mean *national* fertility figures released by a United Nations study in 1994, which put mean rates per woman in Rwanda (prior to the civil war) at 8.5; Saudi Arabia, 6.4; Bolivia and Mongolia, 4.6; Argentina, 2.8; U.S.A. and Sweden, 2.1; Japan, 1.6; Germany, 1.5; Hong Kong, 1.4; Italy, 1.3 (*United Nations State of the World Population Report,* 1994). It was remarkable that the younger Badaga women, even if uneducated, took an active part in controlling their fertility and health by seeking the services of scientific medical doctors and modern clinics. Men, though somewhat better educated, tended to be more conservative in this regard—even though in other matters they were well informed through the newspapers and village discussions. Modern attitudes are very much a part of women's thinking.

This book is laid out in four parts. The first (Chapters 1–3) serves to introduce the Badaga society and detail the research procedures that have been used. Since the structure of households is a central concern, Chapter 3 is devoted to the finer points of Badaga kinship reckoning. The second part of the book (Chapters 4–5) attempts to counter the somewhat *recherché* nature of my kinship analysis by demonstrating different aspects of Badaga households in operation. First I present (Chapter 4) one particular informant's life history; and this is followed (Chapter 5) by an analysis of how mortuary rites are performed. The major quantitative findings of the study make up the third part (Chapters 6–9), and form the demographic core of the book. Finally, a fourth part (Chapters 10–12) explores selected aspects of contemporary Badaga life—the economy, the mass media, schooling, migration, farming — in order to understand what the nature of their modernization has been.

NOTES

1. I am much indebted to Sara Boskovich for her computer analysis of this material, and to Kulvinder Kaur for a preliminary sorting of my census data.

PART I

THE BADAGA HOUSEHOLD IN CONTEXT

Chapter 1

THE BADAGA SOCIETY

People will not look forward to posterity who never look backward to their ancestors.
— Edmund Burke

The Origin of the Badagas

The word 'Baḍaga' has three distinct meanings. (1) It is the largest indigenous community in the Nilgiri hills of Tamil Nadu (formerly Madras state; Maps 1.1, 1.2). They number perhaps 150,000 today, but are no longer enumerated separately by the Census of India. Their name, meaning 'Northerner', was given because they migrated from the plains of Mysore District, just to the north of the Nilgiri hills, in the decades following the Muslim invasion that destroyed the great Hindu empire of Vijayanagar in 1565 A.D. (2) Badaga is also a Dravidian language spoken only by these Badagas. It is now a distinct language, but was derived from 16th century Kannada (or Canarese). Today it contains many words of English, Persian and Tamil origin, as well as many ultimately derived from Sanskrit (Hockings and Pilot–Raichoor 1992). Although the language has an extensive oral literature of plays and ballads, as well as hundreds of proverbs, prayers, omens and curses, it was never a written language (Hockings 1988, 1996). (3) Badaga is also a common term for the Gauḍas, who are by far the largest phratry in this community.

In their medieval homeland they had been settled farmers, living in villages which in a few cases are still identifiable today. Although Badaga legend does refer specifically to their 'wandering in the wilderness', even to an apocryphal pursuit by Muslim soldiers whose advance (like that of the Pharaonic forces against the Children of Israel) was cut off when the Moyar river closed in on them; yet it does not appear from these same sources that it took the Badaga settlers more than a few weeks at most to find forest clearings where they could build their huts and settle in peace. The picture of their initial two centuries on the Nilgiri̤ hills is a hazy one, for they had no chroniclers then; indeed, it is safe to assume that nearly everyone living on the Hills in those distant times, including the various local tribes, was non-literate. Occasional medieval inscriptions have been found in the foothills, carved on rocks, but these inscriptions (in the Tamil or Kannada languages) were evidently the handiwork of lowland warlords and chieftains, not of early Badagas (Zagarell 1996). The first place to be settled by Badagas was a site called A:nekaṭṭi, at the foot of the northern edge of the plateau. The grandson of their leader at that time, a man called Hućći Gauḍa, later established a settlement up above on that northern rim, which became Tu:ne:ri village, hence in later times the permanent home village of the Badagas' paramount chief. Even today this personage still exists, and his family records indicate that he is the eighteenth[1] to succeed to that position, popularly called 'Tu:ne:ri headman' or, more formally, 'four-mountains headman' (*na:ku beṭṭa gauḍa*).

One might ask how it is possible to know anything about the history of a people who were all non-literate until the mid-19th century, and who thus lack written documents from early times? Fortunately, much of their legends are a fairly believable (or at least not supernatural) kind of oral history. Beyond this, it is possible to argue from internal cultural evidence about, for example, the date of their arrival on the plateau. Since the birth of the latest incumbent of the paramount chieftaincy occurred in the mid-20th century, and since the average generation among Badagas today spans 26 years, we have a tool for calculating the date of Tu:ne:ri's founding. However, it should be assumed that prior to this century, when schooling did not delay the age at marriage and first pregnancy, people started reproducing at a younger age, but also died younger, and so we may reasonably guess at a generation prior to 1900 as having spanned only 20 years. This assumption does allow us to count back from the birth of the present headman to conclude that the very first Tu:ne:ri headman was born about the year 1600 A.D. He was said to be the grandson of one man who fled with his family from the Muslims invading Mysore district, and this fact accords very closely with my presumption that it was the break-up of the Vijayanagar empire (covering roughly the modern Karnataka state), which followed the historic battle of Talikota in 1565, that prompted a flight into the visible nearby hills by some of the rural Hindu peasantry living southeast of Mysore city. It would have been altogether appropriate for them to rec-

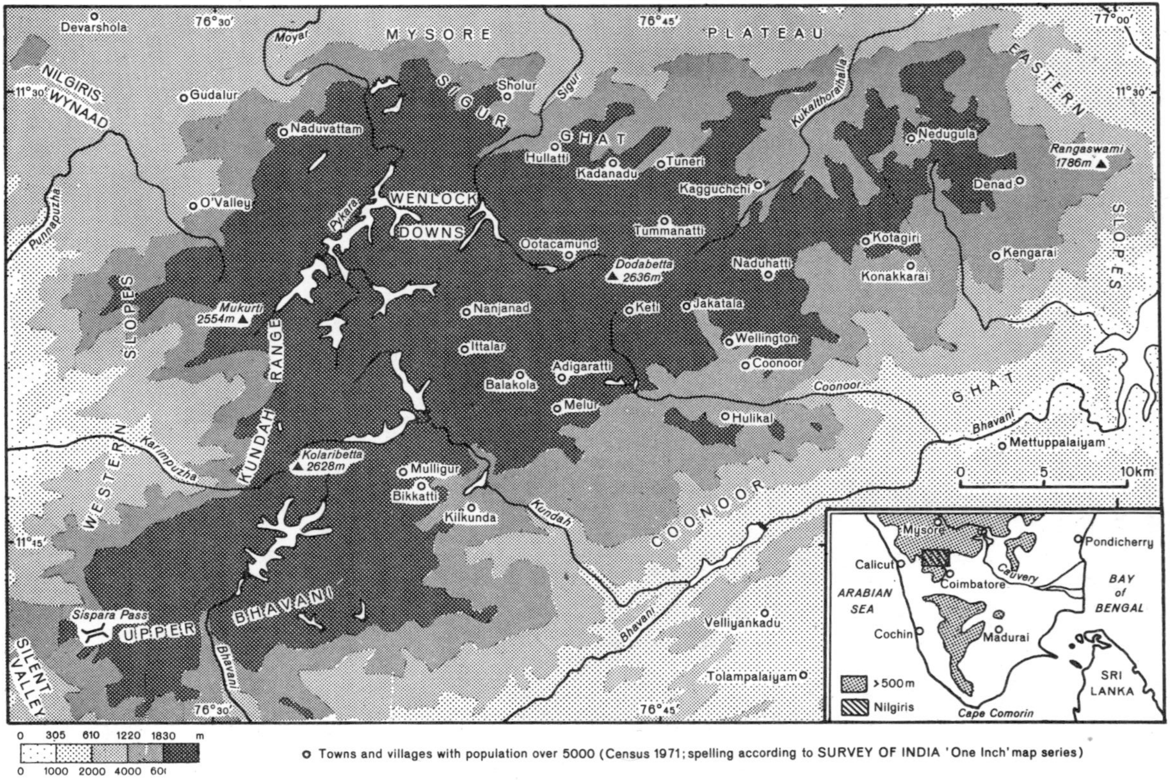

Map 1.1. THE NILGIRI MASSIF

cognize as their leader a male elder, and once they had settled at Tu:n-e:ri it would also be natural to their way of thinking for the eldest son to succeed his father to the office. This was, after all, the most normal way in which offices had been acquired throughout medieval India, and is still common.

Having a headman and a spokesman was essential for the newcomers. They carried a remembered peasant culture in their heads, but now needed to negotiate a *modus vivendi* with the surrounding tribes, specifically the Todas, Kotas, and Kuṟumbas. Although questionable as history, a Kota legend records this:

> ...in the night, at midnight, secretly...they came and arrived at our...district. Having held a big meeting, (the Badagas) begged and asked, saying: Because of the trouble that the Mohammedan made for us... we have come, making ourselves to escape. This country is yours.... We are helpless. You must help us. (The Kotas) decided, saying to all the Badagas who had come to the Todas, the Kotas, the Kurumbas, these three people: If you are to go on making cultivation on the land of our ... district and eating and prospering, to us Kotas you must give a tax of grain (said to be one quarter of the yield). To the Todas you must give a winnowing basket (of grain to each house). To the Kurumbas you must give the village tax (four annas and a meal paid by each house) .... They made a decision, saying: The Kotas must give to the Badagas iron things and wooden things and must make help to them. The Todas must give them winnowing baskets and cane and churning sticks, all these. The Kurumbas must keep watch so that no one at all must come making the Badagas fear. Eating food in the houses of the Badagas, they must keep watch .... (Emeneau 1944–46, IV: 257)

In this short extract from the translation of a much longer tale recorded in the 1930s, one also finds the charter for the peaceful inter-tribal relations that have been extensively discussed in previous ethnographic accounts of the area (e.g., Hockings 1980a: 99–133). The subsequent social history of the Badagas after crossing the Moyar river meshes more closely with a new African model of a permanent 'inter-frontier' which existed in zones of weak political control between established polities (Kopytoff 1987: 3–84). This was the sort of 'no man's land' in which the early Badagas found themselves eking out a living on the Nilgiri hills—albeit surrounded by the other tribes, for they were now to become a tribe among tribes, as they slowly lost their former Mysore caste identity (mainly Okkaliga). They represent perhaps the only well-documented case in Southern Asia of a former caste group adopting a tribal social model for emulation, since usually cultural change has been in an opposite direction: tribes there emulate and sometimes enter caste society. (In modern times, however, the Government of India has not designated the Badagas a Scheduled Tribe.)

It would seem that from the very outset these newcomers distributed themselves through the Nilgiri hills as a result of marrying outside the settlement (i.e., village exogamy). In modern times this principle is regularly expressed as hamlet exogamy, but at the outset there were probably no real Badaga hamlets, only individual houses. Typically a man and his family, perhaps with his brothers' families alongside, settled in their chosen forest clearing during the 16th–18th centuries. Incest prohibitions brought with them from times already long past meant that this small residential unit was always an exogamous unit too. As their population expanded into a regular hamlet, they grew in numbers and social organization from one extended family to one lineage, which later split into several minor lineages. Yet all knew that, if they were not themselves wives who had come from elsewhere at the time of their marriage, they were descended from the founding male of that place. When young people wanted spouses, they had to look for them in other Badaga hamlets. Elopement or marriage by capture were sometimes resorted to. Yet always certain rules applied, for those other affinal hamlets could not be descended from the founder of one's own hamlet (i.e., belong to the same clan), and they certainly could not be hamlets of the neighbouring Kota, Toda, Kuṟumba or Irula tribes either. These patterns of lineage, clan and settlement exogamy still operate among the 150,000 Badagas of today, but they were already being formulated four centuries ago when there were only a few hundred Badagas on the hills altogether (Finicio 1603).

The isolated style of life followed by early Badagas was related to their method of survival. In medieval Mysore their ancestors had lived in ancient villages that were within walking distance of Mysore city and the nearby pilgrimage centre at Nanjangud. Settled agriculture on permanent fields was usual there. On the Nilgiri hills, in contrast, Badagas had no fields available until they had cleared them; and indeed cultivation in small swiddens, following a process of slash-and-burn, was one common form of agriculture on the Nilgiris (as elsewhere in the hilly parts of India) until the mid-19th century. A swidden is a patch of ground cleared of its forest cover for cultivation over the next few years: such a practice is called shifting or slash-and-burn agriculture (or in northeast India, *jhuming*). Not only the Badagas but the neighbouring Kotas too practised such cultivation; indeed, we may presume that much of the highland culture of the Badagas was less an adaptation of lowland traditions they had brought with them than a borrowing of useful features from the material cultures of the Kotas and Todas who had long been there. One old tale makes this point quite explicitly: the earliest refugees were fearful that their daughters would be taken away by Muslim pursuers, usually identified as soldiers. So, to make the girls look unattractive to urbane Muslims, the refugees adopted the ruse, once on the hills, of tattooing the brows and arms of their girls with patterns that would make them resemble the tribal Kota or Toda women. Young girls were still being tattooed in the traditional way as late as the mid-20th century, using a barberry thorn and a solution of soot (Hockings 1980b: 98–99).

Subsistence

As a community of refugees, the early Badagas thus had to cut their farmsteads out of the forests on the Nilgiri plateau, and continued with such activity there until the 1870s. In general, they nowadays use fields around each village (Figures 7.3 and 7.4), practise mixed farming of millets, barley, wheat and a variety of European vegetables, two of which—the potato and the cabbage—have recently assumed major commercial importance. Badaga farmers have virtually no irrigation, but rely instead on the rainfall of two regular monsoon seasons. During this century the farmers have gradually shifted from subsistence cultivation of traditional grains to cash-crop farming of potatoes and cabbages, even with irrigation in some places. After several seasons of disease, the potato fields were sometimes replaced in the 1970s by numerous small plantations of tea (which was first introduced here by a British settler in 1835, and had come from China).

Badagas also have herds of buffalo and cows for dairy purposes, but never kept for meat even though most of the people are not vegetarians (Plate 7). Over the past century there has been an evident decline in the importance of animal husbandry, consequent on the conversion of much former grazing to farming and plantation uses. This slow change has affected the appearance of the countryside. Poultry are still sometimes kept, and ponies occasionally, but not sheep, goats, donkeys or elephants.

This community is well known in anthropological literature for its complex symbiosis with the Toda, Kota, and Kuṟumba tribes of the Nilgiris. It is also true that some Badaga villages maintain exchange relations with the Irulas, Uralis, Paniyas and Cheṭṭis of the surrounding slopes (Hockings 1980a: 99–133). The closest ties are with the seven nearby villages of the Kotas. Until about 1930 every Badaga family had a Kota associate who provided a band of musicians whenever there was a wedding or funeral in that family, and who regularly furnished the Badagas with pottery, carpentry, thatching, and most leather and metal items. In return for being jack-of-all-trades to the Badagas (who had no specialized craftsmen in their own community), the Kotas were provided with cloth and a portion of the annual harvest by their Badaga associates.

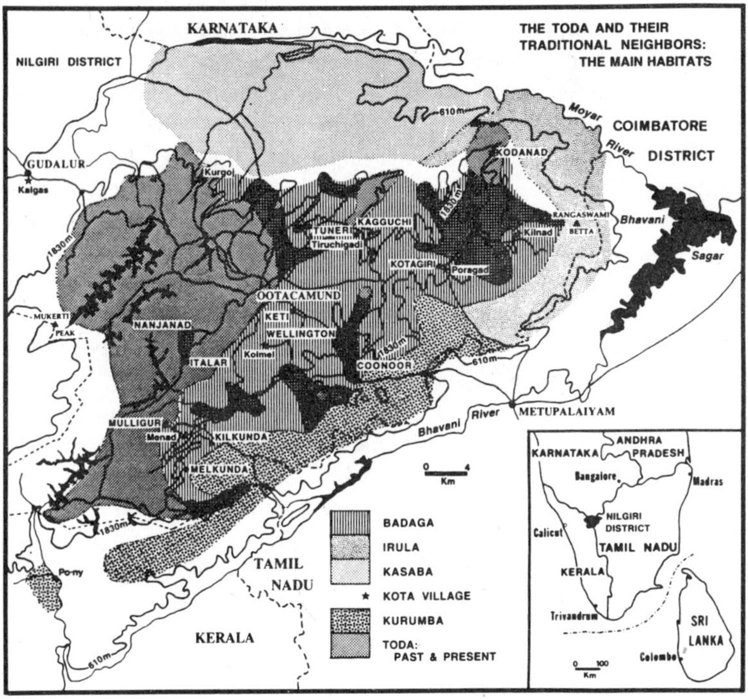

Map 1.2. DISTRIBUTION OF THE NILGIRI TRIBES

The Todas, a vegetarian people numbering barely a few hundred, were the one group in the hills whom the Badagas were willing to accept as near-equals. The two communities used to exchange buffaloes and attend each others' ceremonies. A few Todas still supply their associates with baskets and other jungle-grown produce, as well as clarified butter (*ghee*). In return the Badagas give a portion of their harvest. Since 1930 the relationship has become attenuated, as with the Kotas, largely because the Badaga population has increased out of all proportion to that of the Todas and Kotas—but also because it is distinctly more modernized than theirs, and prefers market to barter relationships.

The Kuṟumbas are a cluster of seven tribes of jungle gatherers, gardeners and sorcerers on the Nilgiri slopes. Each Badaga commune (or village cluster) used to have a 'watchman', a Kuṟumba employed to protect those particular Badagas from the sorcery of other Kuṟumbas. He also took part in some Badaga ceremonies as an assistant priest, and supplied his Badaga friends with baskets, nets, honey and other jungle products. The Badaga headman would levy for him a fixed quantity of grain from each household in the commune.

There are other tribes of slighter importance to the Badaga economy. Irulas and Uralis were thought to be sorcerers like the Kuṟumbas, if less effective ones, and were treated similarly. Some Cheṭṭis from the Plains were itinerant traders who sold knick-knacks on a fixed circuit of Badaga villages once a month. They also had minor ceremonial connections with the Badagas. Paniyas were agricultural serfs on the land of certain Badagas and Cheṭṭis who inhabit the Wainad plateau directly west of the Nilgiri plateau proper.

The settlements, usually holding no more than several hundred people, consist of parallel rows of stone or brick houses with tiled rooves (Plates 1, 2, 3 and 5). They generally lie along the slope of a hill on its leeward side, for protection from the westerly monsoon. Each row of houses is fronted by a set of level rectangular work spaces that together look rather like a street, but are not (Plate 8). The fields spread out all around. Up to a half-dozen temples and shrines for different Hindu gods are to be found in each village. The 19th century descriptions of villages, as well as the large-scale land tenure maps of that time, regularly show one or two large, round, stone or fenced cattle kraals (*to:*) on the outskirts of most villages. By early in the present century most of these had disappeared, to be replaced by cattlesheds (Figure 7.4). Modern villages have piped water to communal taps (Plates 16 and

23), but not long ago the water supply was a nearby stream or at best an open channel running into the village from a stream. One other universal feature is a village green, important as a council place, playground, dancing ground, funeral place, and general grazing area for the calves.

The commonest form of Badaga house consists of two oblong rooms joined in the middle by an arched open doorway. The outer room has the main entranceway at one end, with a heavy door, while at the other a small bathing area (*himbara*) is normal. This outer room (*ida mane*) has a wide plank shelf along one side, used for seating in daytime and sleeping at night. The inner room (*o:ga mane*) contains, at the back, a bed or sleeping platform, and towards the front a hearth for cooking as well as a storage area (*ha:go:ṭu*) for milk. A broad veranda (*ere, ba:gilu*) on either side of the entranceway may be used for storage, or keeping a calf, but a part is usually converted into another bedroom or closed storeroom. While only the very modern houses may have a second storey (Plate 14), most traditional houses had a loft (*aṭḷu*) for storage purposes. Now some of these are being converted into television rooms. Several typical houses are illustrated in Figures 1.1, 1.2 and 1.3.

Political Organization

Characteristic of any 'inter-frontier' like the Nilgiri plateau is that it has historically been something of a power vacuum. This was certainly the case for the earliest Badagas: they had walked out of the realm of Mysore but were not entering any other realm. It was only around 1820 that British people began settling in small numbers on these hills from Coimbatore and Madras, developing the first towns, roads and markets; and the Badaga lands were thereafter effectively brought under the administrative hand of the Madras Presidency, a huge territory covering much of southern and eastern India that was governed at the time by the East India Company. Before that date the early Badagas had themselves been slowly filling this political vacuum on the Nilgiris, for each hamlet founder not only became the head of a micro-economic system, but with the passage of the years he would become a respected elder with a political influence that could easily reach well beyond the confines of his relatives' customary swiddens.

Traditionally therefore Badagas lived in what anthropologists call a chiefdom, for they were under a paramount chief. The filling of the

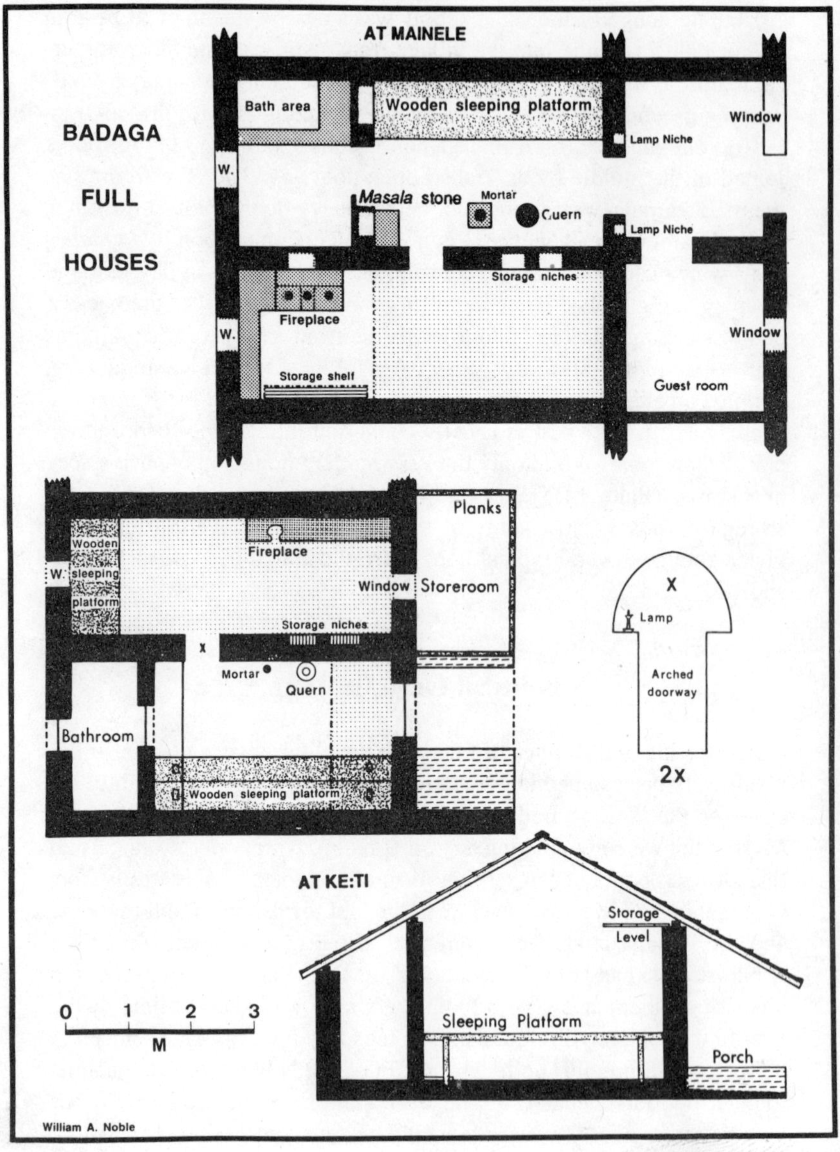

Figure 1.1. BADAGA FULL HOUSES, AT MAINELE AND KE:TI

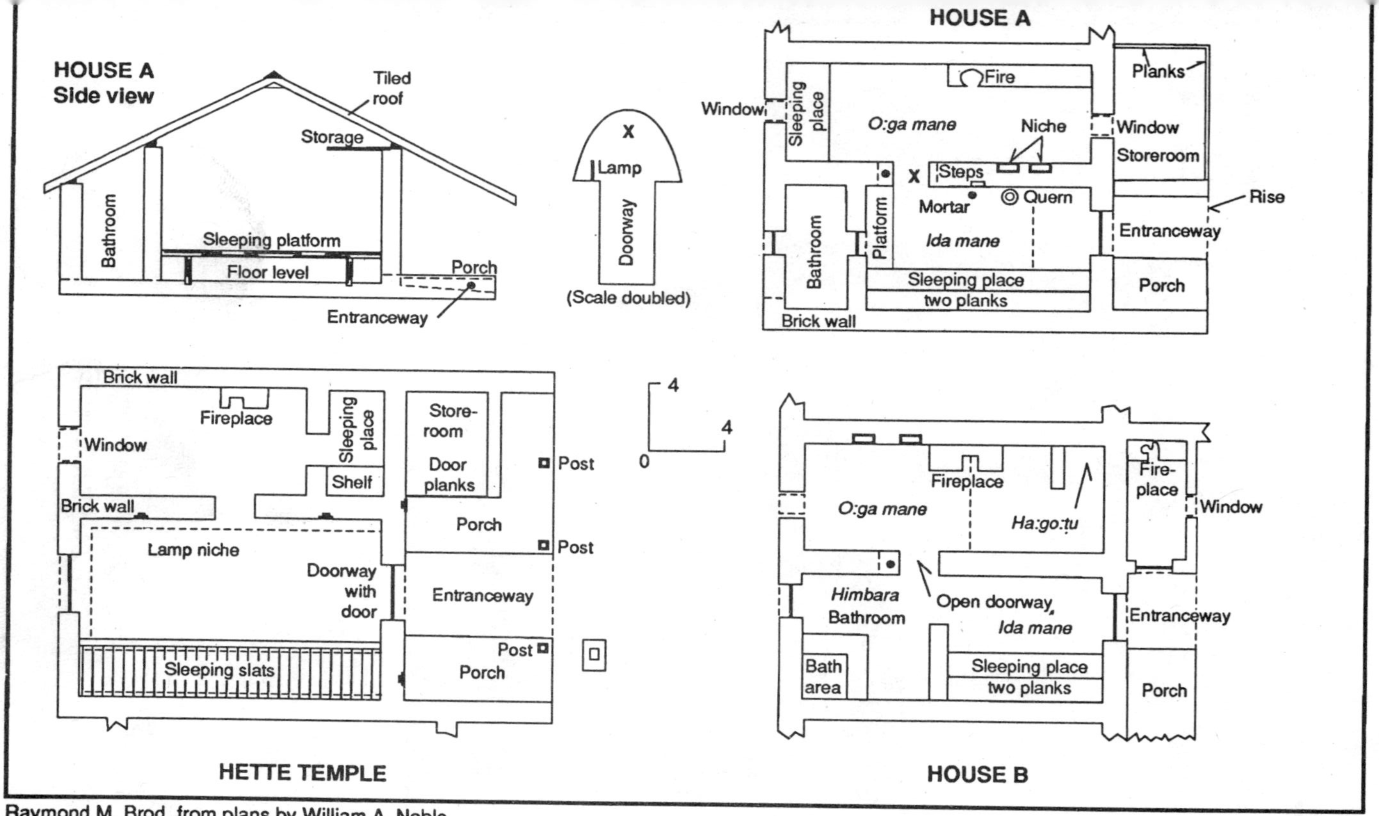

Raymond M. Brod, from plans by William A. Noble

Figure 1.2. BADAGA FULL HOUSES AND A TEMPLE, AT KE:TI

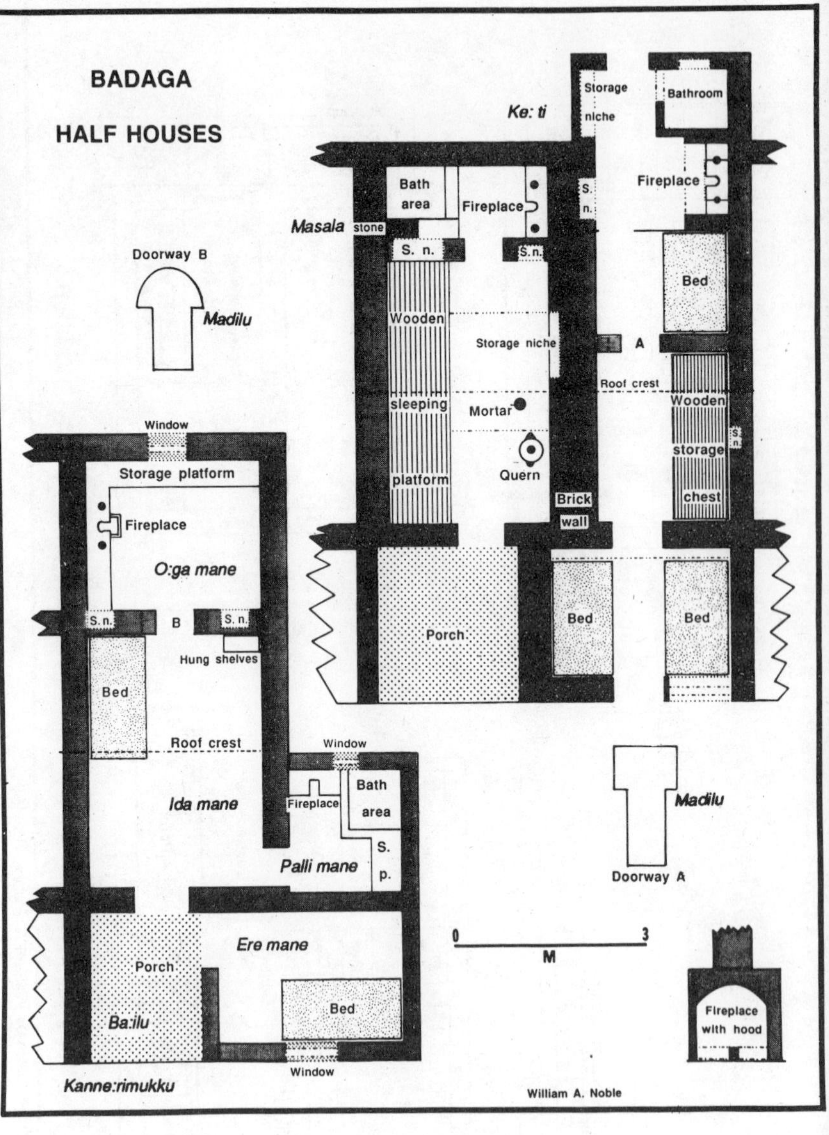

Figure 1.3. BADAGA HALF HOUSES, AT KA:NE:RIMUKKU AND KE:TI

power vacuum just referred to had its small beginning when the first settler, Huććí Gauḍa, founded the first settlement at Tu:ne:ri (Map 1.1), and thus became the ancestor of that village's 18 successive headmen who were also the paramount chiefs for the entire community and even for the Kotas, as well as a court of last resort for the Todas. Initially such hamlet headmen only controlled the loyalty and labour of the younger men and women in their family; but, with the growth of their status and that of their entire family and lineage, they came to control the patterns of marriage and even the fates of wrongdoers on a much wider scale, through their headship of a judicial council. Each hamlet had a headman and a council of elders (Plate 28), and these headmen, like others in neighbouring hamlets, also constituted a higher-level council at what can be called the commune level. A commune was and is a cluster of neighbouring hamlets (any number from 1 to 41) that recognize the headman of one as head also of the entire commune. The Nilgiri hills were further divided into four segments—Todana:ḍu, Me:kuna:ḍu, Poranga:ḍu and Kunde—with recognized boundaries radiating out from the central peak of Doddabetta (2637 metres; Map 1.1). Each of these segments contained a dozen or so communes, and had a divisional council made up of the headmen of these communes, under a divisional headman. In turn, at the highest level, there was an all-Nilgiri council ('four-mountains council') made up of all the headmen of all levels, and of course under the supervision of the Tu:ne:ri headman who, as we have already seen, was also paramount chief. The Badaga council system still has some influence, although its judicial authority has been greatly undermined by modern lawcourts and the Indian legal system. Each headman still has his council; but the paramount chief's council is rarely called together nowadays.

The traditional legal procedure required that a dispute or crime be considered first by a hamlet council—the headman's judgement being final—but that an unacceptable decision could be appealed up the hierarchy of councils. Major land disputes and cases of murder would formerly have been brought to the paramount chief after consideration by councils at lower levels. In early times the headmen could dictate severe punishments, including ostracism and hanging. Today the headmen are mainly involved in small disputes and in ceremonial duties.

Social Organization

The community is divided into a number of phratries, a standard term in anthropology for a social unit made up of a cluster of clans.[2] I feel it would not be preferable to call these units subcastes, since not all are endogamous and they have no forms of occupational specialization. They are, however, like subcastes in forming a hierarchy, with the conservative Lingayat group, the Woḍeyas, at the top and the commune's official servants, the Toreyas, at the bottom. Between these two extremes there are one phratry of vegetarians and three others of meat-eaters, all of them Saivite Hindus. The Christian Badagas, a group started by the first Protestant conversion in 1858, now constitute a separate meat-eating phratry ranked below the Toreyas but still respected for their progressive habits. Each phratry is made up of several exogamous clans — two each in the case of the Toreya, Be:ḍa and Kumba:ra phratries, three in the case of Woḍeyas, and rather more in other cases (Figure 1.4).

A successful family head, even a hamlet head, was effective only if he were fertile. The more sons a man had, the more daughters-in-law he would acquire; and, since both sexes worked on the land according to a set division of labour, the more agricultural productivity would result. But nature being what it is, it was inevitable that the more sons a man sired, the more daughters he was likely to have as well. By the time these girls had attained puberty they would have to be married off to other hamlets and their labour would thenceforth be lost to their father. Nonetheless his daughters were useful to him in the frontier setting, for he could use the very fact of offering their hands in marriage, as well as the resultant kin ties, as a basis for extending his own influence. At the same time this affinal net could become a safety net when a man fell on hard times, for his in-laws might be relied upon to lend him grain or money when really necessary. The strength of affinal ties among the Badagas has always been expressed in the marital preference for a spouse who is a cross-cousin: a youth should marry his father's sister's daughter (FZD) or else his mother's brother's daughter (MBD). At the same time his sister might well find a spouse who was her mother's brother's son (MBS) or father's sister's son (FZS), and perhaps the brother of her own brother's wife. This latter situation is called brother–sister exchange, a very durable relationship. Repeated marriage arrangements between two families linked in this way lead to strong ongoing ties between affines living in separate hamlets, usually some

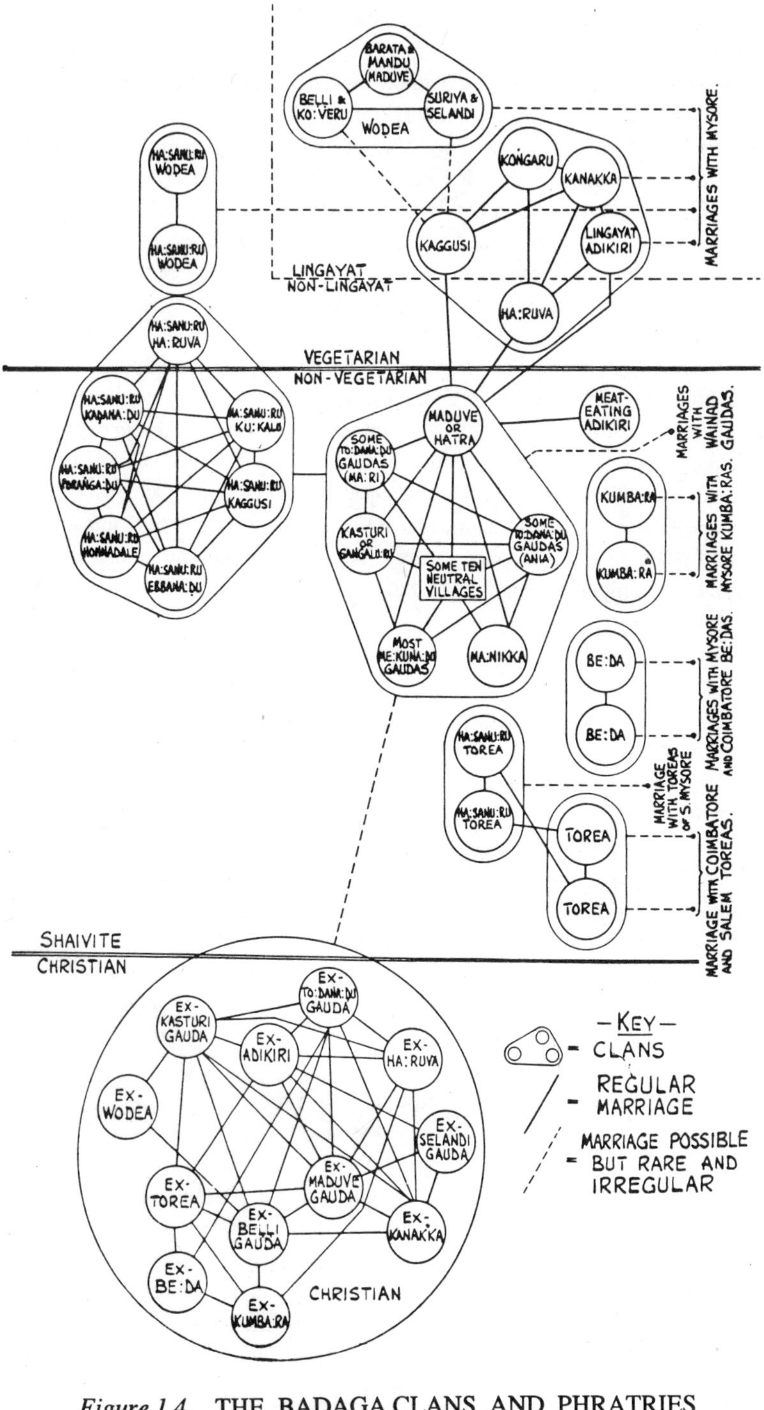

Figure 1.4. THE BADAGA CLANS AND PHRATRIES

miles apart. Married women at their confinements, especially the first one, regularly return to their natal home for the birth, perhaps staying on there for as long as 3–5 months, and thereby re-emphasizing the social bonds between the two villages. Clearly the head of a family is not only the manager of a production system but of reproductive possibilities too, since nearly all marriages are arranged by the parents.

Success or failure rested in the hands of such a manager. As has also been observed for frontier societies in Africa,

> ... the direct expression of and means to wealth is the control of persons, their reproduction, and labor .... [P]roduction is geared toward the maintenance of current social relationships, that is, toward strengthening and supporting the family in its existing social matrix .... [Hence] the importance of being first as a salient cultural feature .... Through their relation to founder ancestors, those lineages that are first in an area have a strong claim to political importance and resource control. Those that are latecomers often have more limited power and rights. (Nyerges 1993: 863)

In short, there are ecological and political dimensions to establishing one's family in a new place.

Every Badaga village belongs to one particular clan or another, and hence is exogamous. In exceptional cases (and there are many) a predominantly Gauḍa village contains a few Ha:ruva, Kaṇakka, Adikari or Toreya families too. As a general rule, at marriage a bride has to leave her natal village and move to her husband's. Beyond this the Badagas have what are, for Hindus, some unusual social regulations. Most remarkable perhaps is that hypogamy (women marrying downwards) is as acceptable as hypergamy (women marrying upwards): in other words, marriages may occur between couples coming from certain clans of differential status, yet in these cases it does not matter whether the groom is from the higher or the lower clan. Economic considerations are likely to be of more importance here.

Although a dowry has become a requirement during the past few years, it is not a traditional part of the Badaga marriage arrangements. Instead a bridewealth of up to 200 rupees was, and still is, paid by the groom's family to the bride's. This sum does not purchase the girl but is payment for the ornaments she will bring with her to the wedding, and hence has increased over the years with the price of gold.

The favoured marriage partner is a cross-cousin, preferably FZD or else MBD. But other more distant relations are acceptable, provided that they belong to an appropriate clan. Generation level is recognized as a distinguishing feature of men alone, and women may actually change their generation levels as they perhaps marry successive husbands belonging to different generations. Though I never identified such a case, it is said to be theoretically possible for a man to be married to a woman and her daughter and granddaughter simultaneously, provided he has not thereby married his own offspring. All three wives would thus attain the generation level of their co-husband. Gerontogamy—old men taking young wives—was traditionally not at all uncommon (Metz 1864: 61). Polygyny is acceptable, though not nearly as common as monogamy, as we shall see. In one extreme case a man had five wives at once; I recorded cases of men with three wives in the sample villages. Divorce and remarriage are easy for men, even for women, and are acceptable practices. Furthermore, widows can remarry without adverse comment in this society.

Figure 1.5 offers a simple schematic representation of major social divisions in Badaga life which have been outlined in this chapter.

Religion

Except for several thousand Christians (some 3,000 Protestants and 700 Roman Catholics), all Badagas are Hindus of the Saivite persuasion: they honour numerous gods, but see Siva as the pre-eminent one, and most other gods as aspects of Siva. Brahma is mentioned in an important funeral prayer, but otherwise neither Brahma nor Vishnu is acknowledged in worship. A sizeable minority however are of the Lingayat sect, which today is almost confined to Karnataka state (formerly Mysore). This was a sect founded in the 12th century which took Siva as the only deity for them, and which still worships him through a phallic emblem, the *linga* (Plate 21). Among Badagas the sect is represented in the entire membership of several clans, namely Adikari, Kaṇakka, Kaggusi, Kongaru, and three more which make up the Woḍeya phratry.

The Hindu Badagas, including these Lingayat clans, worship quite a number of gods, all of which are sometimes explained as 'aspects' of Siva, or members of his family. These include Mahalinga and Ma:riamma (the smallpox goddess), together with many lesser deities hardly known outside the Nilgiri communities, among them the ancestral Hiriodea and his consort Hette.

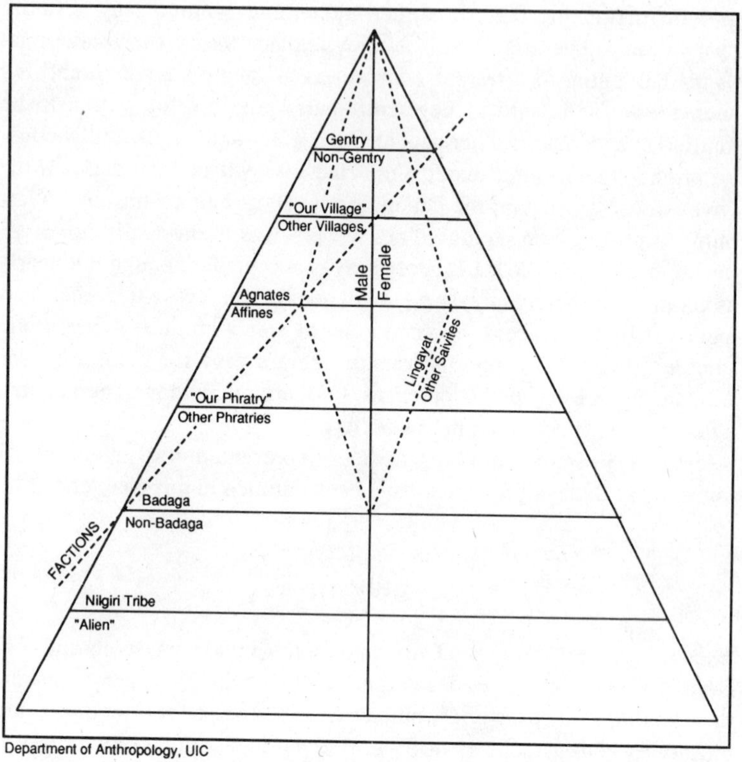

Figure 1.5. SCHEMATIC REPRESENTATION OF MAJOR BADAGA SOCIAL DIVISIONS

Each village celebrates about a dozen festivals during the year. The most important are the Great Festival (*doḍḍa habba*) which begins the agricultural year in February or March, and the God Festival (*devva habba*) which celebrates the harvest in July or August. For non-Lingayat villages, the Hette festival venerates a communal ancestress. Ma:ri Habba is intended to keep smallpox away for the year, and is celebrated in a few villages (such as Hulla:ḍa) by a dramatic fire-walking ceremony in which devotees walk unscathed across glowing charcoal with no protection for their feet.

The complex of deities which Badagas worship is fairly typical of the polytheism to be found in most Hindu communities throughout India, Sri Lanka and Nepal (Elmore 1915). One deity—in the Badaga theology, Siva—is pre-eminent, and is not only worshipped by all Badagas (except for those few who are Christian), but is worshipped in a number of 'forms' or aspects; in other words, is recognized under different names. Some of these aspects of the god are considered to be his family members: of these, his wife Parvati is the most widely worshipped one. The kinship principle is the most usual way of organizing and relating Hindu deities. But the Badaga complex includes other sorts of deity that do not fit into this universal pattern. Hence the occurrence of numerous purely local deities, including what might loosely be called nature spirits, demons, and ancestral spirits. One early missionary observer who knew the villages intimately (Metz 1864: 61) claimed that there were 'no less than 338 idols on the Hills', which may not have been much of an exaggeration. He was of course mainly counting such localized entities, and their stone images, many of which were only worshipped at one place, if indeed they had a cult site at all.

Badagas are commonly aware that a deity known by a special name at a particular place may well be a variant of the supreme god Siva. Thus a god with the extraordinary name of Kakkayya (literally 'vomit Lord'), who is worshipped at three places, is actually an aspect of Siva, who according to some legends swallowed poison which he later threw up. But with other deities there may be nothing more than a vague assertion to link a particular god or goddess somehow with the family of Siva. This is a likely scenario in the case of minor figures that are the ancestral spirits of particular clans. Anganadesvara (the *-esvara* is a name of Siva) is a god worshipped by one Woḍeya clan and some Adikaris. Angamasti is a goddess worshipped only by certain Woḍeyas. Some gods have a particular and fairly restricted function to perform in the scheme of things. Thus Maleya Madappa (or Halevi:raso:mi) is a minor deity who protects cattle. Mallesvara is an aspect of Siva to whom Badagas pray that their cattle will be protected from disease; every cattle-shed is a shrine to this deity. And Mallima is another aspect of Siva who protects people from attack by wild elephants.

Some of the deities are essentially nature spirits. Of these Gangi (or I:rama:sti), the water goddess, is of crucial importance in an agricultural society; she is also equated with Siva's consort, Parvati. Some nature spirits are now scarcely remembered unless a reference to them is preserved in some placename or prayer. There is, for example, a hill called Ammadiṭṭu Beṭṭu ('goddess-boundary mountain'), which certainly contains such a reference, but we know nothing further of that particular goddess today. Another similarly named hill, Ammanmuḍi Beṭṭa ('headland-of-the-goddess mountain') has an ancient shrine on its summit devoted to a lineage ancestress. Evidently the worship of mountain peaks was in general an ancient form of worship in this part of south India. Even today the foraging tribe of Hill Pandarams, living some 175 miles SSE of the Badagas, worship mountain peaks as deities—but without any shrines or iconography (Morris 1992: 100). The Todas too recognize certain sacred peaks; and there is plenty of archaeological evidence in the Nilgiris showing that before the Badagas had come there the hilltops were the favoured sites for the burial of prominent tribal people (Noble 1976).

If nature spirits embody the powers of the land, there are also 'demons' who may have to be propitiated at specific places simply because of the dangers they are thought to pose. A good example is the shrine of a deity called Muniyappa ('teacher, father, Lord') next to the Ketti railway station, which adjoins our sample village of Hulla:ḍa. Although it is a fairly substantial building today, when I first saw it in 1963 the shrine was merely a few rough stones set against a rock face. An annual offering of liquor and chicken flesh is made to Muniyappa to avert his anger and malice. This worship must date back, in his particular case, only to the beginning of the century, when the first steaming carriages chugged their way up the newly laid track, their noise, steam clouds, size, novelty and power posing a seeming threat to all the thousands of villagers who had to cross the railway at this very point in order to walk up to the main road. Badagas were in such awe of these early self-propelled trains that they used to pay off their debts and settle all their worldly affairs before risking a journey down to the plains below on this Swiss rack-and-pinion system. Needless to say, they soon became as familiar with the twice daily trains as all other railway passengers; and yet the cult of Muniyappa has remained at this crossing-point and his shrine has recently been growing in impressiveness, thanks to some non-Badaga neighbours who patronize it.

Another kind of entity that has the status of a minor deity, but is of human origin, is the ancestor or ancestress who is venerated. Among the Badagas, by far the best known of these spirits is Hette, and a close examination of the legends about her shows how she is an instructive role model for Badagas, virtually the personification of Badaga ethnicity (Hockings 1989a: 223–28).

As in all societies, certain transitions in life are marked by ceremonies. For Badagas these events are the naming, the first tonsure or head-shaving, the first milking of a cow (for boys only, and now rarely done), onset of menstruation, the wedding and the funeral. On rare occasions too each Badaga commune used to hold a huge memorial ceremony (*manevale*) in honour of a whole generation of the dead, once the last member of that generation had passed away. This was last performed in 1936, however, and has since been viewed as too costly to repeat.

In a peasant society work is organized by two principles: the technical procedures are organized according to a certain division of labour, primarily by sex; but there is also a mystical organization of production that is handled by priests and their accessories, which rationalizes the division of labour and links it conceptually to an ancient tradition. The Badaga people, like peasants everywhere, do not think of the fruits of their labour as dependent entirely on themselves, on their knowledge and skills. Nor is the outcome of an agricultural season wholly attributable to what the Westerner might label chance, fate or luck, nor even good management. There are deities who symbolically can work on behalf of the farmer, but this is a reciprocal relationship: the farming community must also work for the deity, by feeding and honouring him or her.

Values and Modernization

The analysis of the various myths surrounding the ancestral figure of Hette shows that they are something more than a handful of brief just-so stories. Badaga myth is a metalanguage which permits talking about some very basic facts of life: what it means to be a Badaga, to be distinct from other communities, and how this way of life can be maintained. Ritual is similarly concerned with the lives of real people, and not merely with the presumed requirements of the gods. It too can be subjected to structural analysis.

Very few of the 'classic' ethnographies written in the first half of the 20th century have anything to say about ethics as such, and one will certainly search in vain for that word in their otherwise thorough indexes. It is not that non-literate peoples are or were lacking in ethical principles, but rather that Western anthropologists had no agreed-upon tools for revealing what those principles were, or were perhaps not sufficiently fluent in the language of their subjects to grasp the ethical subtleties of their thinking, comment and behaviour. Nonetheless, there are some good approaches to the question that have the advantage of not relying too heavily on the value judgements of anthropologists themselves.

A value is a selective orientation towards experience, some ideal which prompts the actor to behave in one socially acceptable way rather than another functionally possible way. But such a guide to conduct has to be embodied somehow, if people are to learn and to remember each value of their culture. Embodied values are, perhaps surprisingly, readily apparent though often overlooked by scholars in any traditional culture, such as the Badaga one; for they are spelled out in proverbs, prayers, omens, blessings, curses, and various longer forms of oral literature such as poems, songs, dramas and folktales.

This is not the place to offer even a slight sampling of all the different kinds of oral literature produced by the Badagas: much has already been published elsewhere (Hockings 1988: 14–17, 39–46, etc.; Hockings 1997: 293–315). We may however note that the ethical values of these people can be discriminated into several hundred categories. Some of the categories are very broad, in that they differentiate right from wrong, good from bad. But most of the categories are quite narrow and specific, dealing with potential rules for such matters as using the hearth, choice of a bride, how to plough, and indeed hundreds of other points of day-to-day guidance that any Badaga might find useful from time to time.

As a Badaga child grows up he (or she) begins to appreciate that there are two sorts of cultural given that preceded and surround him, seemingly omnipresent and unavoidable facts of life. One is a set of historical traditions about the community, traditions which are largely of a religious and legendary nature. A second set of cultural givens forms the social network into which a child is born. He can in no sense choose parents and grandparents, nor the village which is home, the lineage, clan or phratry to which he belongs. Membership in such groups is immutable for boys; it is ascribed membership, the sociologists would say. For girls the situation is rather more fluid, since while they start off in the same family, lineage, village, clan and phratry as their brothers, most of these affiliations change upon a girl's marriage.

For the present I will concentrate on the male Badaga. As he grows up and takes his special position in the society, he probably has no particular understanding of a 'purpose' to the social institutions and cultural traditions in which he participates; and yet they do have a sort of function to perform, in that through the man's interpretation of what his cultural heritage is, and his understanding of what sort of people his family are, he makes daily decisions about what he has to do with his life. These are not vague career plans, but specific acts that the person will follow through with as he brings the known technology to bear on the land. For, as we have seen, nearly all Bad̆agas have traditionally been farmers: their peasant technology had directly to do with the production of food for their families. Nowadays when many of them are growing potatoes and cabbages for the Indian market, even tea for the world market, money has become a mediating factor. Their crops are often sold for cash, to be used in the local markets to buy food for the family. Such, however, was not the traditional way.

As the crops have slowly changed over the years, farming technology has also changed. The very relationship of people to the land and its fruits has also changed, entailing changes too in the structure of the social fabric. For each Badaga individual, male or female, the end result of his or her daily efforts is the provision of food for the family and ultimately the perpetuation of the society and its cultural traditions.

It does not matter too much that this cultural perpetuation is less than perfect: doubtless no historical tradition, however well substantiated, is ever transmitted to later generations in its entirety. Memories are selective, and what any one man may choose to perpetuate in his thought and family life is likely to be what he considers relevant somehow in the present day. In short, anything, any idea, that might be of utility is valued; but there is differential evaluation in different sectors of the society. What holds it all together is a complex pattern of specific values that are often repeated, because they are actually embodied in many hundreds of proverbs, prayers, idioms, blessings and curses, omens and rituals (Hockings 1988). Nobody can live in a Badaga village without encountering these statements of values on a wide variety of occasions, from infancy till death. As Pandian perceptively says, 'People everywhere use representations or symbols, and connect them to create meaning-systems. These are shared, or public, and are used in everyday intellectual discourse and social interaction as well as in mythological discourse and ritual action' (Pandian 1985: 37). Goodenough (1963, Chapter 7) was another anthropologist who explored the idea of belief systems, a concept that is directly relevant to the investigation of proverbs, prayers and certain other idioms. As he saw it, a belief system consists of percepts, concepts, a code or language for manipulating them, and those propositions about the percepts that are held by the believer to be true. In another paper (1957) he defined culture in much the same terms, as 'the end product of learning ... not things, people, behavior or emotions, but the organization of these things ... that people, have in their minds, their models for perceiving, relating and otherwise interpreting them'.

The quality of social relationships definitely affects the quality of daily life, including work; and when a man applies himself to the technology at his disposal in order to get some work done, he is also likely to modify his activity in the light of his perceived obligations to his kin, of other role expectations too, of moral teachings that he has encountered, as well as of personal needs which the man hopes to gratify. One does not simply do work for its own sake.

For many years now the Badagas have been adapting to their own use certain alien customs and techniques. Nowhere is this more evident than in agriculture, where crops of European origin are nowadays being grown on machine-made terraces (Plates 1 and 2) with the help of chemical fertilizers, truck transport, scientifically improved seed, and even crop insurance; and in the tea plantations, which must maintain standards necessary to ensure that the leaf can find its way into Indian and world markets. Such progressive attitudes mark the Badagas as an unusually successful farming community. Population figures from the official censuses bear out this success: in 1812 there were reportedly only some 2,207 Badagas; by 1901 there were 34,178; today there are at least 150,000. By developing intensive cash-crop cultivation they have managed to accommodate this greatly increased labour force and still improve their standard of living and of public hygiene. The traditional relationships with neighbouring tribes have been all but abandoned. There is now a sizeable middle class living in the four main British-built towns on the plateau, and the community can boast several thousand college graduates. Badaga doctors, lawyers, teachers and government officials are very numerous, and there are also a few professors, agronomists, engineers, military personnel and politicians, (even among some recent settlers in the United States). A remarkable fact is that fathers have so often been willing to invest the profits from cultivation or labour contracting in college education for their sons and, more rarely, their daughters. Badagas, though still largely a rural population, today have as high a rate of literacy (in Tamil and English) as one might find in Madras city, the state capital.

Modernization is a very broad term for what are really a variety of processes of cultural change. One form of modernization is industrialization, but in the Badaga case this has hardly occurred. Another aspect is urbanization, which has occurred to a slight extent: the few hundred highly educated professional people and their nuclear families tend to live in the few towns, if indeed they are able to find work in the Nilgiris at all. Finally, another quite pervasive form of modernization is what we call westernization. This is the adoption of selected cultural traits, of certain behavioural patterns, from what modern Western society and business have offered the world at large. Modern transportation, radio, newspapers, television, are just a few of the most obvious items in the Badaga repertoire of cultural borrowings.

For 20th century Badagas, as for many other Indian groups, the westernizing patterns that have affected daily life have included the following three important factors:

1. *English literacy*: Being able to read, write and argue in English is today the mark of an educated Badaga. For over a century-and-a-half the English language has been taught in schools in the Nilgiris district, and so one finds tens of thousands of local people, of all ages, fluent in that language. It is in fact quite as much a lingua franca and a window on the outside world as is Tamil, the official and dominant language of Tamil Nadu state.
2. *Christianity*: Although only a few thousand Badagas were ever converted to one or another sect of Christianity, the impact of European missionaries since the late 1840s has been an important one. In the past many thousands of Badaga children, who were to remain Hindus, nonetheless attended mission-run schools where they learnt to read and write English, Tamil or Kannada, acquired some mathematical and geographical knowledge, and so learnt how to locate themselves in a modernizing world. Even Christian values were not altogether alien to their way of thinking, as many of their own proverbs indicate and as my discussion of early schools (in Chapter 11) will make clear; and it is probably true to say that in many respects the small Christian community which arose from the first conversion (in 1858) has recently served as a positive role model for many non-Christian Badagas, especially in matters of education, occupation and family life.
3. *European agriculture*: Early in the 19th century British settlers or local officials introduced the garden fork and numerous European vegetables, including the commercially important potatoes, cabbages, car-

rots and turnips, among numerous other crops. To these items may be added tea, which was introduced to India from China in 1835. Its cultivation, together with that of Australian eucalyptus and the main introduced vegetable crops, has transformed Nilgiri agriculture and the landscape; so much so that the indigenous millets which were the Badaga staple up till the beginning of the 20th century are rarely grown anywhere today. Those Badagas who are still farmers—certainly the majority of all workers—are now growing tea or vegetables for a regional and national market, with the help of such key paraphernalia as irrigation pumps, chemical fertilizers, and crop insurance.

These three factors should not be viewed as simply external influences, for with the passage of time they have become a part of Badaga culture, through a process of public discussion and internalization that has shown the Badagas to be the masters of their own destiny and never mere pawns in some colonial scenario. It was they who decided to send their children to school in the mid-19th century, and it was they who decided to plant tea (initially stealing the cuttings from large commercial plantations run by British planters). This changing of traditional values and adaptation to the modern world has been going on for over a third of the entire time the Badagas have been on the Nilgiri hills, and it has, if anything, been quickening its pace since the British administration of the nation came to an end in 1947. The popularity of videotape machines and national television since the decade of the 1980s is bringing further irreversible changes in the Badaga worldview. In fact, by 1990, television, introduced in the Nilgiri area around 1984, had become sufficiently widespread in rural communities that its presence could be regarded as a useful measure of relative conservatism or modernization. Thus in 1990 Ki:y Odeyaraṭṭi, by other indicators the most conservative of the four sample villages, had one TV set per 159 people; O:rana:yi had one TV per 104; Hulla:ḍa had one set per 57 people; while Ke:ti Toreke:ri had one set per 49 people. The ranking of these villages by this criterion roughly corresponds with their distance by road from the nearest town, and is precisely in inverse proportion to their social status, i.e., the lowest ranking had the highest number of sets per 100 of population.

NOTES

1. The Badaga antiquarian M. K. Belli Gowder (1938–41: 5–6) stated in his unpublished manuscript however that '…the present Moniagar [i.e., headman] of Thuneri gives the names of 21 generations of his forefathers'. If true, this might push the arrival of the first Badagas back by a century or more; but it probably includes three generations prior to their arrival on the hills.
2. 'Thus, there may be two or three clans which recognized relationship to each other. It is common to call such groupings of related clans *phratries*.' (Fox 1983: 92). My Figure 1.4 here is reproduced from Hockings (1980a: 76, Diagram 7).

Chapter 2

RESEARCH DESIGN

The tools to him that can handle them.
— Thomas Carlyle

The Chosen Villages

In mid-1963 I did the first of four nine-yearly censuses of four contiguous Badaga villages centrally located on the Plateau (Figure 2.1); they were chosen as a 1 per cent sample of that community because they represent four hierarchically differentiated strata, namely Toreyas, Gauḍas, Adikaris and Woḍeyas (ranked here from lowest to highest). That they have been slightly more effective than average in the Badaga community when it comes to population control is suggested by my estimate that in 1963 these four villages contained 0.983 per cent of the total Badaga population, whereas in 1990 this percentage was probably down to 0.937—and not because of emigration.

The purpose of these censuses was to produce a longitudinal database that would reflect, both statistically and qualitatively, the structural changes that have been occurring in Badaga households during recent times. No such controlled study of a comparable sample has been done anywhere in South Asia before, and the few longitudinal studies that do exist are mostly the work of different people with diverging interests (see Appendix II). My censuses, taken in 1963, 1972, 1981 and 1990, cover essentially all persons (and not just a sample) living during the study period in these four nearby villages. Cumulatively, they are intended to cover one generation of cultural change, since a generation in this community is now 26 years (though it was shorter in earlier centuries).

For comparative purposes it also proved possible to use a complete set of the baptismal and death registers covering local Christian Badagas during the period 1860–1914, i.e., roughly a century prior to my own set of observations. These dealt with the entire Christian population of the immediate area, namely Ketti Pastorate and some outlying villages. The entries cover every case of baptism and of death there between 1860 and 1914, and indeed went on beyond that date down to the present (the later records, however, included numerous Christians who were not Badagas). Interestingly, these early observations record considerable detail on social status, whether the person was a Badaga or not, parentage of the newborn, place of residence, probable cause of death, etc.; and they thus allow me to extend my own observations backwards in time for a sample of the population quite comparable to my own, yet living a century earlier.

A generation prior to the first Badaga conversion in 1858, Capt. Henry Harkness, the very first of a long stream of amateur ethnographers to puzzle over the Nilgiri communities, recorded the following comments about our sample area and his lodgings in 'Kaultray', his quaint spelling of Ka:ṭe:ri (which I suppose is *my* quaint spelling of Katery; Plate 15).

> Proceeding on our route, we came to the village of Kaultray, situated among fields of ripening grain of almost every description. On the road we had been overtaken by a storm, which still continuing, and our tents not having come up, we were obliged to pass the night here, and to accommodate ourselves in the best way we could, in a Burgher [Badaga] verandah ....
>
> The inhabitants of this, and two or three other little villages at a short distance, consisted of some three or four families of Lingavants, about the same number of Arrvars, Kanacars, Adikaris, and common Burghers, and also a few families of Toriahs [i.e., Lingayats, Ha:ruvas, Kaṇakkas, Adikaris, Badaga Gauḍas, Toreyas—P.H.]. The surrounding scene showed them to be an industrious people; and as far as their notions could be made applicable to us, we found them hospitable. Small as the place was which we had for our evening accommodation, we were obliged to allow of the claims of the quern, the winnow, and the garner, to a share of it; and had we put up in the Toriah village [i.e. Ke:ti Toreke:ri—P.H.], the distaff and the wheel.... (Harkness 1832: 111–12).

(By later in the 19th century the Toreyas had altogether abandoned the craft of weaving.)

Household types, according to my censuses, are quite varied and, although the nuclear family is the numerically dominant type and the extended family the ideal type, I will identify many categories of house-

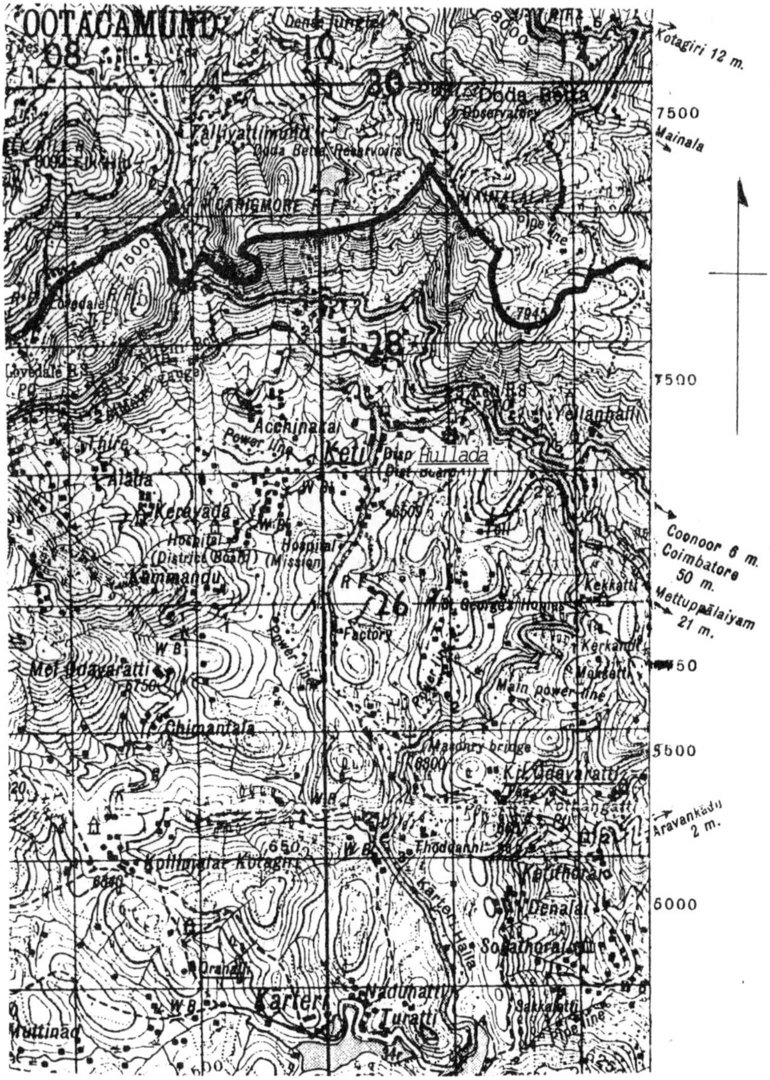

Map 2.1. MAP OF THE STUDY AREA
(with the four villages underlined*)

* Ke:ti is near the centre, Hulla:ḍa just to its east, Ki:y Oḍeyaraṭṭi towards the southeast, and O:rana:yi in the southwest.

hold structure in the four villages under study. It may be noted here that the household, rather than the family, has been chosen as the unit of analysis throughout because, despite its many variations, it lends itself to direct and repeated observation in the field. The Badaga household is clearly definable because in every instance it lives in one village house with one front door and one hearth; families may be more dispersed. Each village itself has been historically the locus solely of Badaga residence. My emphasis on the household as the primary unit for data collection in no way obscures the structure of the Badaga family. Indeed, that structure emerges from a comparison of the four sets of data from the four successive censuses of each particular household.

The four chosen villages are all at roughly the same elevation in the middle of the Nilgiri massif: O:rana:yi is at 2400 ft., Ke:ti Toreke:ri at 2425 ft., Hulla:ḍa at 2460 ft., and Ki:y Oḍeyaraṭṭi (the highest in status as well) at 2590 ft. (Plates 1, 2, 3, 5, 13 and 14). Two of the four are hamlets (*haṭṭi*) within the commune that is headed by Ke:ti (Ke:ti *u:r*). A third, Ke:ti Toreke:ri, is actually a sector of Ke:ti itself. The fourth, O:rana:yi, is not linked administratively to Ke:ti, for an unmarked boundary places it as a hamlet of So:gatore *u:r*. As we have seen, the hamlet represents the lowest level and the commune the next higher level in a traditional Badaga hierarchy of politico–juridical units having councils.

All four had acquired electrification before my study began, but at that time only Ke:ti and Hulla:ḍa had a serviceable road connecting them with the towns. Halfway through the study period the other two villages got improved roads and their first bus services. None of the four villages ever had a traditional fair connecting it with the wider region, although Hulla:ḍa's annual firewalking festival does attract many itinerant traders and sightseers from other villages. Ke:ti has long had a small post and telegraph office, two more are within a mile, and the Ke:ti valley has 126 telephone connections (1993) including 14 lines within Ke:ti itself. It is quite near the railway station which adjoins Hulla:ḍa (which had another three phone lines). Other public facilities already in Ke:ti in 1961 included a co-operative society, a rural health centre, a veterinary dispensary, a maternity and child welfare centre, and a medical dispensary; there were two medical practitioners then. By contrast the two Lingayat villages of the sample were at least 2 km away from any such facilities, only some of which were to be found in the nearby Ka:ṭe:ri, Pa:la:ḍa or Adigaraṭṭi villages. While these latter had a number of telephone lines and small post offices, there were none at all right in the two Lingayat villages.

Evidently then the four villages had differential access to modern communications; but given that they lie so close together, within an area of scarcely 10 sq. km, and are all inhabited by Badagas of various sorts, it would be legitimate to ask what cultural factors hold the four villages together? The answer is that there are specific juridical and ritual ties linking them, but *no* marital ones. Because I have chosen four villages representative of four different Badaga phratries there could not be intermarriage, since (with minor exceptions that do not here apply) the phratry is definable as the largest *endogamous* unit within the total Badaga society.

There are some calendrical ceremonies that may only be performed by the head village of a commune for all its constituent hamlets, in this case by Ke:ti or So:gatore. (Elsewhere one finds them being celebrated by individual hamlets. In the past a hamlet was often too tiny to mount a festival, because of the cost of materials.) Such communal ceremonies normally include the God Festival (*devva habba*), the Great Festival (*doḍḍa habba*), the harvesting festival (*ka:ṇike habba*), and in former times the costly memorial ceremony (*manevale*), etc.

But there is another sort of ritual linkage between the four chosen villages. Many of the Badaga villages have several kinds of priestly functionary. These (depending on the circumstances) may be (1) a member of the same phratry which inhabits a village; (2) a Ha:ruva man; (3) an associate from a Kuṟumba tribe; and (4) a Woḍeya Lingayat. Ke:ti commune, for example, makes use of all four types of priest (and I saw them all in operation there during 1963). The Woḍeya who services this area—including O:rana:yi—is a member of the Woḍeya priestly clan (Oḍeyar/Ma:ntu) who resides in Ki:y Odeyaraṭṭi (Plate 20).

Census Design

As we have seen, the four villages chosen for my study were no more than 4 km distant from each other (the closest two being under 1 km apart; see Map 2.1), and they represented four stratified phratries of the Badaga society. By picking representative villages so close together in the centre of the Nilgiri massif, I considered this would hold constant geographical and historical variables that otherwise might have gone some way towards explaining differences between any of the four villages located at a greater distance from each other; and it would also obviate any effects of being marginal to the area of Badaga culture. Three of the four villages were actually within sight of each other, the fourth being hidden behind a hill. It was intended that any differences perceived between the four should be explained as social differences and not environmentally induced ones or an effect of different historical circumstances. However, the four villages did not only differ in their social ranking: another significant variable was their absolute size. Judged by number of households, the lowest-ranked Toreya village was also the smallest, having about two dozen households. The two high-status Lingayat villages were each more than twice as large as this; while the medially-ranked Gauḍa village was twice as large as these latter two. (Actual numbers of households are given later, Tables 7.4 and 8.1, on pp. 162, 174)

One aspect of the research design, which explains the unusual nine-year periodicity of the censuses, was a desire to be able to link up my data conceptually with the national Census of India in one year, namely 1981, when both it and my own census were to be taken. Thus the work on the Badaga villages might not be statistically isolated from larger datasets. In the event, this strategy did not prove to be especially fruitful. My census was done a mere 2–3 months after the national operation, which could have made little difference to any statistical comparison. The problems lay rather with the units of analysis.

I was unable to guess that the Census of India officials would — erroneously, and contrary to all precedent — decide that the Badaga language, the one definite marker of Badaga ethnicity, should now be considered as equivalent to Kannada, even though previously it had not been. Consequently, the 1981 and 1991 Census publications gave no separate break-downs for Badaga speakers but obscured them in the much larger category of Kannada speakers. This error has thus made it impossible for me to link my findings with those of the national Census at many points where, in earlier years, it would have been possible.

The 1981 Census of India did make it clear in numerous publications that it was looking at units called Buildings, Census Houses, Households, and Rooms on a nationwide basis. A Building in the Badaga case would however be, by the national definition, a whole row of adjoining houses, perhaps 10 or more of them, each with its own entranceways and internal partitions (see Figure 7.4). A Census House was defined nationally (in numerous official publications) as 'a building or part of a building having a separate main entrance from the road or common courtyard or staircase, etc., used or recognized as a separate unit. It may be occupied or vacant. It may be used for a residential or non-residential purpose or both.' I too was looking at such houses, each of which had one or two entrances. But it was the Census definition of Household which was most crucial, for here I could at least follow the idea in spirit if not in detail:

> A Household is a group of persons who commonly live together and would take their meals from a common kitchen unless the exigencies of work prevented any of them from doing so. There may bc a household of persons related by blood or a household of unrelated persons or having a mix of both. Examples of unrelated households are boarding houses, messes, hostels, residential hotels, rescue homes, jails, ashrams, etc. These are called 'Institutional households'. There may be one member households, 2 member households or multi-member households. For census purposes, each one of these types is regarded as a 'Household'.
>
> If a group of persons who are unrelated to each other live in a census house but do not have their meals from the common kitchen, they would not constitute an institutional household. Each such person should be treated as a separate household. The important link in finding out whether there is a household or not is a common kitchen.

My censuses did not encounter any of the 'Institutional Households'. In the final analysis, the failure to identify Badaga speakers as a national Census category since 1971 has meant that I have largely been left to my own devices, with little leverage on the national data.

Family or Household?

These two terms should not be confused: a family is a unit created by a kinship system, a culturally shared and patterned way of organizing biological relationships; whereas a household (as just defined) is a residential unit which, in Badaga society, is created solely by the family system. Thus there is a relationship between family and household, but it is one of causation rather than of identity: the family creates the household, and a joint family will sooner or later create more than one.

Much empirical research on the family in India is in fact concerned with the domestic group or household, because it is the household that is the visible unit of data collection and analysis. The present research too takes the household as the prime unit of observation, but at the same time recognizes that this unit is the concrete historical expression of ideology, namely the Badaga kinship system. One certainly cannot be fully understood without reference to the other.

In research on the European household a necessary distinction has been made between family and household by social historians who frequently encountered cases where the household included non-relatives, like servants. Such a factor lends clarity to the distinction; but it does not hold water in the Badaga case since I never encountered a household with any non-relatives. There *was* one entire household of strangers living temporarily in Hulla:ḍa in 1990 — a Badaga policeman and his family; and another in 1963–1972 — the family of a Muslim merchant; but in both cases these people moved on elsewhere. Another family of Malayali cultivators had lived there for many years, but their home was on the outskirts and is not included in this study. O:rana:yi was the other village in my sample which had one or two families of non-Badagas living in separate households out in the fields for periods of many years (Plate 6): they were Harijan farm-labourers. But while they may have rented their homes from local Badagas it would have been unthinkable for them to have shared occupancy because of the large status difference. Until some decades ago it was customary for more well-to-do Badaga households to include some unrelated children as hirelings or bonded servants; but this benign servitude had stopped before the Second World War, and indeed I have no direct evidence that the practice occurred particularly in my four sample villages, (though it probably did).

An early comparative effort to study Indian family structure was compiled by Kolenda from 26 published case studies in 1968 (reprinted somewhat erratically in 1987). In what is primarily a statistical analysis, and necessarily a rather crude one, she grapples with the fact that the many authors whom she relies upon have no agreed-upon typology of Indian families, and indeed vary in their definitions of such a basic concept as the joint family. Undaunted, Kolenda cobbles together a set of widely occurring categories which she defines in the following way (Kolenda 1987: 11–12), and which I shall make use of later, as have several other researchers as well as the most recent Censuses of India:

1. *Nuclear family*: a couple with or without unmarried children.
2. *Supplemented nuclear family*: a nuclear family plus one or more unmarried,

separated, or widowed relatives of the parents, other than their unmarried children.

3. *Subnuclear family*: a fragment of a former nuclear family. Typical examples are the widow with unmarried children, or the widower with unmarried children, or siblings—whether unmarried, or widowed, separated, or divorced—living together.

4. *Single-person household.*

5. *Supplemented subnuclear*: a group of relatives, members of a formerly complete nuclear family, plus some other unmarried, divorced, or widowed relative who was not a member of the nuclear family. For example, a widow and her unmarried children plus her widowed mother-in-law.

6. *Collateral joint family*: two or more married couples between whom there is a sibling bond—usually a brother–brother relationship—plus unmarried children.

7. *Supplemented collateral joint family*: a collateral joint family plus unmarried, divorced, or widowed relatives. Typically, such supplemental relatives are the widowed mother of the married brothers, or the widowed father, or an unmarried sibling.

8. *Lineal joint family*: two couples between whom there is a lineal link, usually between parents and married son, sometimes between parents and married daughter.

9. *Supplemented lineal joint family*: a lineal joint family plus unmarried, divorced, or widowed relatives who do not belong to either of the lineally linked nuclear families; for example, the father's [widowed] brother or the son's wife's unmarried brother.

10. *Lineal–collateral joint family*: three or more couples linked lineally and collaterally. Typically, parents and their two or more married sons, plus the unmarried children of the three couples.

11. *Supplemented lineal–collateral joint family*: a lineal collateral joint family plus unmarried, widowed, separated relatives who belong to none of the nuclear families lineally and collaterally linked; for example, the father's widowed sister or brother, or an unmarried nephew of the father.

12. *Other*: Some researchers—Woodruff, Kulkarni, Bose and Saxena, and Mencher—included an "other" class of families which they did not define, or about which I could not make reasonable guesses …

Essentially, Kolenda has identified three main family types, namely subnuclear, nuclear and joint, and has further qualified them as lineal, collateral, or supplemented. To these, and following Berreman, she adds certain categories only applicable in those villages having some polygyny:

> ... a simple polygynous family is composed of a man, his two wives, and their unmarried children. A supplemented polygynous family is composed of the simple polygynous family plus some unmarried, widowed, or divorced relative of the head or of his wives, other than their unmarried children. A sub-polygynous family is usually composed of a woman, one of the wives of a man living elsewhere (perhaps with his other wife), and her unmarried children. A supplemented sub-polygynous [family] is such a household plus an unmarried, divorced, or widowed relative other than one of the children. A polygynous lineal or collateral household includes at least one component family composed of a man and two wives. (Kolenda 1987: 25)

Throughout this lengthy study Kolenda is talking about families as commensal or hearth groups, which as she correctly puts it are 'the only way to define the functioning family group' (1987: 79). It is possible therefore to compare the disparate data that she has gathered with those from my Badaga households, since in nearly all cases observed in the four villages the architecturally circumscribed space which is a household is the locus of a functioning family group, with one hearth.

The studies mentioned in the next section and Appendix II are of special relevance because even when they are talking about 'the family' they are usually referring to the household. Their approach thus comes close to my own:

> ... an approach which gives 'ethnographic priority' to the household. The strategy entails an analysis of the household, including definitional issues, which attempts to reveal its particular characteristics, whether relational, structural, conceptual, and/or behavioural, which recognizes that these characteristics are not merely manifestations of the encompassing society writ small in the domestic domain, and which focuses on the centrifugal implications of domestic relations and processes for social domains of a larger scale (Gray and Mearns 1989: 13).

My own definition of a household, for the purposes of this study, may be worded as follows: *An architecturally defined space habitually occupied by a small group of people who are related to each other as a nuclear or extended family (with the possible addition of one or two widowed relatives or servants). Its working generates an ongoing domestic domain of social, economic and kinship processes.*

This is not radically different from the way other social anthropologists have defined the South Asian household; for example, Gray and Mearns:

> ... the household in South Asia is a specific confluence of three forms of social relations—kinship, production, and consumption—including the functions and meanings co-implicated by them. Together they entail a territorial dimension, which is usually manifest in 'co-residence', as the locus for the practise of these relations. (Gray and Mearns 1989: 22)

Comparable Village Studies

While South Asia has generated many dozens of village studies, very few of these have been able to use a diachronic framework (see Appendix II), as the present study does. It may be useful nonetheless to survey briefly several longitudinal studies done elsewhere in India that will be used here for comparative purposes.

First, there is one north Indian study, published in numerous fascicles by Stanley and Ruth Freed between 1976 and 1993, which has some points of similarity with my own, although it deals with only a single peri-urban village near Delhi. In their words:

> The analysis is based on censuses and holistic ethnographic studies that we made in 1958–1959 and 1977–1978 and a sterilization survey that was undertaken in the latter part of 1983 .... The interval between the two studies was in all likelihood long enough to permit the identification of significant demographic trends. It is especially noteworthy that the study straddles the important demographic watershed between pre- and poststerilization periods. (Freed and Freed 1985: 232–33)

The village had 176 families in 1977/78, belonging to a number of distinct endogamous castes. Since the 1985 paper concentrated on fertility and population growth, it will be of some comparative utility here.[1]

Obviously there could never be a study that was at all points comparable with the present Badaga study, for it would become almost a duplication. On the other hand, and very fortunately, there *is* another study that is in many ways quite comparable to my own, and done in an adjoining state in the same period, and so some space is devoted here to mentioning its major features because I have cited it repeatedly.

The study referred to was carried out in rural Karnataka, in Tumkur district, during the years 1979–1984 by three demographers of an anthropological inclination (Caldwell *et al.* 1988). In an attempt to examine demographic change at what they call a 'micro-level', they chose one major and eight smaller, outlying villages on the Mysore Plain at a place some 75 miles WNW of Bangalore city (and due north of Mysore city). At the time of study these were still non-mechanized farming communities growing primarily Indian finger millet and sorghum, but also keeping cattle for milk and traction.

All of the villages under study fell within 'an elliptical area with a longer axis of about seven miles and a total population in late 1979 of 4,773' (ibid.: 10). The smaller hamlets ranged in population from 62 to 543, and in some cases only contained one caste. The main village, on the other hand, was multi-caste and had a population of 2,557 at the time of study. Measured another way, the main village contained 413 households, while the other hamlets ranged from 13 to 100 households. These smaller hamlets were to some extent dependent on the larger central village for certain economic facilities, especially its weekly market. Of the eight hamlets, the one furthest from this village was five miles away. All of the villages were close to a main road with frequent bus services to larger towns; but there was no railway nearby. During at least some parts of each year the research team consisted of the three principal investigators and anything from eight to 12 other trained collaborators. They combined the varied approaches of participant observation with more formal census and survey techniques. By their definition, the total number of households they were dealing with was 786, with a mean size of 6.1 persons.

This is perhaps sufficient information to illustrate the comparison between the Caldwell–Reddy study and my own. I, of course, studied agricultural people of a single community in a hill zone where crops other than *ragi* and *jowar* were being grown. I only worked in four neighbouring villages, and with only one local research assistant at any given time. But the total number of households in my database was eventually 283, a number which had been increasing through time, and was on a similar scale to the Karnataka study just referred to. In my case I did study every household in each of the four villages over 27 years; whereas Caldwell, Reddy and associates concentrated at first on the 194 households of their large village which had 'one or more couples, with spouses living together, where there were three or more living children, and where the wife was 30–39 years of age .... We found that we could cope with this number and we later used the same method of selection for the smaller villages' (ibid.: 15). While their kind of sampling, common in micro-studies, is quite defensible as a way of getting data on fertility and some other demographic characteristics, it is clearly less than adequate for identifying all forms of household structure. The Badaga study was, in this regard, not so restricted. The Caldwell–Reddy team evidently became somewhat disenchanted with their procedure because, before they had finished the work, 'we reverted to systematic sampling, usually of every second household' (ibid.: 15).

On the face of it the four-year study of villages by the Caldwell–Reddy team should not yield the kind of longitudinal data that my 27-year study might. As it happens though, whether by good luck or by design, the large village of their study had also been included in the Economic Survey of Mysore State that was conducted in 1941 as part of the official Census of Mysore in that year. The Caldwell–Reddy team thus had at their disposal for *one* village data for a 40-year span, 1941–1980, which of course overlaps considerably with my own study span of 1963–1990 and invites comparison of changing demographic phenomena in the two neighbouring regions.

Yet another study was completed in the Tumkur district in 1963/64, midway in time between the two studies just discussed; but it is not referred to by the Caldwells and their associates, and was possibly not known to them. This was a study of communication in three villages located about 10 miles from the town of Tiptur, and was done by Selden and Audrey Menefee (1964). Their control village was only some 15 miles from the large village of the Caldwell–Reddy study, in very much the same cultural setting, and so their findings are highly relevant to the later study. Beyond a typed report it has never been published, but I will use it here where appropriate. The Menefees' interview schedule was much shorter than the one I had administered in the Nilgiris some six months before, and dealt fairly directly with matters of communication of information (in a total of 24 questions).

Some Questions of Reliability

Before presenting the main body of my findings, it will be worth exploring several methodological problems that have dogged my work, that of the Caldwell–Reddy team, and other demographers too in South Asia. (This section may take the wind from my critics' sails; cf. Guilmoto 1992.)

(1) *Age*: A person's age in India can always be problematic, and regrettably it is the least certain aspect of all our census data, my own included. The current truth is that, except for a small minority of professional-class or Christian birth, the fact of a childbirth is not formally registered anywhere, as it is in many countries: birth certificates do not exist except at the more prominent hospitals, where childbirth rarely occurs. While a very few Badagas may have kept some written records on their children, it was for the most part just a matter of 'common knowledge' within a village when a boy was old enough to go to school, or a girl old enough to get married. Age cohorts are recognized, and a useful mnemonic tool has sometimes been 'my child is the same age as so-and-so: they went to school together'.

In the latter half of the 20th century the law has repeatedly raised the minimum age at which a young man or woman might marry, in an effort to decrease the number of childbearing years, and the near-universal education of Badaga children has certainly delayed the time of marriage. A phenomenon reported from elsewhere in South Asia, wherein a girl's age has been inflated to give the impression she is legally old enough to marry, does not seem to have occurred in my four sample villages. Although some of the Woḍeya girls did appear to have married in their middle teens, several years below the current legal minimum of 18 years for women, for Woḍeyas this was of no consequence.

In the Badaga case manipulation of a woman's age, less for my benefit than for the ears of others standing around while I conducted an interview, did seem to occur quite often with women aged *over* 18. I noticed a marked tendency for their male relatives, when acting as informants of mine, to understate the age of unmarried female relatives in their 20s or 30s. A quite typical conundrum that arose from the data was where a woman's age of 18 or 19 seemed well established in one census, but then her male relatives would tell me at the next one nine years later that she was now 22. Of course, the older such a woman is known to be, the less are her chances of making a really desirable match. While during the period of study a number of young men moved away from their parental villages for employment, there was a noticeable number of women in every village who were well into their 20s but unmarried. A few of these had indeed been married for awhile, but divorce had resulted. For most, though, the right marriage opportunity had not yet come along; or more exactly, the increasing demands for dowries on the part of families of young men with a promising future had created a greater potential expense than the parents were capable of shouldering. It is certainly something new, but not particularly uncommon, to encounter households here that contain one or more unmarried daughters aged as much as 30. One might suspect that such women have secret lovers, but the facts are apparently otherwise and (in contrast with much earlier times) it is likely that such unmarried women are chaste. In each village there were also one or two elderly men and women who reportedly had never been married.

Elderly people were another source of reliability problems where age was concerned. Quite often they had not been to school, and thus could not be linked up with an age cohort of one-time classmates. Their own memories were commonly not very reliable, unless perhaps their birth had occurred at about the time of some significant event, which was rarely stated to be the case. Their younger relatives simply knew that these people were older than anyone else in the family, and so perhaps exaggerated just how old these people were. Thus my own records sometimes indicated that a man described somewhat haphazardly as 70 or even 80 was in fact in his mid-60s. But there is no doubt each village did at times contain some really old people, and it seems very likely that the oldest man in O:rana:yi, for example, was indeed 93 when he died.

Elderly Badagas in the 19th century used to estimate their age according to how old they had been at two major historic events: the death of Tipu Sultan in 1799 or the arrival of John Sullivan on the hills in 1819. At the beginning of the present century there were still a few Badagas and Todas alive who claimed to have 'seen Sullivan', the founder of Ootacamund and the first modernizer of the Nilgiri hills (Hockings 1989b: 334–42). This somewhat bolstered their credentials as being truly old. An account of the *manevale*, a very infrequent memorial festival, in the local newspaper in 1905 illustrates how one such aged crone stole the show away to the point where the reporter told us very little about the festival itself:

> The most notable figure in the gathering was an old woman, who declared that the present celebration is the third she has witnessed in her life time. The first was when she was a girl of 14, the second 50 years later, and this 60 years after the last. If her statement be reliable she must be 124 years old, and quite a unique specimen of human longevity. She says that her children, grandchildren and great-grand-children, number 105. In appearance, she is

> healthy and her rememberance [*sic*] of events of the past is quite phenomenal. She can remember the first European carried up the old Kotagiri ghaut in a chair, which must be either Messers Keys or Welsh [i.e., Whish] or Mr. Sullivan. The old lady quite enjoyed the prominence given to her on the occasion, and was proud of being introduced to several of the European visitors as a curiosity.... (South of India Observer 1905; note that Keys' visit was in 1812, Whish's in 1818, Sullivan's in 1819).

Such instances remind us that indeed there were exceptional cases of centenarians in both the Badaga and Toda communities.

My assistants and I were probably most careful over the age matter in 1963, at the first census we did.[2] The last census, in 1990, was another in which I tried to be especially careful about recording ages. For those people who survived through the whole period of the study, there was no getting away from the fact that at the end of it they were 27 years older than when we began, and I was fairly confident that I knew how old they had been in 1963. Yet because of the problems outlined above, it is not possible to make exceptionally reliable statements about mean age at first marriage, mean age at first live birth, or even age at death. It would not be unreasonable to assume a margin of error of ±2–3 years for every individual's age above 2, regrettable though this may be. The Freeds reported a similar experience to this in the conduct of a census and the collection of data on ages (Freed and Freed 1985: 237). One has to assume that the national Census of India was never immune from this problem.

(2) *Naming*: Actually the problem of just how old a person was begins to pall when compared with the problem of *who* he or she was: people often changed their names between one census and the next! On occasion, several members of the same household did this during the same nine-year period, at first causing doubts in my mind as to whether I was still dealing with the same group of people. Yet if a household head (who rarely did change his name) had sons Ma:dan 10, A:rjunan 7 and a daughter Ma:di aged 3 in 1972, it was fairly evident I was reporting on the same people when in 1981 he gave the names of his children as Krisṇan 19, Kallan 16 and Pa:rvati 12.

No doubt there are several reasons for such (annoying) name changes. One certainly might be fashion or personal preference. But another could just be convenience. In the aforementioned example, if Krisṇan brought home a bride also named Pa:rvati, his younger sister might readily change her name, perhaps to De:vi, so as not to confuse the household. Even a Pa:rvati appearing next door might be enough to precipitate such a change of name. The census-taker may well have to inquire if Pa:rvati is the same person as De:vi; but since the latter is a generic term for 'goddess' its choice could seem a logical one to the girl who had previously borne the name of Śiva's wife. Some of the name changes were in the nature of simplification. Thus the name Candrabo:ś (after Subhas Chandra Bose, the Bengali freedom-fighter) given to one boy was at a later census abbreviated to the English 'Sun' (or *Can* ‹ Chandra). Unfortunately most of the very frequent name changes encountered did not even display this degree of logic, however. Some people were known by three quite distinct names (not to mention slight variants) over the 27-year period. In an extreme case, one young man had used four names by the time he was 23: Sekaran, Kuttan, Kumar, and Raju. If this can be taken as suggesting some sort of identity crisis, then it may be relevant to add that at 23 he left his village and (most atypically) disappeared in the city of Tiruchirapalli. His whereabouts are now unknown.

To further complicate the issue, there were many names which recurred with great frequency; so much so that it was quite possible for two or even three Bo:jans in the same village all to be married to Laksmis, or for three heads of household to bear the name K. Nanjan (the initial always being that of their father's name). Ke:ti Toreke:ri, the smallest of the sample villages with a population of about 90, has three men the same age, all named N. Ha:lan. In Hulla:ḍa, a unique case was noted of two brothers living in the same household who were both named Ra:man. This situation had arisen because the younger of the two was a twin and it is customary to name twin boys Ra:man and Laksmaṇan, from the *Rāmayaṇa*—even though they had an elder brother, Ra:man. Nicknames, or better common names (*hora hesaru*), are widely used to avoid such confusions. For me, detailed record-keeping was essential.

(3) *Agẹ at Marriage*: A study done in Mysore before my own study commenced (United Nations 1961) found that girls who married between the ages of 14 and 17 had an average total of 5.9 children; whereas those who married between 18 and 21 produced only 4.7. The date of this study was so early that we can safely assume no modern methods of contraception were then in use in this village population.

Age at marriage is not recorded anywhere in Badaga villages (except for those Christians who have church weddings). Of course, younger adults could tell me with fair accuracy how old they were when they got married; but among the older informants there were serious doubts about the accuracy of their memories. Occasionally people who had in fact taken a bride in her early adolescence elevated her age a little because there has long been in law a minimum age for girls to marry. It is currently 18, but some decades ago was 15.

These reservations apart, the definition of the marriage itself can be problematic. True, the bride and groom go through a public ceremony which proclaims them man and wife in the eyes of the village; but then there is a second ceremony, sometime later, called in English the seventh-month ceremony, when a cord is tied round the wife's neck to proclaim that she is now in the seventh month of her first pregnancy. This event is really the confirmation of the permanency of the marriage and, as we have seen earlier, it tends not to occur in early adolescence at all, for on the average older women in my sample had their first birth at 20.5 years, and younger women at 21.2.

This certainly seems a far cry from the situation among Kanarese villagers in the Caldwell–Reddy study, for there 'nearly all families in the study area believe that attempts to marry daughters should begin at menarche and should be successful as soon as possible' (Caldwell *et al.* 1988: 96). Nonetheless their figures were not so different from mine, since 'In the study area the modal age of female marriage by 1979–82 was 20 years' (ibid.: 240). The authors also note that 'By 1980 ... only 1 percent of 10 to 14-year-old girls were married, 31 percent of those aged 15–19 ..., and 82 percent of those aged 20–24' (ibid.: 82). The fact that 18 per cent of young women of 20–24 there were not married, and were usually living in the parental household, underlines a major change in household structure that is even more prevalent in the four Badaga villages. Legislation to raise the minimum age for marriages, and the requirements of higher education for females, are only a part of the story: the main reason behind the situation of these young unmarried women in both Karnataka and the Nilgiris is the demands now being made for high monetary settlements.

(4) *Absentees*: One minor puzzle was that a few persons who appeared in several census records did not appear in an intermediate one. This could not be explained by a presumed death if they reappeared later. But there was evidence of a certain amount of inter-village mobility. A young man might not feature in one census because at that time he was away at college, or working somewhere in a factory, or temporarily

living with a relative elsewhere so as to have easier access to a high school or college in one of the Nilgiri towns. Widows too showed a tendency to disappear, and not only because of an otherwise unrecorded death. It was fairly common for a widow to stay with several of her adult sons in turn; or to live with an unmarried daughter somewhere. In a number of instances, an entire nuclear family moved to a town for factory work, or even to live in the wife's village because of some farming opportunity or other economic benefit there. And I did record instances where a family simply died out between one census and the next.

NOTES

1. I am indebted to Stanley Freed for sending me a complete set of these fascicles over the years.
2. It is difficult to insist on seeing each individual in the villages and demanding an accurate age. Many residents simply did not know exactly how old they were. Furthermore, in any such agricultural community, many people are out in the fields on any given day or off to town and cannot be found. It was therefore felt sufficient to question one or two residents at each house whenever occupants could be found there, and to rely on my research assistants who were nearly always with me to detect any likely error in the data; for these assistants were always from that very village or the neighbouring one, and knew everyone personally. Had I waited around long enough to see every resident face-to-face, the census operation would have dragged on over too long a period to be acceptable to me.

Chapter 3

MARRIAGE AND DESCENT

We are interested in others when they are interested in us.
— Syrus Publilius

Larger Social Units

For almost any people of South Asia an individual's status is reflected ritually in three major events of his or her life, namely birth, marriage and death. This is certainly a truism of Badaga life, and one worth exploring. Accordingly, the following three chapters will examine all of these important and revelatory topics. The present chapter[1] introduces the Badaga system of kinship terminology, which is Dravidian, and shows how kinship operates, how descent is determined and how marriages should be arranged. Chapter 4 will present the life history of one individual, as it illustrates neatly the interplay between family obligations and personal aspirations. In Chapter 5 we move on to the moment of death and the funeral which follows, in an effort to show kin relationships and the larger social structure in operation; in short, to suggest the workings of the society.

Today, as I see it, we find no castes within Badaga society. These people live in a tribal milieu, surrounded by the indigenous Toda, Kota, Ku̱rumba, and Irula tribes, and their culture has become fairly tribe-like itself. It would not be reasonable to identify the Badagas as a caste if they were not interacting with any other castes. The community is divided into 10 phratries which are mainly endogamous. Two of these are vegetarian; all are primarily agricultural. Each phratry is made up of a number of exogamous clans, anything from two to 16 of them (Figure 1.4), and these clans are in turn segmented into quite a few exogamous lineages. As with the well-known Ghanaian case of the Tallensi (Fortes 1949: 12–43), there are actually lineages within lineages, so that we may need to speak about maximal (*kuḍumbu*), major (*kutti*), minor (*kutti*), and minimal (*guppu*) lineages, though perhaps not every clan currently has all four levels. Segments of the minimal lineages are in fact extended families, counting back for about five generations, and with most of their members still alive (Figure 7.6).

These larger social units have a complicated history and organization (detailed in Hockings 1980a), and they will not be considered much in this present study. It is nonetheless relevant to mention how they fit into the residence pattern. The Badagas live in about 430 exclusively Badaga villages which are normally exogamous. Marriage is virilocal. Each village is thus the home of one or more patrilineages all belonging to one or another clan (and hence, one phratry). But with few exceptions a clan is not confined to a single village.

One particular village, Tu:ne:ri, was probably the first place to be settled, in the late 16th century, as a result of which its headman became the paramount chief. This position, like virtually all Badaga headmanships, has descended patrilineally within the family. Every other village has its own headman, descended from the founder, and clusters of neighbouring villages form a commune around one particular village whose headman is also acknowledged to be the commune headman. Furthermore, the whole of the plateau area has been divided into four quarters, and one man is recognized as the divisional headman in each quarter. At every one of the four levels of headmanship there is also a council, made up of inferior headmen (except in the case of the village council, which consists of lineage elders who work with the traditional headman there).

The society is relatively homogeneous in the sense that, although the 10 phratries are ranked into a widely accepted hierarchy, all families were traditionally subsistence farmers of millets and all lived by essentially the same kinship rules and obligations. We will therefore be able to explore the meaning of these rules without constant reference to exceptions and alternatives found only in certain sectors of the society.

Kinship Behaviour

It is not possible to present the Badaga kinship system here in such a way that it fully explains Badaga behaviour, even that sort which we anthropologists usually call kinship behaviour. Any actions occurring in the social setting of two or more persons who consider themselves to be 'related' may well have motivations that lie in such spheres as the practice of agriculture, the accumulation of political power, the acquisition of wealth, or the display of education—as well as in so-called kinship obligations. One can thus argue that the presentation of a system of kinship terminology does little in the way of explaining behaviour, even though it is concerned with the labelling of actors in a wide variety of interactional situations.

I will confine myself, in the following pages, to two interconnected facets of kinship: (a) the system of terminology by which Badagas identify certain others as sharing ancestors and responsibilities with them, i.e., 'being related'; and (b) the manipulations of this system so as to arrange marriage, transfer ownership of land, and assign responsibility for performing life-cyle rituals amongst one's 'relatives'. That familial interaction is not necessarily dominated by kinship obligations or guided by high ideals of behaviour has been illustrated by an example published earlier (Hockings 1982: 853). Even if that example proved inaccurate in some details, it could be paralleled by similar stories from any number of villages. In each case we would find that while rules for intrafamilial conduct do exist, as one central part of the Badagas' cultural tradition, personal considerations of one sort or another will very often modify the behaviour in quite unpredictable ways. The distinction between rules, i.e., institutional norms, and practice, i.e., the behaviour of individuals, will be a theme running through much of this chapter.

The extensive analysis of Dravidian kinship over the past half century, especially at the hands of Louis Dumont, Kathleen Gough, E.R. Leach, Thomas Trautmann and Nur Yalman, has rarely been insistent on maintaining a distinction between rules and practices, and authors have tended to shift from one kind of data to the other whenever it suited their argument, usually leaving the reader to assume that kinship practices are the rules in action. This may or may not be so in a particular case, but no identity between rules and practice should be presumed.

In Badaga kinship practice we certainly find that a great deal of accommodation of behaviour becomes necessary in daily life beyond the realm of kinship rules, since many of these have not been elaborated sufficiently to provide for all possible eventualities. Take, as an example, the ritual requirement that a daughter (and in fact her husband) must make a gift of one embroidered shawl at the funeral of each of her parents (see Figure 5.2): that may be identified as a rule, one that can be stated by informants and is normally followed; but if there are several daughters, some married and others not, who presents that one shawl? Here we can find no rule to guide behaviour. In one instance that I noted, the several daughters were married to men of differential wealth, and they had to agree to split the costs of one shawl evenly between them. In this situation the poorest of the husbands would press for a lower contribution, and the wealthier husbands would have to agree to his figure and contribute the same amount themselves so as not to embarrass him; then they jointly got a cheap shawl.

In another case three brothers each had one wife. The eldest had three sons and no daughters, the second three daughters, and the youngest one daughter. This meant that there would eventually be four married daughters available to present—with their husbands' financial support—six embroidered shawls at the six funerals expected at the parental level. But before any of these deaths occurred, one daughter was divorced. The husbands of the three daughters remaining married agreed that each would make himself responsible for the purchase of two shawls, and then they designated which two funerals each would contribute these to. Brothers sometimes divide up responsibility for their living sisters in a similar way, each thereby making himself responsible for the ceremonial and other requirements of one, two or more sisters, whether these women are married or not. In all of these examples, which I cull from recorded occurrences, there are no specific rules to guide behaviour in every eventuality. What we find instead is a rational attempt to compromise where necessary and fulfill kinship obligations where possible. Family enmities, premature deaths, lack of interest, divorce, absence, or poverty may all enter into the modification not only of kinship rules but of agreed-upon arrangements such as we have just instanced. Egalitarianism between siblings of the same sex is certainly one guiding principle here, even if circumstances make it difficult or perhaps impossible to honour.

Many of the Badaga kinship 'rules' are preferences rather than prescriptions. Take the 'rule' of cross-cousin marriage, for example, which is typical of Dravidian kinship systems generally. In the Badaga case a youth may marry (amongst others) either his FZD or his MBD, but there is a marked preference for a FZD and some good reasons for it. (Standard abbreviations are used here for kinship terms, viz.: B = brother; D = daughter; F = father; H = husband; M = mother; S = son; W = wife; Z = sister: thus MBD is mother's brother's daughter. Ego is our reference point.) One reason for the preference involves a feeling of status congruence. Families, it is believed, demean themselves somewhat by becoming bride-givers. This is acknowledged nowadays by the payment of a dowry, a new custom among the Badagas. But a young man's spiritual guide is not the family priest in this community; instead it is always his mother's brother, whom he calls *guru* and also accords much respect. It thus becomes incongruent if that particular man should give his daughter in marriage to the very youth he has counselled. Marriage with a FZD, or with the daughter of a mother's brother other than one's *guru,* gets around this emotional problem.

Patrilocality is another preference that is usually spoken of as an unbending rule. Yet there is in point of fact a term, *aḷiya se:tu,* for the live-in son-in-law, a young man who opts to live with his wife's family after their marriage. This has been considered an undignified and pitiful thing to do, but nevertheless it can bring real material advantages to a man whose wife has no brothers, and is a necessary alternative to virilocal residence in such a family. The epic ballad *Ba:la Sevana* deals with a man who moves into his father-in-law's village to help with the buffaloes, leaving his own mother in her village lamenting the loss of her only son, and bemoaning her fate since 'there will be nobody to set fire to her corpse'. It is interesting to note that Ba:la Sevana married into the Kunde (or Kunda) region, one that used to be so economically distressed that its children were often sold into bondage for a period of years, thereby becoming the household servants of Badagas in other parts of the Nilgiris. The live-in son-in-law was one institution that helped make up for the loss of male children in those bad years, when bondage was the only answer to the threat of starvation in that locality.

Patriliny and Patrilocality

Today the Badagas are successful cash-crop farmers, and those of the Kunde region are some of the wealthiest tea growers in the district. Until the early part of this century, on the other hand, they were all mainly farmers of millets and several other grains, which together with dairy produce provided their subsistence. When one delves further back in their history, to the 17th and 18th centuries when they were already well established on the Nilgiri hills but with a population of under 2,000, one finds that the Badagas were already millet farmers yet thought of themselves as primarily buffalo herdsmen. (This is reflected very clearly in a number of their epic ballads, which never mention agriculture.) Since each family or lineage used once to have its own herd of buffaloes, then it is legitimate for us to consider the kinship system in the Badaga case as having developed as a means of assigning and transferring ownership of and rights in property, especially cattle and houses, but to a lesser extent land too. We must remember that in the early days Badagas practised swidden agriculture, and the Nilgiri population density was so low that land really had no market value there and was apparently easy for a few hundred farmers to come by.

Now, keeping a herd of buffaloes requires adequate grazing and certain other conditions. One is the presence of a number of active men, typically brothers, who will keep the herd together while grazing and fend off tigers when possible. Women could not do this work: indeed, the epic poem *Ba:la Sevana* ridicules the mother of the hero for trying to drive the family's herd out to graze with a stick in her hand. Both swidden and ordinary plough agriculture also called for the combined efforts of several men (as well as a number of women), and so here too Badagas found a good reason for cultivating their fields as a joint family. Many still do so today. The point to be noted is that both the buffalo-herding and ox-ploughing and swidden cultivation were economic conditions that favoured patrilocality, the joint family, and brother/sister exchange at marriage—this latter a preference which maintained a balance of manpower between two intermarrying families or small settlements. If a youth married his FZD and her brother in turn married his MBD, brother/sister exchange would result, the ideal of cross-cousin marriage would be honoured, the two families involved would have asserted their equality, and close relations would continue between them. Where brother/sister exchange has occurred, divorce becomes rather more difficult because it places great psychological strains on the other couple, those who are not getting divorced.

The girls in this system invariably used to go off to another village in marriage shortly after menarche, where they would be needed to do housework and look after small children; do some sowing, weeding and reaping in the fields; and raise a new generation of farmers and buffalo herdsmen. In this married situation, the birth of a son means that a woman has largely fulfilled all three of her obligations to the family she has joined—for on marriage a Badaga girl relinquishes membership in her natal family, lineage, and village, and joins those of her husband. Her membership in them is made especially manifest when her husband dies and a son continues to support her in her husband's village; and when she too dies it is her husband's village and its headman who are responsible for conducting her funeral, with the collaboration of her husband's family.

The economic decision-making rests with the adult men: when to sow, what to plant in each kind of soil, when and where to move the cattle in search of new grazing, when to buy or sell them, when to harvest, and, in former centuries, when to shift the swidden. These decisions call for accurate topographical knowledge, and it is thus both appropriate and necessary that the detailed local knowledge which boys acquire in work and play should be put to good use when they become householders—in their natal villages, that is. Women are never expected to make such decisions. Hence patrilocality is a principle of survival, a fact which is only reinforced by the phenomenon of repeated divorces that might take one woman in her lifetime as a bride to two or three different villages, in each of which she would be something of a novice with regard to the local ecological conditions.

For a male, membership of his father's lineage—whether maximal, major, minor, or minimal—is inalienable. There may nowadays be little or no assertion of the solidarity of an individual with his lineage during his entire lifetime, but yet the tie remains. Some lineages do however still maintain in common a herd of buffaloes.

For females the descent situation is rather less clear. A woman at marriage joins the family and hence the lineage of her husband. This connection is not inalienable, on the other hand, for divorce may easily rupture it. The term for affines (*nantan/natta*) is applied by a man's family to all of his wife's natal family and lineage; it is similarly applied to all the agnatic relatives of any potential wife. This is a commonplace in Dravidian kinship systems. Among Badaga women we also find that a wife calls her own parents and brothers *natta/nantan,* and in anticipation of a certain married future may even use this term in reference to them while she is still a small, unmarried girl, just as her potential husbands would.

The Affines

The community based on patrilocal residence is a moral entity in which deference is enforced by authority. Relationships with one's agnates are always extensive and carefully maintained, and this contrasts with the narrowness of affinal relationships. The two categories are further differentiated in behaviour by the fact that a male can be fined by the village headman if he does not show the proper respect due to an agnate, and primarily to a member of his own village; but there is no fine for lack of respect to an affine.

Badagas have a saying, 'Although she is our sister, is her husband ours?'—i.e., there is no relationship among affines (Hockings 1988: 89, no. 9a–b). This means that Ego does not always recognize generation levels among his affines.

What is important, here as elsewhere in the kinship realm, is the age differential. Take, for example, the unexpected situation (Figure 3.1) of two men, Ego and 'N', who find that they are 'sons-in-law' to each other, because Ego is FZH to 'N' but is also a classificatory BS to the wife of 'N'. (Note: the letters placed here in single apostrophes, 'A', 'B', 'C', etc., stand for hypothetical people and so are like personal names. Letters placed in double quotation marks, e.g., "M", "F", etc., indicate classificatory rather than actual kin relationships, and should be read as 'in the category of mothers, but not actual mother', and so on.) Thus, if the permitted marriage that Figure 3.1 illustrates takes place, the two men do not know how to treat each other according to the rules that normally guide behaviour towards affines. The problem is resolved by determining which man is the older one and is thus entitled to the deference of the other.

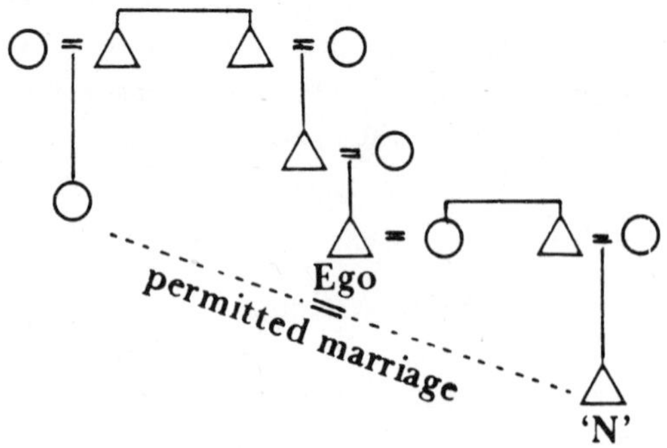

Figure 3.1. SONS-IN-LAW TO EACH OTHER

The same point about the non-recognition of affinal generation levels is brought out in a second example. In Figure 3.2 Ego should not show respect to 'M', although the latter is of a superior generation level, because it is permissible for 'M' to marry 'N'. Ego therefore calls 'M', his potential son-in-law, by name instead of by a kin term, as he would otherwise do in addressing an older person. It is important to note that in a society where remarriage is common and polygyny does occur, any married couple can quite probably trace the kin relationship linking them through two or even three different connections. In such a situation, aggravated as it is by the commonness of 'cross-generational' marriages, affinal generation levels really become unmanageable concepts, since Ego's spouse could conceivably be assigned to several different generation levels, from his point of view, depending on which way her relationship to him was traced through their kinship field.

Rights over the wife as genetrix rest fully with her husband and his lineage. Upon divorcing her he assumes control and responsibility for all of the children she has produced for him, boys and girls, and she is sent back to her father's house.

The fundamental principle of patriliny finds biological justification in the Badaga theory of conception. In their traditional view, a foetus develops solely from the semen of the father. The only biological role of the mother is a nurturing one, seen as rather analogous to manuring a field. Blood comes to the fœtus from the mother's stomach, where it has been made from digested food; and after the delivery her milk also comes from digested food in the stomach. While the mother's role is thus a crucial one in that she feeds the foetus and baby, it is not considered to develop from her flesh at all.

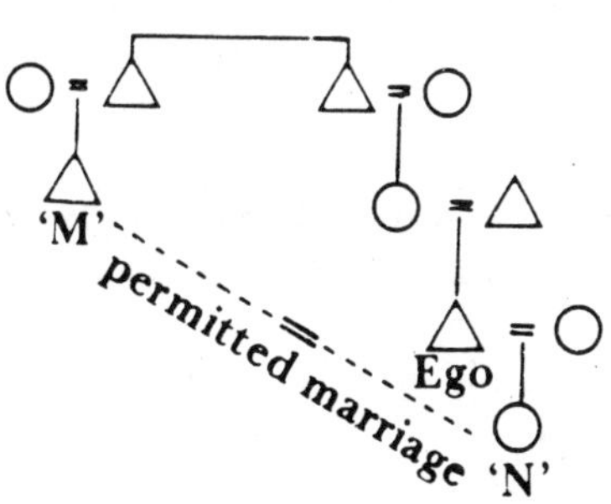

Figure 3.2. NOT RESPECTING HIGHER GENERATIONS

Visiting the Relatives: A Kin-based Institution

All Badagas are expected by their families to visit affinal and agnatic relatives with some regularity. The effect of this requirement is to keep the joint family ideal alive even after a household has broken up, and to sustain the ties with affines from whom one may at some future time need either a spouse or a loan of money.

One such rule is that all Badagas must eat with their close relatives at least once a year. 'Close relatives' here means those with whom one is involved in the performance of family ceremonies: it hence includes both one's closer agnates and some affines. Accordingly, a family either sends a message that the members are coming to visit some relatives, or will send an invitation for them to visit instead; and such visits involve minimally the eating of one meal. Everybody recognizes that if relatives do not eat together within a 12-month period, it means that there is some ill-feeling amongst them. Steps may even be taken by village elders to locate and rectify the source of the friction, so that it may not impede the performance of public ceremonies later on. There may of course be other reasons, such as distance or occupation, which make it impossible for relatives to get together; in this case they may still send gifts of food to each other once a year. In the modern day when business or study obligations can make these family feasts difficult to attend, some Badagas go so far as to prepare a special foodstuff before the 12-month period since the last such feast has elapsed, a foodstuff which can be kept indefinitely and be offered to relatives whenever convenient, even after the 12-month period is over.

A man visiting his wife's natal home is always an important guest whether or not he has received an invitation to come. Her family are all very respectful to him for fear he decrease the amount of his wife's contacts with them, which he is certainly in a position to do. For all family ceremonies or festivals in their village, they make sure he is among the first to be invited. When younger siblings of his wife are ready for marriage, he is consulted about a spouse, and may intensify the ties between the two families by suggesting his own sibling or parallel cousin. Hence, any villagers noticing that a man does not attend the ceremonies in which his wife's father is involved will conclude that he is snubbing his father-in-law for some reason.

Visits in the other direction, to the house of a married daughter or sister, are much more circumscribed. Her parents will not go to her husband's home without a good reason. They will however make occasional visits there just to emphasize the bond between the two families and to show that the parents still have affection for their daughter. Her brothers should equally have an invitation or a definite purpose for visiting her. In general, her natal family consider it rather lacking in dignity to visit her too often, and they will try to restrict the visits of any brother who seems especially fond of her. Her husband's family may well feel that very frequent visits from her brothers waste a woman's working time and can even become something of an economic drain on the household.

Adoption and Inheritance

Upon the death of a family head only his sons inherit his property (despite national laws giving daughters an equal right). The farmland and cattle are divided between sons, or else maintained undivided as joint family property. But with regard to the house, the Badagas have the inheritance institution of ultimogeniture: it is the youngest son who gets the house and who usually keeps his ageing mother and unmarried sisters in it. New houses might have to be built for the elder brothers. The ultimogeniture makes good sense in a society where often a girl was married by the age of 12, and where consequently the oldest son of an elderly widow might be no more than 13 or 14 years her junior. Her youngest son would more likely be a young man in the prime of life, more vigorous, with fewer dependents, and better able to provide for his old mother. By the time he has grown up, his elder brothers have commonly married, cleared fresh farmland (in earlier times), and built themselves new houses near this land (Rivers 1906: 560; Frazer 1918: 81).

Since the Badagas were until modern times non-literate, and even now write wills only in rare cases, there has always been a series of rules to handle the transmittal of property from the dead to the living, whether lineal male descendants or adopted sons. Their substitute for a written will is the *sa:la jo:li,* a verbal statement made by the dying man. Each wish or 'due' (*sa:la*) in it is normally followed by his relatives, but if any wish seems unfair they will immediately question him about it. Unfairness should here be construed as meaning an unequal division of property between the male heirs or too much generosity towards the wife and/or daughters. These people may try to reach a compromise with the dying man so that his wishes can later be followed without further argument.

There are no rules about particular kinds of property going to particular categories of relatives, with the one exception that when the head of the household dies his main house goes to his youngest son. Even so, the value of that house has to be divided between all the sons, so that the youngest may well have to give something to his elder brothers. The rights of the youngest son in the house are absolute. It is true that he must be ready to shelter his widowed mother there; yet if he wants to he can sell the house without prior consultation. The funerals of his father and mother will be held there, under the superintendence of their eldest son. Yet if the eldest son wants to bring Kota musicians to perform at the funeral, but the youngest son prohibits this, his will must prevail since it is now his house.

In 1963 I interviewed a sample of 301 Badaga males (aged 15 and above), and a further sample of 119 adult females. These people came from all parts of the Nilgiris district but included 101 from two of my sample villages; and one of the questions asked concerned the number of houses that they 'owned'. In Table 3.1 it will be seen that 38 per cent of the men did own houses, but only 19 per cent owned more than one house. The percentages of women 'owning' houses were at nearly all levels less than for the men, a fact that is explained by the presence of some uncared-for widows in the sample, and also some unmarried

Table 3.1
BADAGA HOUSE OWNERSHIP

Houses owned	Adult males	Adult females
Owns no home, or shares part of one with other relatives	61.8%	72.3%
Owns 1 house	18.9%	13.4%
Owns 2 houses	6.6%	3.4%
Owns 3 houses	3.0%	–
Owns 4 houses	2.7%	4.2%
Owns 5–9 houses	0.8%	–
Owns 10–29 houses	0.3%	0.8%
'Owns 30 or more houses'/d.k.	6.6%	5.0%
	(*N* = 301)	(*N* = 119)

daughters who did not feel like saying they 'owned' their fathers' houses. (I fear half-a-dozen young women were being facetious by saying they owned some unbelievably large number of houses.)

If a well-to-do man has built a subsidiary house somewhere, that one can be inherited by his eldest son. Failing that, the family home which is inherited and thenceforth owned by the youngest son may still be partitioned between his brothers. They would then be expected to give some rent or property to him in return.

Property is impartible until the owner's death, and then land is to be divided equally between his male heirs. The agreement on partition of the land ought to be written down and signed by the beneficiaries. Each gets a registration document (*paṭṭa*) from the state government, attested by the village accountant. For partition of other moveable property no documentation is called for: the beneficiaries simply agree to the division in the presence of the headman and some village elders. Occasionally a sick old man may choose to arrange the division amongst his sons while he is still alive.

If a man should happen to die when his wife is pregnant, his property will not be divided until after the delivery; and if a son is born, he too will become one of the inheritors. Thus a young widow will be watched by her husband's relatives for a month after her bereavement to see that she menstruates. They then declare that she is not pregnant, thus ensuring that she does not afterwards try to pass off an illegitimate son as an heir to her late husband's estate. Occasionally a son who is to inherit is considered insane or otherwise incapacitated. Under such circumstances a village headman and council would give his share of the inheritance directly to his son or else to whichever person was supporting him.

Inheritance problems most commonly arise when an ageing man has no sons. He may then marry a young woman, probably his second or third wife, in the hope that she will produce a son. (In early times, I was told, he might even encourage a younger brother to sleep with her.) Alternatively, he will adopt a son. At its simplest, this could involve bringing his brother's son or another agnatic male into the household. The latter could even begin to run the household and enjoy the property before the owner's death, and if the headman and the relatives accepted this situation the property might be fully transferred to this person before the old man died. Where no male descendant exists, and none has been adopted, the dead man's property is divided equally between his brothers, who are then obliged to apportion some of it for the support of his daughters and/or widow. Once she dies that portion reverts to the brothers. It may of course happen that one or two of his brothers have already died before a childless man dies. In that case the sons of those dead brothers would still inherit their portions. Several sons of one dead brother divide their father's share equally amongst themselves, but it is altogether no larger than the share that each of their living uncles receives.

The brother of a dead man does not formally adopt the orphaned children, but it is he who should bring them up and arrange their marriages. Once the male orphans are adults they take over their father's property from their uncle who has been managing it. In this situation the village council would nonetheless award a part of the property to that uncle in recompense for his services.

When brothers are dividing up an inheritance among themselves, they give a share called *tale ku:ru* ('head share') to their eldest brother's eldest son provided that he is older than every other brother's son. In effect this person is treated by them as a younger brother rather than a nephew except that his share is smaller than that of the brothers. When his own father, the eldest of the brothers, dies, his property is divided in equal portions in the usual manner amongst all of his sons. Since his eldest son already owns the 'head share', that is not touched. The end result is that the eldest son of an eldest brother often inherits a bit more property than his younger brothers do.

Kinship Vocabulary

It is a feature of Badaga speech that a third party is referred to by his connection to the person addressed. Thus when a man is speaking about his own wife, he does not say 'my wife', but refers to her by her relationship to the person he is addressing, even though this may involve quite complicated vocabulary. However, in the case where the man is talking to his FF about her, he will still not refer to his wife by her relationship through the speaker to his own FF, and so instead of calling her 'your grandson's wife', Ego will describe her as "'X's' mother" where 'X' is Ego's own child. The same terms are used for children by both male and female speakers, but the reference may link a speaker to a child through either of its parents. It is interesting in this context to note what happens when two brothers marry two sisters, as in Figure 3.3.

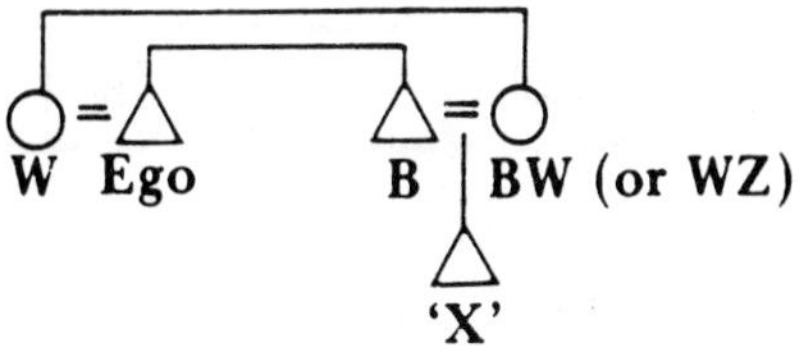

Figure 3.3. TWO BROTHERS MARRYING TWO SISTERS

In this situation we find that Ego calls 'X' his BS, while Ego's wife calls 'X' her ZS. It is one small reflection of sibling solidarity.

The near universal distinctions of sex are mirrored in the terminology (see Table 3.2). Thus a term ending in *-i* (*mammi* for the first ascending generation collaterals) will connote a female while the same term ending in *-a* (*mamma* for the first ascending generation collaterals also) will be used for a male. (This suffix differentiation is general in the Dravidian languages and not reserved just for kinship terms.)

Generational division is prevalent and especially obvious for the second and third ascending and second descending generations. All grandfathers and great-grandfathers—paternal or maternal—are referred to as *ayya*, all grandmothers and great-grandmothers as *hette*. Sons, grandsons as well as all small boys tend to be called *ma:ti* or *tamma*. Granddaughters and grandsons are also referred to in descriptive terminology.

Inheritance and respect patterns within a single generation place emphasis upon who is elder (e) or younger (y) and this too is reflected in the kinship terms. An elder brother is *aṇṇa*, a younger one is *tamma*. An elder sister is *akka*, a younger one *amme*. Even in generations other than Ego's *a* prefix (*doḍḍa* for elder, *kunna* or *cikka* for younger) is applied to some terms to emphasize whether a relative is younger or older than the person through whom Ego is related to him or her. A few examples are these: *appa* is father, and a FeB would be called *doḍḍa appa* while FyB would be *kunna appa* (*ha:lappa* is also common); the mother is *auve*, and a MZS would be *doḍḍa auve ma:ti* or *cikka auve ma:ti* depending on the relative seniority of the MZ; *ayya* is any male of the second or third generation ascending, but a FFeB is called *doḍḍa ayya* while FFyB is *kunna ayya*.

Agnates of generation levels senior to Ego are addressed by him using a kin term. Those who are of generations equal or junior to Ego's

Generation	Lineal agnates	Collateral agnates	Affines
third ascending second ascending	FFF, MFF *ayya* FFB, MFB FF, MF FM, MM, FMZ, MMZ, FFZ		WFF, WMF MMM, FFM *hette* WFFW, WMFW
first ascending	*appa* F *auve* M	*appa* FB *mammi* FZ, MBW	*mamma* or *appa* MZH *guru* MeB *mamma* FZH, WF, WMB, WFB *auve* FBW, WFZ, WMZ *mammi* WM, WMZ
Ego's generation	Ego *aṇṇu* eB *tamma* yB *akka* eZ *amme* yZ	*aṇṇa* FBeS *tamma* FByS *daidaka:ra* = parallel cousins *akka* FBeD *amme* FByD	*gaṇḍa* H *ba:va* ZH, WB, H *ba:maida* ZH, WB, MBS *heṇḍru* W *amme* WyZ *akka* WeZ, WFZ *attige* BW, WBW, FZD
first descending	*ma:ti* S *heṇṇu* D	*aṇṇa ma:ti* eBS *tamma ma:ti* yBS *aṇṇana heṇṇu* eBD *tammana heṇṇu* yBD	*aḷiya* DH, BDH *ayyabeṭṭa* DH, BDH *akka-* or *ammeya ma:ti* eZS, yZS *sose* SW, BSW *akkana heṇṇu* eZD *ammeya heṇṇu* yZD
second descending	*heṇṇuna ma:ti* DS *ma:tina ma:ti* SS *ma:ti na heṇṇu* SD *heṇṇu na heṇṇu* DD *mammakka* = grandchildren, brothers' grandchildren, of both sexes		*mammaku:su* = spouse of a grandchild
third descending	*marumakka*/ *mammakka* = great grandchildren of either sex		—

Table 3.2

BADAGA KINSHIP TERMINOLOGY

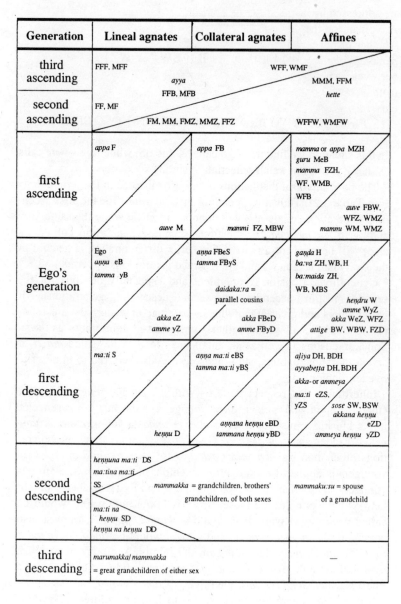

are addressed by name, even when the individuals are older than Ego is. A woman, on the other hand, should never utter her husband's name, whether or not he is present. If asked for it, she may describe another person altogether, and then add, 'It's the same name as his.' She does not even refer to her husband by the standard kin term, *gaṇḍa,* but instead says *enna mane avaka,* 'my house-keeper' or more usually *enna maneyama, enna gaṇḍumaga,* 'my male person'.

The Badagas display what Murdock (1949: 223–36) has termed a Dakota-type terminology. They also have the Iroquois terminology (bifurcate-merging) which emphasizes Ego's lineage by: (1) equating father and his brothers (*appa*) but separating off mother's brothers (*mamma*): (2) equating mother and her sisters (*auve*) but separating off father's sisters (*mammi*). The Iroquois bifurcate-merging cousin terminology specifically separates out the cross-cousins who can be married (FZD—*mammi heṇṇu*; MBD—*mamma(na) heṇṇu*) from the sisters (eZ—*akka*; yZ—*amme*) and parallel cousins (FBD—*akka, amme,* and MZD—*doḍḍa auve heṇṇu* [e] or *cikka auve heṇṇu* [y]) whom one cannot marry. By calling Ego's Z and FBD by the same terms, Ego's patrilineage is also emphasized. Dakota-type terminology also assumes patrilineages and patriclans which, as already stated, the Badagas possess.

It should be noted that the generational level within the agnatic group is extremely important. This importance is stressed even to the extent that if Ego's DD is married to a man related as "F" to Ego, then she has to be treated as a "M" by Ego. And if ZD marries a "F" relation to Ego then she is considered "M" to Ego even though he is *guru* to her. Females automatically assume the generation levels of the men they marry (Figures 3.13 and 7.6). In the example illustrated (Figure 3.4), if 'A' marries 'B', which may happen if 'A' is younger than 'B', then she calls 'C' 'father's wife', not 'brother's daughter'.

The same general principle is illustrated by another possible though hypothetical situation. In Figure 3.5, 'B' marries 'C' and later dies, leaving her with several sons. The widow 'C' is then encouraged to marry 'A', probably a widower himself. If she has a son 'D' by him, then 'D' is one generation senior to 'E', 'F', and 'G', although he is younger than any of them. 'E' thus has to call 'D' "father". Later at the inheritance of 'A's' property, 'D' gets one half of it, while the other half is shared by 'E', 'F', and 'G'.

Another possible situation does give some weight to female generation level. Here (Figure 3.6) 'A' has married 'B' but then produced no

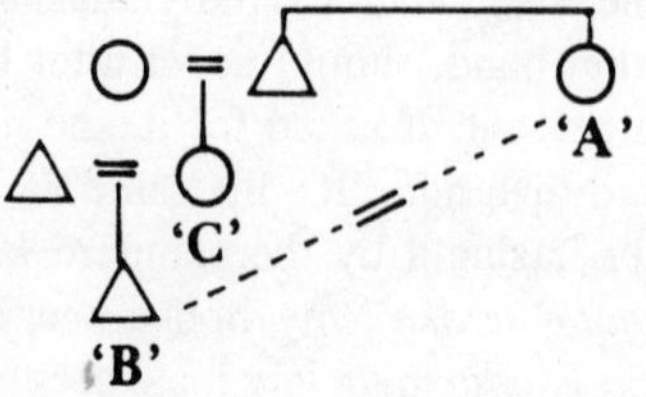

Figure 3.4. WOMEN ASSUME THEIR HUSBAND'S GENERATION LEVEL

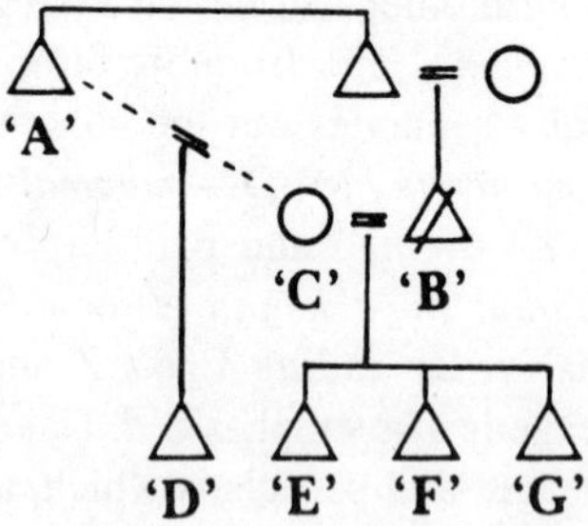

Figure 3.5. HALF-BROTHER BECOMES A FATHER

children, so 'B' arranges for a second wife, and marries 'C', his first wife's niece. A son 'Y' is then born to 'C', but subsequently to this 'A' also produces a son 'X'. In this situation 'Y' must always call 'X' 'elder brother' although in point of fact 'X' is younger than 'Y'.

Yet another instance of how relationship is determined by one's husband's generation level is found in the following case (Figure 3.7). 'B's' wife died and so he married 'C', who is classified as a 'daughter' to his son-in-law 'D'. She therefore calls 'D' 'father' and he calls her

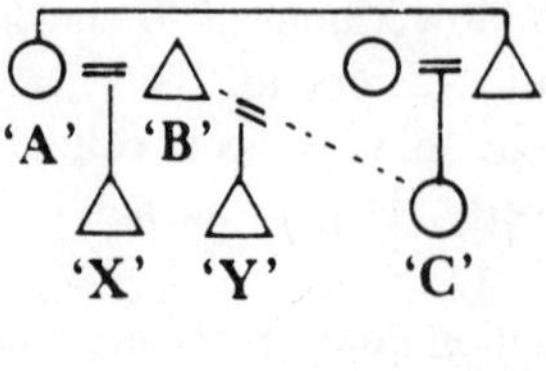

Figure 3.6. FEMALE GENERATION LEVEL

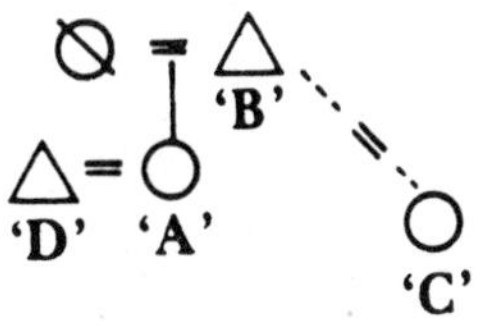

Figure 3.7. REMARRIAGE AFTER THE WIFE'S DEATH

'daughter'. 'C' also calls 'A' 'mother' since she is seen by her as a 'father's' wife, but at the same time 'A' calls 'C' 'mother' too, because 'C' is also a father's wife for 'A'.

Marriage Patterns

While there is a hierarchy among the various phratries that make up Badaga society, and while there are definite marriage rules linking particular clans (i.e., clan P tends to find most or all of its spouses in clan Q of the same phratry, and *vice versa*), this hierarchy and set of marriage preferences is not supported by a belief concerning purity and pollution of the individual. In fact, one can argue that hypergamy and hypogamy are equally acceptable to the Badagas—something that is perhaps unique for any Indian community. Thus a girl *or* youth of the high-status vegetarian Ha:ruva clan may marry a person of a non-vegetarian Gauḍa clan without any adverse comment; nothing worse in fact than some inconveniences at mealtimes. Instead of purity/pollution considerations, it is shame or prestige that becomes important during marriage arrangements. Thus everybody wants to marry a headman's child but nobody wants to marry an orphan. A large joint family is considered a strong and respectable social unit—even if a new bride sometimes feels less than welcome in it—and people do seek marriage connections with it for their daughters.

Badagas will state that the preferred marriage partner is a FZD. However, one can also marry a MBD or a WZ. They will also explain that the following cannot be married: Z, FZ, FW, FBD, BD, SD, half-Z, WBW, WMZ, WM, WZD, MZD, FBW, BW, SW, ZD, DD, WBD, MZ, and MBW (see Table 3.2). Males do not generally marry women older than themselves although they can marry a woman in an ascending generational position so long as she is in a 'potential wife' category.

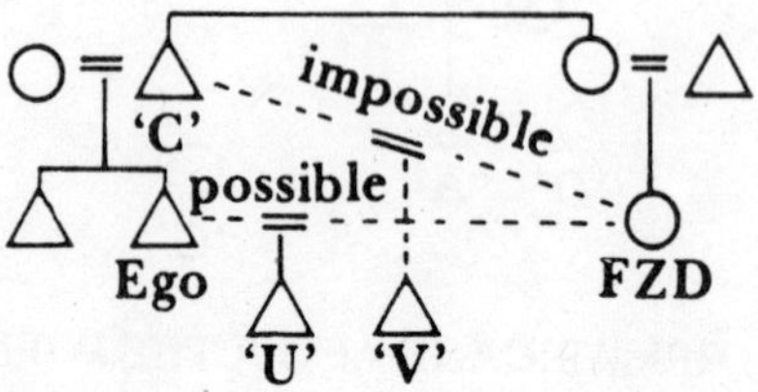

Figure 3.8. INHERITANCE OF THE FATHER'S PROPERTY

Given that Badagas prefer marriage with the cross-cousins, and given further that most property is to be divided equally between all sons of a man, ZD-marriage—found elsewhere in south India—appears to be an impossible preference for them (with the exception of the anomalous case illustrated in Figure 3.12). It cannot be tolerated because it could lead to ambiguities concerning descent and inheritance. Picture the situation (Figure 3.8) where Ego marries his FZD, which is indeed the prime Badaga preference: if Ego's father 'C' has two sons, then Ego inherits half of his father's property. If Ego marries his FZD and also has only one son, 'U', the latter inherits all of Ego's property. But if Ego's father were to have sexual access to his ZD when she was his own son's wife living in his house, and if further Ego died before his father and then the woman gave birth to a son 'V' shortly afterwards, some serious questions would arise about inheritance. For if 'V' were considered the son of 'C', then Ego and 'V' would each inherit a third of 'C's' property, and 'U' would inherit all of Ego's property. But if 'V' were considered the son of Ego, Ego would inherit a half of his father's property, and 'U' and 'V' would each inherit a half of Ego's. To avoid quarrels over the inheritance, and further quarrels over sexual access to a woman living in the joint family, a man cannot marry or have relations with his SW, even when she is his own ZD, and even though the son may have pre-deceased his father.

There are four basic groups into which males cannot marry. They are:

(1) *Females of Ego's own patrilineage*: This would include women who are born into his patrilineage: Z, FZ, FBD, MBW, BD, SD, half-Z (when the common parent was the father), WBW, WMZ, WM, WZD. All females marrying into Ego's lineage would also be included here (including M, MZ, FBW, and FW), for a woman becomes part of her

husband's lineage when she marries. When brother/sister exchange does in fact occur, a WBW would be equivalent to Ego's own Z; a WMZ or a WM or a MBW would equal FZ; and WZD would be Ego's own daughter if he had married his WZ.
(2) *Parallel cousins*: MZD could be Ego's half-Z if his father had married the MZ. FBD is included here but has also been mentioned under the previous heading.
(3) *Daughters of offspring and of siblings*: A SD, ZD, DD, and WBD (who would be a ZD when brother/sister exchange occurred) are in this category.
(4) *Wives of other lineage males*: FW and FBW, FFBW and FM are encompassed in this category. As already stated, these women become part of Ego's lineage once they marry into it.

The basic people Ego can marry (FZD, MBD, BWZ and WZ) are cross-cousins, ideally with brother/sister exchange linking two families.
Badagas see all of their phratry as either affine or agnate. As a woman is assimilated into her husband's lineage when she marries, she therefore becomes an agnate to the husband rather than remaining an affine. An affine could basically be described then as a potential wife or an actual or potential wife-giver.

Marriage Possibilities: Some Interesting Anomalies

Owing to the fact that the ideal marriage partner—actual FZD or MBD—is not always available, certain unusual marriage possibilities have been noted among the Badagas. In the following section I will examine them, using hypothetical examples offered by my informants.

The first thing to understand in Figure 3.9 is that although 'Y' is of an earlier generation than Ego (seemingly his great-grandmother), she should be of younger age than Ego if he is to marry her. Ego's mother was not in 'X's' lineage after her marriage, thus her father 'X' and his father would be of a wife-giving lineage and the marriage would hence be unusual but still permissible.

I can combine two other cases (Figures 3.10 and 3.11) because basically they are the same: a man is marrying his father's second wife's sister. Although this would put the bride in a classificatory "M" role, the marriage would be permissible for the following reasons (I will use Figure 3.10 to illustrate): Ego's father's second wife was not in Ego's

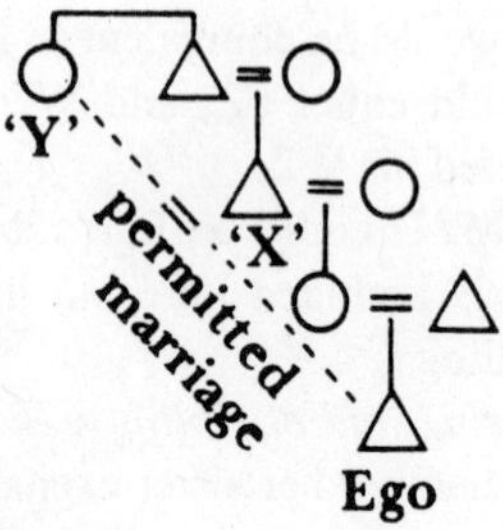

Figure 3.9. MARRYING A GREAT-GRANDMOTHER

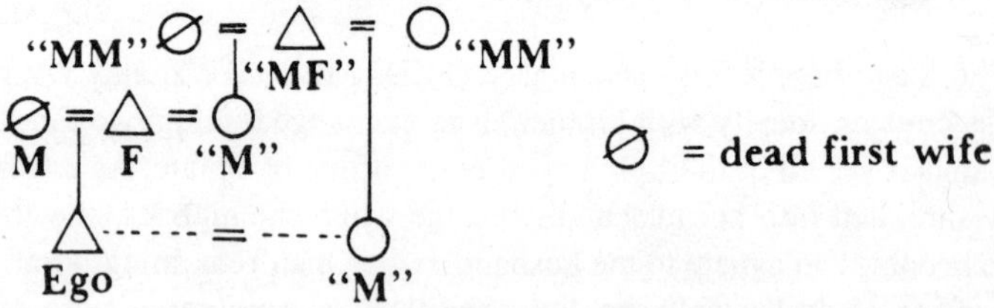

Figure 3.10. MARRYING THE FATHER'S SECOND WIFE'S SISTER (*i*)

lineage before her marriage, thus her parents would not be in Ego's lineage. It is assumed that Ego's father's second wife's father's second wife ("MM") was not a member of Ego's lineage before marriage but was a member of some third lineage. Thus, as long as the daughter of this woman in no way fits into a category of people that Ego cannot marry because of agnatic relationship to a member of Ego's own lineage, she is a permissible marriage partner, although considered "M".

In Figure 3.7 we find that while Ego's son 'P' can marry the ZD of Ego, his other son 'Q' by Ego's "ZD" cannot marry Ego's actual ZD, as this would be considered tantamount to mother/son incest (i.e., a MMD marriage). What is technically called 'uncle/niece marriage' is possible, but only under certain special circumstances. In Figure 3.12, Ego cannot marry his actual ZD because he is always a *guru* to her, and has to perform certain ceremonies for her which preclude his being her husband too. He could however marry his sister's step-daughter, a classificatory "ZD", since she will have someone other than Ego to act as her *guru*; this would be permissible provided the second wife of the ZH

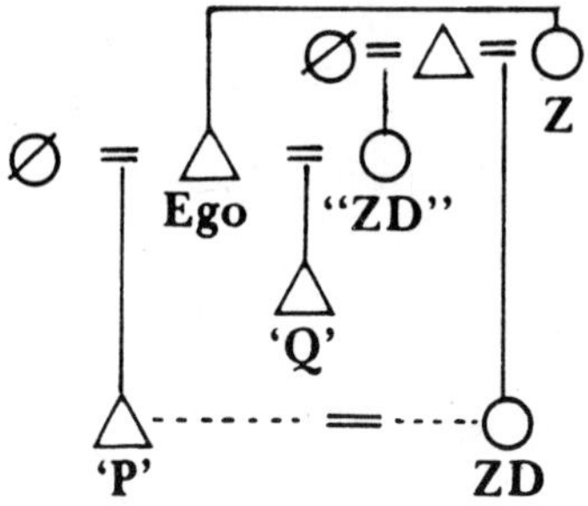

Figure 3.11. MARRYING THE FATHER'S SECOND WIFE'S SISTER (*ii*)

had been taken from a lineage other than Ego's.

Figure 3.13 simply illustrates the fact, mentioned earlier, that a male Ego may marry women of different generation levels all at once or one after another. Badagas generally do not marry women older than themselves, so it is to be assumed that all of these women are younger than Ego. As relationship is only counted on the paternal side, any or all of these marriages would be permissible, simultaneously or sequentially. If 'Q' has a son 'Y' by Ego, while 'R' has a son 'X' by some other man, 'X' will call 'Y' 'father'. If Ego subsequently marries 'R', 'X' will then start to call 'Y' 'brother'.

Even though 'Q' (who is married to 'R') is, in Figure 3.14, in a classificatory "M" relationship to 'R', Ego can still marry 'X'. The FM of 'X' is not of Ego's lineage. Assuming that the FFZSW is no longer of Ego's lineage and is not related through any members of Ego's lineage in such a way as to preclude the marriage, then this union is permissible. It should be pointed out that there is more than one way to 'skin a cat' and

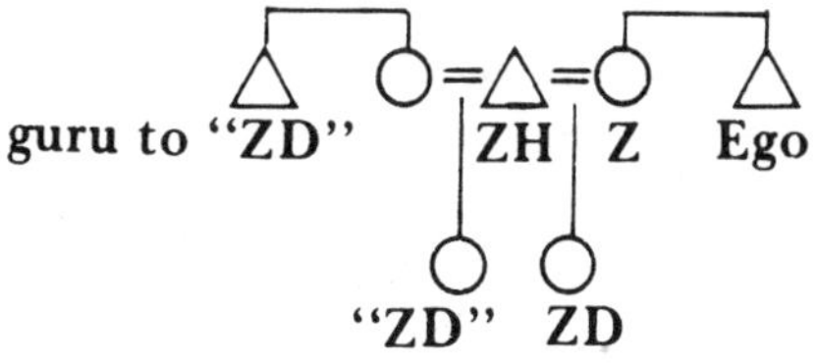

Figure 3.12. UNCLE/NIECE MARRIAGE

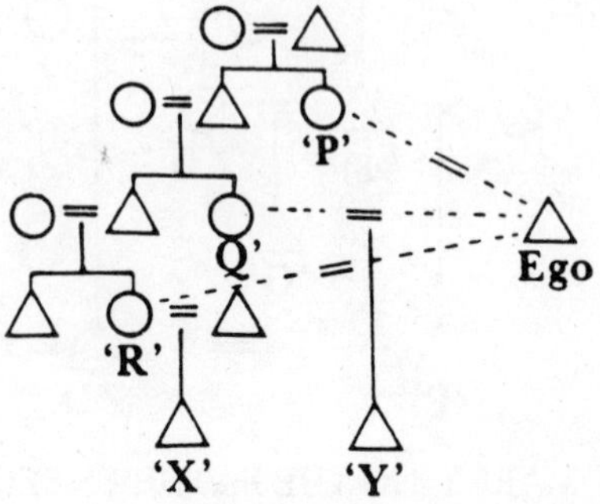

Figure 3.13. MARRYING WOMEN OF DIFFERENT GENERATION LEVELS

in any of these marriage situations the relationship between the two potential spouses can be figured in such a way as to allow the marriage. If in fact Ego were related to 'X' so as to prohibit the marriage with her, but if this relationship were distant enough, it might simply be overlooked provided no one protested.

Pervasive Patterns of Exchange

In the larger phratries the Badagas have a generalized system of marital exchange, a preferential pattern of bilateral cross-cousin marriage. Such a system allows some of the clans to differ in status from others. In the smaller phratries consisting of no more than two clans, however, restricted exchange occurs, still with the bilateral cross-cousin marriage.

Because of their theory of patriliny, namely that every infant is formed solely from the semen of its father, the two prime cross-cousins who constitute potential spouses are in an equivalent relationship for Ego. From a Badaga male's point of view, these possibilities are MBD and FZHD—in other words, the daughter of a bride-taker (or bride-giver) who belongs to another lineage and clan. Once married, a brother and sister belong to different but linked clans, and so it is appropriate that their children should marry each other. If the pattern of brother/sister exchange continues for more than one generation the MBD *is* also a man's FZHD. Marriage between such cross-cousins thus has the effect of balancing out the bride-debt in alternating generations: in

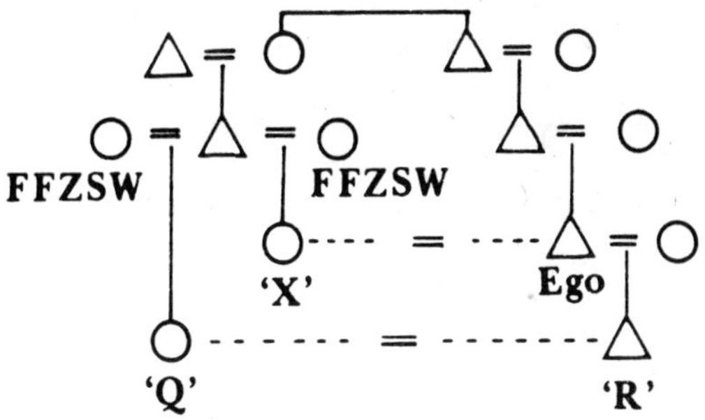

Figure 3.14. MARRIAGE MUST BE OUTSIDE ONE'S LINEAGE

every generation the males take brides from those lineages to which their fathers had sent their own sisters in marriage. This reciprocity can be demonstrated statistically. Table 6.1 (on p. 132) takes the example of Hulla:ḍa village, which is centrally located on the Nilgiri Plateau, and traces all available information on the number of wives who have joined it from other villages and the number of Hulla:ḍa girls who have gone in marriage to other villages, up to 1990. There had been (in 1963, at the first census) 98 women who had married into the village from other clans. Ten of these people were elderly widows whose connections with their natal villages had been broken off by death and time. Sixty other women, born in Hulla:ḍa, were known to be married elsewhere and still kept up some social ties, such as periodic visiting, with this, their natal village. Four women born there had done something quite atypical by marrying within Hulla:ḍa itself; but this situation was acceptable because it did not contravene the rule of clan exogamy. In each case either the husband or the wife belonged to a family of a 'Badaga Outsider' lineage and another clan who had settled in this village fairly recently from elsewhere. By 1990 the number of cases was distinctly larger but the aforementioned proportions similar. It should be pointed out that there was a tendency among the villagers to forget all about old widowed women, originally from this village, who had been living elsewhere for periods of up to 70 years; and this explains why the first pair of columns in Table 6.1 (p. 132) generally has a lesser number of women than does the second pair.

It is remarkable that, out of well over a hundred suitable villages, a mere four of them account for about 60 per cent of Hulla:ḍa's marriage ties. The normal practice here keeps the number of villages and families

Table 3.3
RECIPROCITY IN MARRIAGE, BY LINEAGES, IN 1963

Hulla:ḍa lineages	Women from:	Known women to:	Women from:	Known women to:	Women from:	Known women to:
	Tumanaṭṭi		Mainele		Kundesappe	
Doḍḍa Mane	3	1	3	0	2	1
Me:l Ke:ri	9	1	5	0	2	3
Naḍu Mane	3	3	4	4	3	3
Osa Mane	6	4	7	5	2	3
'Outsiders'	8	4	2	3	2	3

involved in its marriage network down to manageable proportions. There is definitely an ideal and a strong tendency towards reciprocity between two Badaga villages in the exchange of women. Thus 56 per cent of all wives coming to Hulla:ḍa by 1990 came from the first four villages named in Table 6.1; 60 per cent of the daughters married away from Hulla:ḍa who still maintained social ties there were also living in those same four villages. This reciprocity is felt to be the responsibility of each lineage, and it is to some extent reflected in the data of Table 3.3 concerning the marriage patterns of each Hulla:ḍa lineage, as well as in the fact that the referred percentages in 1963, one generation earlier, had been 54 and 61 respectively. (For simplicity, only the villages with which Hulla:ḍa was linked by more than 20 marriages in 1963 have been included in Table 3.3.) This table shows that at that time Naḍu Mane lineage had a perfect record of reciprocity with those villages. Osa Mane and the 'Badaga Outsiders' (relatively recent settlers from elsewhere) manifested at least a tolerable degree of reciprocity. In fact, complete reciprocity is not often attainable because nubile women may not have been available in a particular village when needed for a marriage, or required in Hulla:ḍa when available elsewhere. When a lineage has sent a disproportionately greater number of women in marriage to another village than it has received brides from that place, a sense of uneasiness with the situation is usually felt, as might be the attitude towards Doḍḍa Mane and Me:l Ke:ri lineages.

Cross-cousin marriage does sometimes take the form of sister exchange, an ideally reciprocal arrangement. If a young man does not marry his ZHZ (who might be either a MBD or FZD to him), he commonly marries a related neighbour of his ZH. This alliance offers an easy resolution to the practical problem of finding a go-between and arranging the alliance: if his relatives do not disapprove, the youth has the excuse of visiting his married sisters while getting a chance to contact and evaluate prospective brides in their village, and the fathers of these girls can feel more secure about arranging a marriage with a family already linked to their village and perhaps the joint family through previous marriages.

NOTES

1. This chapter is little changed from Hockings (1982). I am indebted to Othmar Gächter, editor-in-chief of *Anthropos*, for permission to reproduce that article here. Kathryn L. Cooper and Sayoko Morioka did preliminary analyses of the kinship system for me.

PART II

LIFE AND DEATH IN THE HOUSEHOLD

Chapter 4

M.N. THESINGH: A LIFE STORY

One life; – a little gleam of Time between two eternities.
— Thomas Carlyle

In order to suggest a more dynamic view of how the household operates, Part II will first present the life story of a single farmer as a palliative to any over-generalization. Then, in Chapter 5 I examine a crisis which arises from time to time in virtually every household: the death of one member. Death is part of the dynamic—along with marriage and birth—by which household structure conventionally changes. To illustrate the preceding generalizations (see Chapter 3), let me now present the short life-story of one informant, a farmer, in his own words.

M.N. Thesingh (Plate 11) was born in O:rana:yi on 28 August 1912. A month later, during the naming ceremony for the infant, he was given the name of Isvarayya; but the baby made a great fuss, and this was taken to mean that he did not like the name. So his father's mother called him Thesingh, after a mythical warrior, and he used no other name. (M.N. were the initials of his grandfather and father.) When he grew up he learnt that he was in fact the hereditary headman (*gauḍa*) of his village, though he never chose to occupy the position; but it meant that from his family connections he had a thorough grasp on the kinship and social organization of the Badagas, and also a certain amount of influence. As an informant to me, one of his best qualities was that if he did not know the answer to a query he said so, and then worked out who would be the best people to search out for that topic. Lesser men would have made up some sort of answer. Although he had rarely heard a lecture in his life, he was quite capable of giving one, extemporizing for hours on a topic: here was one informant who never needed 'pumping'. As he had a clear understanding of what anthropology was, he would go into lengthy ethnographic detail, citing and translating appropriate proverbs and covering the subject in a well-ordered way with scarcely any prompting. While his intellectual qualities proved to be quite remarkable, and he was the ideal anthropologist's informant — eventually working with David G. Mandelbaum, M. B. Emeneau and Christiane Pilot-Raichoor, as well as myself — his life as a Badaga farmer was no doubt unique but was not particularly unusual. He described it to me in the following words.

*

I am Thesingh. I was born on 28th of August 1912. It is said so, and also it was written by my father in a book, and I found it. But until, say, about the fourth or fifth year of age I was not aware of anything. I cannot remember it, and I know that. I think it may have been during my fifth year I was sent to school in Kolmel. Kolmel then was the nearest school to our village; because in those times there were no schools as nowadays. When I went to the school I saw that my relations were the masters there. My maternal uncle was the infants' class teacher and the other uncle was the headmaster. And so I was not troubled in going to school. And usually in those days the last class teachers must come to the villages and must collect students and then go to the school with all the students: it was because the students were not going to school in those days, and further, the parents also were not interested in sending the children to school. So my uncles came to my house, and I remember that my maternal uncle was carrying me on his shoulders to school. And after leaving the school every day I would trouble my uncle to give me some pictures, otherwise I wouldn't come to school tomorrow. In that way, I remember, I went to school and I studied. When I studied in the school, there was infants' class first. (Nowadays it is first standard, second standard, and so on. In those days there were only infants' class and then first standard.) And so for infants' class I remember that there was no boy from O:rana:yi except me, and the other boys were only Kotas: so, among the Kota boys, I was studying, and I studied up to fifth class in the Kolmel school.

Because it is very near our village, we are all very friendly with the Kotas, and in those times were having Kota music for a funeral, and all that. Now some people do not call the Kotas, and I am on their side: that means I don't require Kota music for a funeral. When we rejected the Kotas the friendship was broken; but we are not enemies. With K. Sulli, yes, there is a difference, because he is an educated man [see Mandelbaum 1960]; and so whenever I go to Kolmel he will stop me for some 5 or 10 minutes, and we will sit together and talk about civilization and all that. Even if we happen to meet in

Ooty [i.e., Ootacamund] or some other place we will talk for some 10 or 15 minutes because he is my friend. That is a separate thing, an individual thing.

And when I was studying in the third class or so my father died. And to my grandfather there were only two sons: my father and his brother. And when I was about 9 or 10 my father died and all the properties were not divided. So my uncle—that means my father's brother—and my grandfather, they were managing the whole property in a combined manner.

And after I passed the fifth class year, there were 13 students. That means from Me:l Oḍeyaraṭṭi and from Tambaṭṭi and Muttina:ḍu, and even one or two students from Ka:ṭe:ri, they were all coming to the school at Kolmel. And when we were examined, I remember there were 13 students: out of 13 only two passed. At that time Panguli Menon was the inspector. He gave me a certificate saying that I was first, and J. Beḷḷan from Tambaṭṭi was second; and all the other 11 students they failed. And then I was sent to the Ke:ti school: at that time higher elementary only was in Ke:ti. And so I had to walk from here to Ke:ti when I was 11 or so. Then I was walking all that way for three years, and I studied there and completed eighth standard. When I was studying in the eighth standard there were 18 students. Then there was the inspector (I think I remember Sambasiva Pillai), and he examined us, and only two had passed out of the 18. Out of the two I was first and A.K. Hiriyan from Accanakal was second.

But then before I passed the examination—I think the examination was during June, after the vacation—during April, April 1st, my grandfather died. When he died I remember very well that he called my uncle, that means my father's brother, and told him that he had enquired from the teachers in Ke:ti if I would pass. 'So if Thesingh passes the school, please send him to the high school, to Ooty, and educate him as far as you can.' And thus saying, he died.

After the death of my grandfather, the property was still a combined one. It was not divided because we were children, very small boys. I was the first son to my father and I had two other brothers and one sister: leaving the four, my father had died. So if it is divided we cannot manage the property; so my uncle was keeping all the property in a combined manner and he was managing it. And he took me to the high school and I produced the certificate for the headmaster. At that time there was only one high school in the Nilgiris: it was the Municipal High School; (and now I think there are maybe 65–70 high schools). In those days only some moneyed men, some well-to-do men can afford to send their children to the high school. And my uncle took me there and he kept me in a lodging hotel, a Brahmin hotel, because we are vegetarians, and I was admitted in the school. When my uncle showed the certificate to the headmaster, he didn't accept it. They again placed an examination, and we had to write the examination, and not only that, but also they examined orally. When we were examined there were 22 students with me. They all applied for the fourth form (there was a form system at the high school); and out of the 22 only two passed; and out of them I was one, and I was admitted in the school.

And it was very curious to me, because till that time I was not in touch with towns; and so I was left in Ooty, and my studies and the standard also were not fitted to that high school. So I had to work hard, and my uncle made an arrangement with the master there, Mr Ramachandra Rao, to give tuition for me. I studied there, and once a week I would come to my house, in O:rana:yi, that is: on Friday evening I would come and on Monday morning go to school again. At that time there were no buses or anything of the kind: only the train. So I had to walk to Lovedale for the first train, and the first train was about 10:00 in Lovedale and it would carry me to Ooty by 10:15. The school was at 10:30, so I was hurrying to the lodging room, as I had to take all the books, and then hurry to the school. Sometimes I would be five minutes or so late, so my uncle made an arrangement with the headmaster that I must be excused if I was late 5 or 10 minutes because I cannot walk from O:rana:yi to Ooty and reach there at the usual time. In that way I studied, and the next year I was promoted to the fifth form. (I want to say that nowadays it is Tamil medium up to Pre-University Course; but in those days from the fourth form up it was all English medium. Every subject except the vernacular was in English.)

Nowadays students are going to school in shirts, and bush-shirts, and all that: in those days a student must come to the school with coat and trousers or *dhōtis*; and even in wearing the dress it must be in the right manner: if a student is to wear a cap it should not be slanted, it should be straight. And all the buttons must be buttoned up: if one is not, he will be fined by the teacher. That was the way.

I want to tell you one thing, that in those days I was having my hair knotted, because we should not crop the head. (We are Lingayats and vegetarians, you know, so we should not crop the head: if we have to cut the hair, it is below our caste.) But in the fourth form, when I was sitting there I was a little boy, about 14 or so, and there are three benches all around. On the first bench are only little boys, the second bench a bigger size of boy, and the third bench were the biggest boys. And so I was sitting in the first row because I was small, and so the big students behind me would make some mischief by catching my hair and pulling it down. So I was troubled, and when I came to the village weekly I told my uncle all this trouble, and he was laughing at that. And I asked my grandmother if she would mind, if I could be permitted to crop it, but all the family did not accept it. So there was one man from Ha:laṭṭi who was some relation to me, and because Ha:laṭṭi people always come to Ooty and I was studying there he usually came there every Tuesday and used to see me, and occasionally he gave me two annas. So one day I wept before him, saying that I must get cropped, and so on. So he promised me that he would come one Friday evening, and that I must be ready there. When I would go to my house in O:rana:yi, he would accompany me. On that day he came to me as he promised and he took me to some saloon in Ooty and cropped my head; and then we both came to our village. Without him I could not come because these people would abuse me; so with him I came to my house. At that time my grandmother and my brothers and my mother were living in one house and my uncle with his wife and family were living in another house; but the property was combined property. And on that day, say, about 6:30 or 7:00, we reached our home and when we stepped on the veranda my grandmother—she was awaiting my arrival because on Friday evening anyhow I would come—when she saw that my hair was cropped, she abused me and did not allow me into the house. And till my uncle came I was kept outside. And when he came he made some compromise with my grandmother. I was cuffed outside the house and this thread was cut, and my grandmother took some fire and she put it on my tongue, and then only was I allowed in the house.

When I went to the fifth form there were some optional subjects we should choose; and so I came to my uncle and told him everything, because he—that means, the parent or guardian—must apply to the headmaster that such and such a subject may be granted to me, to the student. So he asked me, 'What are the subjects in the school that you must choose?' I told him that there is a typewriting division in the school, shorthand and typewriting; and so he applied for typewriting and shorthand, that is, business and commercial. There is another division, mathematics and physics, and another, history and vernacular: there were three divisions. And when I applied for this commercial one, the headmaster one or two days after the application was sent called me to the office specially, so I went there. He told me this is a second-grade subject, commercial and business, and brilliant students must choose physics and mathematics, 'So you must apply for mathematics and physics,' and so on. 'Yes Sir, then I will do it; but I do not know about this,' I told him. And so he told me, 'I have entered you to the physics and mathematics division and when you go again to your village you take a sheet, an application form, and have it signed by your uncle, and bring it,' and so on. Thus I was entered because only brilliant students are selected for the mathematics and physics section; and so I studied mathematics and physics, and I passed the fifth form and when in the sixth form there was S.S.L.C., the school final examination. Nowadays if I look back, if I think about these examinations, it was not an examination, I can say. In those days the examination was held, during my period, in the YMCA Hall near the cash bazaar; and at the time we attended there were 76 students: 18 private students—not from the Nilgiris, I may say, but from Coimbatore and other places—and 58 students from the high school: we 76 attended the examination, in 1929 or '30, I don't remember exactly. Out of 76 only nine passed, eight from the school and one from the private candidates; and out of those nine I was one. Of course I got brilliant marks, and in mathematics I got 100 per cent in the S.S.L.C. examination.

At that public examination, you see, when the students are allowed into the examination room they will be checked all over—that means all their pockets and everything and even you must take off your cap and show it. Only a pen and, in some physics or mathematics examination a geometry box, are you allowed—and that too you must open and show to the examiner; and only then will you be allowed into the room. And during the examination, if you want to go to urinate or something two police constables will accompany you. And when the examiner wants to stop the examination—it was two-and-a-half hours—when the second hand comes to the last moment he will say, 'Stop writing! Hold up your hands!' and all students must hold their pens up in their hands. Otherwise if, suppose, there is a sentence, 'He went to Ooty' and you have only written 'He went to' (Ooty you have not yet written); but if you just want to complete that, he will come and write there, 'extra time taken', so minus some marks. And so that way, when he says that, we must hold up our hands. But for myself the time of two-and-a-half hours was more, because early in the examination I revised once, so it was plenty of time for me. And thus I passed the S.S.L.C.

But in those days my parents and my guardians who were above me were not educated: they did not know about all that. In those days in Coimbatore there was no full college: there was only one college and that too only up to F.A. (Fellow of Arts; in those days there was no Pre-University Course and all that: there was Intermediate and B.A. Intermediate, which means F.A. for two years, then B.A. for two years; and in Coimbatore there was only a F.A. college.) Otherwise we would have to go to Madras for a B.A.; and in all Palghat district there was only F.A., no full college. I think I got the results during July and as soon as I got the results, after one week or so, I received a prospectus and a letter and some papers from the Presidency College, Madras. I had not applied at all, but the post came to my address. And when I opened it, it was from Presidency College, saying that, 'If you are wishing to continue your studies in college, we are ready to admit you. Please go through the prospectus and if you are interested come on such and such a date with such and such fees,' and so on. I took this to my headmaster, because we did not know about this. He told me that Presidency College was a first-class college in Madras at that time, so they will select students from the results. 'They themselves select brilliant students and so of their own wish they write to you; so they have selected you themselves. You can go if you want,' he told me. And when I came here I told everything, every detail, to my uncle. And my uncle was not of course a bad man; as far as I know, he was good, and he tried to take me to Madras. When this was happening, my grandmother told my uncle that I should not be sent to Madras, because in those days I think nobody had gone as far as Coimbatore. So she was not prepared to allow me to go to Madras for studies. Anyhow, my uncle made some compromise with my grandmother, and he called some relations from Ka:ṭe:ri, and they all spoke together and made some arrangements to send me to Madras. The last day, when we were to start for Madras, my grandmother suddenly fell across the doorway and she was lying there saying, 'If you want to send my grandson to Madras, let him step over me and let him go, otherwise I won't allow it!'

So on that day I was stopped; and then I was disgusted, so to say, about everything, and I was keeping quiet at home. I would not go outside, I would not go to town, and I did not go to the fields, and I would not do any work. When all this was going on my grandmother made arrangements with my uncle and relations that if I married, then everything would come to some solution, 'otherwise he will go mad,' and so on. And so all the relatives compelled me to marry. I was not ready to marry, and I put off that matter for one year or one-and-a-half years. Anyhow, I was induced by my friends, and I think in 1931, I don't know exactly when, but between November 15th and December 15th I was married. Then I was looking after my fields and my agriculture.

Before my marriage I was interested to give some lessons with English books to the boys here who are nearly of my age, with very many standards: some boys do not even know the alphabet and some have studied up to second or third standard. And so, according to their standard, I gave them lessons, and it was only during the night. My friends would go to work during the daytime, and during the night, after meals, when we should go to bed, we would usually gather in my office room and I was giving them lessons for nearly one-and-a-half years. During that time my uncle wanted to get some girl as wife for me, and my present wife was once called from

Ka:ṭe:ri secretly, and she was shown to me by my grandmother. This was purposely done, but I did not realise it was happening: one day this girl was taken to my house and my grandmother called me from the office, saying something about eating. And when I went into the house I saw this girl. After wasting some five or ten minutes I again went to my office room. Then at once my grandmother came to me and asked me, 'See this girl! She is a fair girl, and I think it is good if you marry her.' But I abused my grandmother and told her, 'I am not going to marry her! Of course this is not the girl: I will choose some other girl,' and so on, just to put off the marriage. But when we were studying and when I was giving lessons to my friends one night, my uncle at about 10 or 11 o'clock came to my grandmother and he opened the door from outside. My grandmother was thinking that it might have been some thieves because it was about midnight. So she knocked at my office room by the secret window-like door: this was a secret entrance from the inner house of my grandmothers' to the office room. In those days they were afraid of thieves because my grandfather was a well-to-do man having some cash, so she—my grandmother—made that arrangement to have a separate entrance into the nearest room; and by that entrance she knocked for me. And by then my uncle outside said with a loud voice that it's not a thief, that he had come with a girl for me, and so he wanted my grandmother to open the door. Thus she opened the door and so we came to know that he has brought a girl for me. And according to our custom, when a wife is brought for a husband, the husband should not be in the house when the wife enters. Because of this my friends, even though it was midnight, went to their houses, and I was in the next neighbours' house. In the morning, at about 4 or 5 o'clock, I came to my office room. And the custom was that when a new bride comes to the house, the husband can see the wife only after she has brought some water to the house. So for this purpose they were arranging to take my wife to the water tank to fetch water in the very early morning. I advised my grandmother, telling her that if the girl is to go for water, the villagers will see my wife, and my wife is now wearing a *dhōti,* but if she is to be my wife she must be in a sari. And there was only one sari-like cloth in my house, and that was purchased for my sister. She was not married at that time, she was of course a little one. Even then I was interested to have some cloth like a sari for my sister, and it was in my house. And I advised my grandmother to give that cloth to my wife and to make her wear that cloth—it would be just like a sari—and only with that must she go to the water, otherwise I won't marry her. On this matter, in those days, there was a quarrel between the people who are interested in wearing saris and people who are against it; because in Ka:ṭe:ri some people were wearing saris, only one or two women, and against that there were some big persons saying they should not wear it: if they wore a sari , they should be outcasted. And when my wife was brought from Ka:ṭe:ri there were two other persons who accompanied her, two affines: they were on the opposite side, so they did not allow my wife to wear a sari. Thus there was a dispute between my uncle and the other two persons, and without eating or staying for the rituals they went away. And ignoring them my uncle sanctioned my want, and the sari was given to my wife and she went for water. And then I accepted her and we married. This was my marriage.

After my marriage, I was not particular about getting any job. I was interested in agriculture. I was, so to say, the head of my family, though it was not divided; and I was in agriculture, and was cultivating potatoes. In those times we generally did not use this artificial manure, only natural manure, but I was the third or fourth person in our village to use the artificial manure. It was from Parry's—they supplied manure; and I cultivated to a large extent. I was cultivating more potatoes and sending them to Meṭṭu-pālaiyam, and I think at that time I had about 10 acres, more than 10 acres. But now I sold nearly all the land, and on some leased land I raised tea. I sold some of the land, even the leased land, as tea estate. Now I am cultivating potatoes, not on my own land but on leased lands. And in 1938 or '39, I don't remember exactly, we made a partition between my uncle and myself, that means my brothers and myself and my uncle. Then I became the head of the family, and we were three brothers.

For five years there were no children. In those days my grandmother was giving medicines for pregnancy as my mother is now doing, and for girls who have no children. For all the other villages and other girls she was giving medicines. For me, after five years, she gives medicine but it is not successful. But during the fifth year, in 1935, my wife got pregnant, and in 1936 my son was born.

And when I was managing this separate family, in 1937, Dr Mandelbaum came to Ooty. I happened to meet him in May, and he called me to Ooty. So I went there once, and he wanted to learn something from me. I was not prepared to tell everything; but Dr Mandelbaum explained, 'I am not taking any secrets from you, but I want to learn these things.' Anyhow, he returned again and he wanted to study the Kotas, so he appointed me as an interpreter, and asked me to bring some Kotas. So I worked in Ooty for about 60 or 70 days with some Kotas; that is, a Kota from Kolmel, and some other day a Kota from Me:na:ḍ (Me:na:ḍ means Kunda), and some other day one from Triciga:ḍ—different Kota men and women. I worked with them, translating what they told. In this way I was with him about two or three months, and he paid me something (I don't remember what), he took down notes, and then went away. And again I was cultivating.

I worked for Emeneau for only 15 days or so. He wanted to learn about the language, that is, he wanted to differentiate some sounds .... He wanted to know the stages and turning of the tongue, and he held up a torch. He learned some such things from me, and then left [see Emeneau 1939]. Dr Mandelbaum, when he left here, promised that he would come during 1941 or '42; but the Great War, the Second War broke out, and he didn't come. In 1948 or '49 he came, and I worked at St. George's Homes with Dr Mandelbaum for a longer time, I think it may have been some three or four months, while he was living there.

And in the meantime I had got children and I was cultivating. During that wartime, in May 1942, I was appointed as a manager in N.S. Iyah's estate. You know there is a high school in Pa:laḍa named N.S. Iyah High School: it is that N.S. Iyah, who had some estates there.[1] And I was paid 400 rupees per month over all the commissions at that time. For four years and seven months I worked there, and I resigned that job, and again I came to cultivation. Around 1948 cultivation failed, year after year: I do not know why it failed, but I was losing my property. Around 1959 Mandelbaum came again, but he did not study anything. In 1959 or '60 the late blight came. At that time I cultivated 50 or 60 bags on the Ooty side, and all failed: I was put to a loss of about 5,000 or 6,000 rupees. After that I was not able to cultivate more potatoes, and year by year the late blight and early blight, potato diseases, were increasing; and moreover my family grew in number year by year, so I was not in a position to support my family. Thus I am not cultivating more now, only these millets: ra:gi, sa:me and wheat, and all these things. Only last year, 1971, I cultivated some potatoes and I had a gain, and this year I am not so poor—I am just increasing.

Now in 1963 or '64 I married a girl from Tanga:ḍu to my son, and my son was employed in the cordite factory during 1960 or '61. He was appointed as a labourer, and now he's promoted from labourer to senior, and so on, and is now a maistry. He has a chance of getting A-grade maistry in six months or so, and then he has every chance to get a supervisor's post. And in the course of three years or so he'll be paid more than 500 or 600 rupees. Then I think there'll be progress for my family; and further, I have got four of my daughters married and now there is no expense, so to say, with only one daughter left.

This is the state, and now I can tell you that I am old: my son is doing everything in supporting the family. Because my old friends come, and I have no duties, and I just go to the fields, that's all. Because it is the rainy season there is no work here now; so that boy is interested to keep me in the house and support me in everything, and he wants me to be in a good state. My duties? I am thinking that only one girl is left: if I get her married, I think that my duty is finished. So I am praying to God, when I do *pūja*, 'Please, I think I have no work here: please, just one thing, the marriage of this last girl, and take me to You. If there are any sins, please pardon all these sins, and hereafter don't give me any births. And I'll come to You, please take me to You', and so on. That is my prayer.

*

Thesingh lived for another 10 years. On 25 July 1976 his mother K. Sithamma died in her 86th year, after having confided much of her therapeutic knowledge to the anthropologist (Plate 10; see Hockings 1980b). She was totally unlettered, yet told me that she thought college education was good for girls. While it might be true, as most parents feared, that a girl could be tempted while away at college, a good girl would not succumb to this. And, she added, many an uneducated girl does give way to temptation in the village itself! In 1977 Thesingh worked as an informant for the French linguist, Christiane Pilot-Raichoor (see Hockings and Pilot-Raichoor 1992). Then in 1981 he conducted two of my four village censuses, as he had done twice before. In that same year he was able to pay off all of his various loans and even purchase an acre of farmland. But then, at the beginning of 1982, he became quite sick, and passed away in his home on May 5, 1982, just before reaching 70—which many long years before someone had foretold would be the time of his death. Following the Lingayat custom, he was buried in a sitting position in the graveyard outside his village.

The story of my friend Thesingh's life, told in his own words, brings out several salient features of the villager's condition. First, there is a clear pattern of the household's fortunes being linked to the vicissitudes of the agricultural seasons and decisions made by the head of household. Second, the costs of getting daughters married are today a pervasive burden. Third, there is a keen awareness of the hurdles in educational advancement and how they are to be handled; similarly, of the phases of promotion in a government job. And finally, one sees clearly how an old lady's whim—that in the absence of a husband or son, she needed her adult grandson to be at home in readiness to officiate at her funeral—stood in the way of that grandson's prospects for serious advancement with a Madras University education (he would have been the first Badaga from his immediate area to go there). His acceding to his grandmother's wishes on this point in 1930 was probably what committed the family to financial instability for several generations to come. A grandson of Thesingh's recently became the first member of this family to acquire some college education locally; yet today a Bachelor's degree no longer brings any guarantee of good employment prospects, as it would have done in the 1930s.

NOTES

1. N.S. Iyah's tea estate, called 'Benukal', contained 64 acs. of plantation.

Chapter 5

THE EBB OF LIFE

Kind Nature's signal of retreat.
— Samuel Johnson

Orientation to the Mortuary Rites

In generalizing about the social life of Badagas I have to present the regularities wherever I have seen them running through daily activities and my quantifications. These regularities, by the very fact of their repetition, appear as the central supports of the social system. They are reflected in the organization and meaning of mortuary rites. A truism of modern studies of the funeral anywhere is that it is viewed as 'a reassertion of the social order at the time of death' (Bloch and Parry 1982: 6). This chapter does not refute that functionalist position, indeed accepts it, but also tries to show just how the social order is supported in the arrangement of the complex mortuary ceremonies to which the Badagas are heir.

It is my view that the funeral is the most complex of all Badaga ceremonies because it is the most important; and it is the most important because, being a communal rather than a family ceremony (as a naming or wedding is), it makes clearer to people than anything else does just what are the key roles, the status differentials, the order of social precedence and the dominant values in the society. In its pre-modern incarnation that society was also preliterate; which means that its youth then lacked any means of formally *studying* how their own society was organized. Ceremonies, I will assert, made up for this deficiency in learning by providing visible demonstrations of the most necessary of all lessons: how to behave correctly in society. One of my informants in Ke:ti hazarded a guess that by the time it was his turn he might have attended something like 300 local funerals—perhaps four or five a year.

Such a repertoire will have shown him everyone he knows acting out a formal role *vis-à-vis* his or her fellows; will show such roles changing through the years; and furthermore will allow him to correlate variations in the performance of the ceremony with the social status of each particular dead person. For children the lesson is crucial.

This kind of subcultural variation is itself important, as the very comparison between any one funeral and others that an individual has previously attended is a subtle teacher about social structure.

This is not to imply that the general function of funeral ceremonies is only a pedagogical one. They certainly have a psychological impact on all participants, because they allow for a socially approved release of emotion, and the ritual locates each individual precisely in the social fabric, while highlighting the power differences, the socio-political structure, that will continue to be fundamental to inter-personal relations in this society. The resultant reaffirmation of status serves to reintegrate each person in the social fabric and to reassert the most general principles of social order.

A brief, and rather sketchy, descriptive account of the Badaga funeral by an Irish priest early in the present century may serve as an introduction to the topic.

> When death is drawing near a gold coin... dipped in ghi is given to the dying man to swallow. If he is too far gone, the coin is tied round his right arm. If the coin slip down or is swallowed easily it is well with him—he needs both gold and ghi for his long journey, the one to sustain his strength, the other to fee the guardian of the fairy-like bridge that spans the dreaded river... If, after death, the coin is still in the man's mouth, it is taken as a bad omen, and is attributed to the unfortunate Kurumbas, who are made to suffer for it ....
>
> After death the corpse is kept in the house till the funeral car [*i.e.* catafalque] is completed and all the relatives have assembled. Cremation must not, however, take place on a Thursday. News of the death is sent to distant hamlets by one of the lower Badagas [*i.e.* Toreyas] ....
>
> On the appointed day the corpse is taken on a charpoy or native cane-cot to an open space, and a buffalo led three times around it. The right hand of the corpse is passed three times over the horns of the animal; milk is drawn and poured into the mouth of the corpse. The funeral car is composed of either five or eleven tiers, decorated with cloths or streamers. One tier is decorated with black chintz. But for this display the poor are allowed to substitute a cot and umbrella. The body, washed and dressed in coat and turban and a new cloth, is now placed in the lowest story. Two silver coins—rupees answer the

purpose—are stuck on the forehead. Beneath the body are placed a crowbar and baskets containing parched paddy, [crude sugar, millet flour], etc. The women now rush to the cot, sit round it, and keep up a long, weird wailing for some hours, one set being relieved by another. Then the Badaga men come forward and salute the corpse by touching the head. The women are allowed to touch the feet only. This done, a dance is formed round the bier to the strains of Kota music. The dancers are dressed in gaudy petticoats and small turbans worn for the occasion. If the corpse be that of a very old man, his feet are washed and the water drunk by the men of the village, who believe that thereby their sins are forgiven. In the afternoon the car is brought near to the burning ground, and is hacked to pieces to make the pyre. The widow of the deceased, now dressed in red, takes off her 'nose-screw,' some wire from her ear-rings, and a lock of her hair, and ties them in the cloth of her dead husband. This denotes the severance of the marriage tie.

The 'after-death confession,' a most touching and impressive ceremony, is next made by an elder of the tribe, who stands at the head of the corpse. By a conventional mode of expression the sum total of sins a Badaga may have committed is said to be thirteen thousand. Admitting the deceased had committed them all, the reciter cries, 'Stay not his flight to God's pure feet,' and the whole assembly chant the refrain, 'Stay not his flight.' The reciter now enters on a long catalogue of misdeeds, such as 'the estranging of brothers', 'shifting the boundary line', 'sweeping with a broom', telling lies, going to sleep after seeing an eclipse, using a calf set free at a funeral, showing the wrong path, ingratitude to the priest, to all of which the audience make answer, 'It is a sin.' At the end of the long enumeration comes the hopeful prayer, 'Though there be thirteen thousand such sins may they all go with the calf set free to-day.' Then follows a series of touching aspirations: 'May his sins be forgiven; may the door of heaven be opened,' etc. Then, amid solemn silence, the calf is let loose and, like the Jewish scapegoat, it may never be used for any sort of work. The corpse is next placed on the funeral pyre, which is lit by the eldest son, while he says, 'Being begotten by my father and my mother I, in the presence of all and the Deva [God], set fire to the head after the manner of my ancestors.' Next day the ashes are searched for the wife's jewels and for the little gold coin, with which the Badagas are very reluctant to part. Two days after the funeral the relatives shave their heads and beards in token of mourning. (Slightly abridged from MacNamara 1912: 151–53)

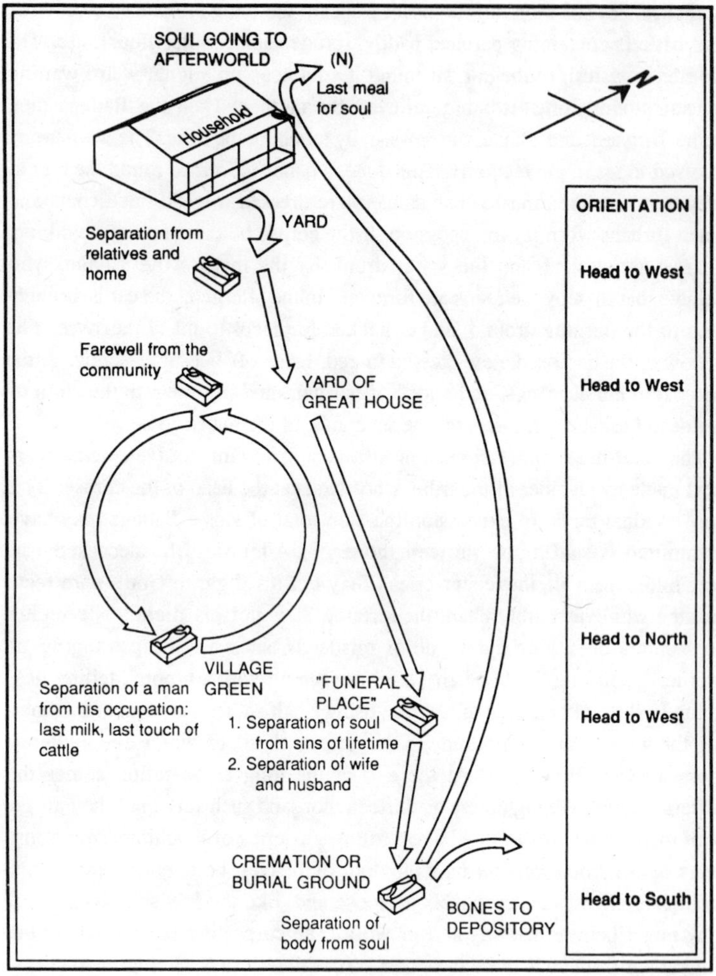

Figure 5.1. MOVEMENTS OF THE CORPSE DURING A FUNERAL

From first to last during such a funeral, the household is intimately involved with the proceedings (which are described in more detail by Natesa Sastri 1892, Noble and Noble 1965, and Hockings 1999). On the first day following the death the corpse lies on a much-decorated cot, first in front of the bereaved house, then on the 'funeral yard' (*sa:vu ke:ri*), while friends and relatives come to pay their respects and comfort the grieving family. Later the corpse moves on by stages to its cremation or burial; but since the soul may still be lurking around the house, the final act of the funeral a few days after death involves putting a parting gift of food on the roof of the Great House to help provision the soul on its journey. The rites of separation which constitute a funeral are plotted schematically in Figures 5.1 and 5.3. They indicate no expectation that the soul will ever return by means of reincarnation, for in Badaga thinking this has been its final worldly birth.

Among Hindu Badagas there are two main forms of disposal: Lingayats, whether Adikari, Kaṇakka, Woḍeya or Kongaru, bury their dead, whereas the other phratries and clans commonly cremate the dead. If a Ha:ruva woman had married a Lingayat she will be given a Lingayat burial as she is united with her husband's family. Christian Badagas only bury their dead, and normally in a designated cemetery.[1]

Analysis of the Funeral

My analysis has been based on the traditional Badaga funeral; but already 30 years ago it was evident that numerous items in the ritual were being omitted, partly through faulty memory, partly through disinclination, and partly to save time. Villagers allowed that the sequence of events was sometimes not followed 'correctly'. Many villages have not seen Kota musicians in a lifetime. It is thus not uncommon for much of the ritual to be omitted today, while some items have been moved in the protocol. Some people now do the grain-placing ceremony with rice on the front yard, others — just very close relatives — actually do it inside the house before removing the corpse. And although women are not supposed to proceed beyond the Funeral Grass, as they have no further rites to perform, I have often seen them throwing earth or food offerings into the grave. Nor does anyone stop them any more if they come to the final *korumbu* rites.

The normal state of a Badaga being is one of purity, *sudda,* which is promoted by daily worship and forbearance from sinning. That state is suspended, or rather replaced temporarily, by one of impurity, *ti:ṭu,* under certain circumstances: contact with menses, childbirth and death. (Impurity could also be acquired in other situations, such as marriage, intercourse, or just eating with a non-Badaga.)

From the moment of death the corpse and all immediate family are polluted, and people remain so until the conclusion of the funeral. Use of the household's milk cupboard (*ha:go:ṭu*; Figure 1.1), if still extant, is now suspended, for milk is a pure substance. There is normally a liminal phase, a transitional period, between the earlier state of *sudda* in the household and the moment of death: this is when the invalid lies, corpse-like, inside the house as relatives come from elsewhere to bless him or her and seek blessings in turn. After the *ti:ṭu* which all (except priests) who participate in the funeral will suffer, a second liminal phase follows immediately on the disposal of the corpse, and continues for the nearer relatives until the departing spirit has been fed at the *korumbu* rites (Figure 5.3).

It is noticeable that, in the Badaga Hindu funeral, unlike the Christian one, priests do not play a central role. A priest will often be present, but only as a member of the village community or a relative of the deceased. He tries to maintain a certain sanctity and residual purity by not eating any of the food offered, for it is polluted by its association with death. He never touches the corpse by way of respecting it. (There is no special procedure for the funeral of a priest.)

The funeral itself, for all its multitude of petty rules and ritual observations, has a quadripartite dramaturgical structure, which is not in a chronological sequence but rather one of themes that pervade the entire observation.

The loss of a member of the community, especially of an elderly one, threatens the stability not just of his household but of the community as a whole; which explains why the hamlet headman rather than a son of the deceased is given charge of the operations. His prime concern is to re-establish the social stability that has just been ruptured. This is done —unconsciously, no doubt—by performing rituals that promote four basic principles of social stability, namely hierarchy and social divisions, auspiciousness, sex distinctions, and kin relationships. A dramatic tension is present throughout the funeral, because each of these principles is associated with a counter-activity of serious import, as we shall see.

A fundamental principle of Badaga society is that each and every phratry is divided into clans; or more specifically into intermarrying categories which anthropologists label agnates and affines. At every point in the funeral this separation is re-emphasized, through quite specific rules about what the agnates must do and what affines can or cannot do. There seems to be a latent tension between the two categories during the funeral, arising from the fact that the local people, the agnates, have either lost a daughter entrusted to them by the affines, or alternatively have lost her husband, which hence raises questions about the widow's future security.

The social hierarchy is threatened by evil spirits which are thought to be attracted under these sorrowful circumstances, and congregate especially near any funeral ground. The idea is common to many cultures:

> It is a belief familiar to anthropologists ... that the body is at certain times particularly exposed to the attacks of evil spirits ...; its diminished powers of resistance have to be reinforced by magical means. The period which follows death is particularly dangerous in this respect; that is why the corpse must be exorcised and be forearmed against demons. This preoccupation inspires, at least partly, the ablutions and various rites connected with the body immediately after death: such as, for instance, the custom of closing the eyes and other orifices of the body with coins or beads; it also imposes on the survivors the duty of keeping the deceased company during this dreaded period, to keep watch by his side and to beat gongs frequently in order to keep malignant spirits at bay (Hertz 1960: 33–34).

Evil spirits (*pe:i*) are the embodiment of ambiguity: they are neither human nor divine, neither male nor female, neither living nor dead, they are present yet invisible. At numerous points in the funeral they need to be thwarted to protect social stability. Thus we see Badaga men and women dancing energetically in front of a gaily decorated, temporary abode for the corpse. The impression is given of a sort of second wedding, with the widow dressed rather like a bride, covering her face up while weeping, and wearing a special nose-ring. Men shout '*o: hau hau*' in jubilation, as they do at auspicious ceremonies. In 19th century reports we read of shots fired in the air, and can still see processions with knife-blades, some of fantastic design, held in the air with points upwards. Even the half limes stuck on some of these blades are believed to 'put lime juice in the eyes' of the hovering spirits. Iron protects the living from evil spirits: so heavy iron tools are carried in procession to the graveyard, though some are not actually used there. The site of the grave is first stabbed with a crowbar. Elsewhere milk and grain are thrown onto the ground. Drums are beaten and horns sounded during the procession to make a frightful noise; while food and coins are thrown in the air. Probably too the giving of a turban to a female corpse, and the ritual requirement that some men dance in what might be viewed as a female dress, a pleated skirt, are further attempts to confuse the evil spirits by sexual ambiguity; some men nowadays dress up as Kotas, Todas, Kuṟumbas or even Europeans, which is considered very humorous (cf. Elmore 1915: 35–40). Throughout the entire ceremony the rigidity of the social hierarchy is re-emphasized by reference to generation levels especially, to the separation of affines from agnates, and the particular role obligations of Kotas and Todas (low- and high-status tribes), as well as Toreyas and Woḍeyas (low- and high-status Badaga phratries).

Second, auspiciousness must be sought in the face of this most inauspicious of events: there are thus many references to it. Three in particular is a lucky number, and nine is the luckiest of all. It is therefore easy to see why so many things occur in threes throughout the entire funeral; and why the Woḍeyas invite nine elders to eat at the *tiṭṭi* ceremony in the bereaved house. All even numbers are inauspicious, however; a belief which perhaps explains a curious saying: 'If death [comes] today, [it will be] three days by tomorrow' (Hockings 1988: 105, Item no. 54). The morrow is of course the commonest day for holding the funeral, at least in modern times. The concept applies equally in counting the days of menstruation, for the second day of that impurity is also considered to be the third; for example in counting when will be the 'sixth' day on which a woman may return to her kitchen duties. (For purposes of calculation, each day ends at the next sunrise, not at midnight.) Considering the day after the death as the 'third' day may further confuse the evil spirits with a sense of auspiciousness and celebration, and so counteract their baleful influence on the vulnerable mourners.

A third basic principle of social life, emphasized throughout the funeral, is the distinction between the sexes. There are different rules of procedure for a male and a female corpse, and different ritual obligations for male and female participants throughout. At all points they stand, sit or walk somewhat separate from each other. Whenever something is done to or for the corpse, it is the men who do it but the women who weep. Yet everyone is polluted, including the corpse. It will only become purified by fire, or alternatively by being sanctified as a *linga* inside the Lingayat grave. Women will be habitually impure, for a few days every month; whereas for men this present impurity is an exceptional circumstance, though like women's pollution it is something quite beyond their control. The insistence on sexual distinctions in role-playing throughout the ceremony is an attempt to evade the levelling effect of pollution and so reassert one of the major principles of social stability. Shaving, the act which separates men from the impurity they have suffered, is not required of women, for they will soon be polluted again. In this respect too, men are different.

Fourth, kin relationships are ruptured by the death of a family member. Virtually all categories of kin are obliged to make some kind of offering, whether food, cloth, implements, money or music, during the course of the funeral, as the diagram makes clear (Figure 5.2). Not only do such gifts reaffirm specific kin ties, but they also reflect the time depth of the community, since they can be regarded as linking one generation with another—in both marriages and funerals. Here it may be mentioned that the materials given to the Badaga corpse are in general very similar to those offered to a dead Brahmin in other parts of India, which are cotton cloth, iron vessels, salt, earth, grain, clarified butter, balls of sweets, and a cow (Stevenson 1920: 140–41). In this respect, as well as in the methods of disposal and the evasive measures directed against evil spirits, the Badagas affirm their Hindu ancestry, (if not an ancient Brahmin connection).

Yet counter to the stated obligations to assert their links with the dead individual, there is a measured process of separation going on throughout the entire funeral, beginning from the moment that life leaves the body, and ending when the spirit leaves the household, after its final meal at the *korumbu*. Counter also to the common Hindu belief, Badagas do not think the soul will be reincarnated anymore. It has already gone through seven births, and only the seventh was as a human. Thus no one expects to encounter the soul again on earth.

The steps in this separation of the deceased from the community seem to be marked by an increasing appeal to God on the part of the latter: this is at least what the incidence of prayer suggests. There is no formal prayer while the body lies in the house, none when it comes outside, and none when it is before the Great House. It is only when the corpse has reached the Funeral Grass on the edge of the village that the first, very long, prayer is pronounced. Then as body and soul move on towards the conclusion of the entire funeral, more and more prayers are

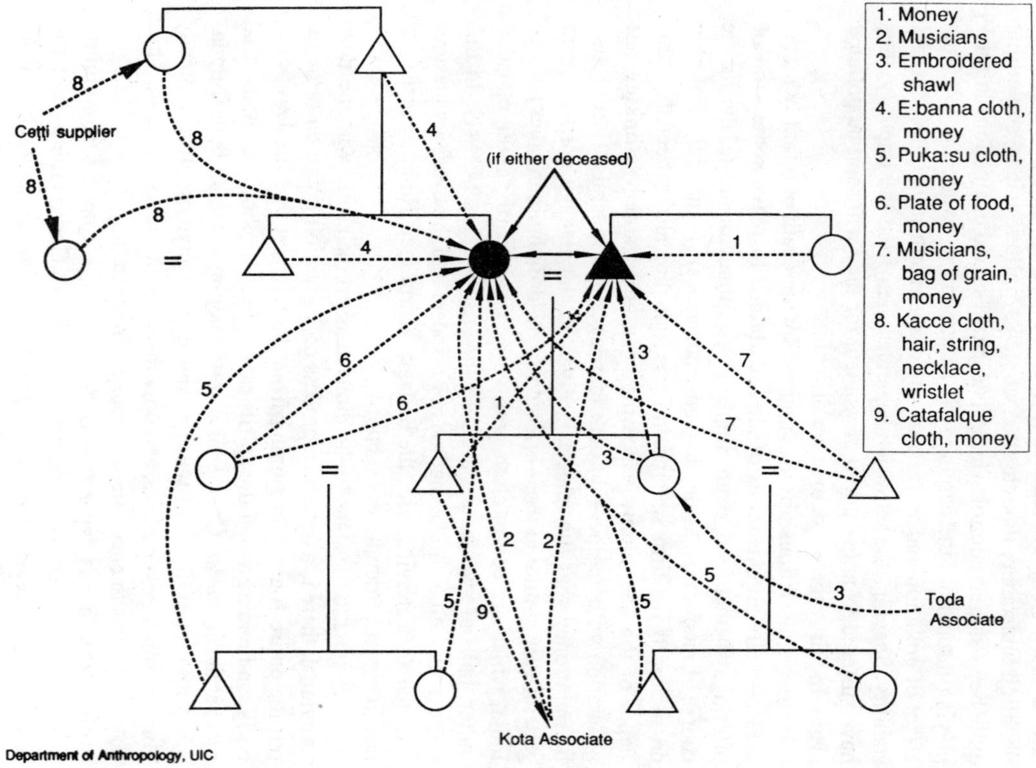

Figure 5.2. OFFERINGS MADE BY SPECIFIC KIN AT A FUNERAL

uttered. All of them are worded so as to introduce and relate the deceased to gods (Siva and Brahma) and especially to the spirits of departed ancestors; and they specifically plead for acceptance of the soul into the supernatural realms. By the end of all the ceremonies the transformation of a personality from household member to ancestral spirit is complete.

The first act of the family at the moment of death is to provision the body, and their last act at the conclusion of the last rites is to provision the soul. This is paralleled by the simple act of placing a small coin in the mouth at the moment of death, and later throwing one into the cremation flames, or into the Lingayat grave as it is about to be filled. In this manner the entire process of disposal of the dead is bracketed in time with two monetary offerings, often interpreted as 'tolls' by Classical analogy. Both kinds of provisioning mark the division between the liminal phase and the period of *ti:ṭu* or pollution: they are both natural, human and everyday. In between, the aforementioned prestations (Figure 5.2) link categories of relations across what I might characterize as the 'great divide' of Badaga social life, that which separates agnates from affines. (Everyone within his phratry who is known to Ego is actually, or potentially, one or the other, for everyone belongs to a clan.)

During the course of the ceremony (Figure 5.1), the dead body is moved to five successive locations in a scenario which, step by step, moves it further away from the household and progressively separates it from the Badaga society. By the time the corpse has reached the burning ground a few people can be heard giving it messages to bear to their loved ones who have already gone: thus, 'Tell my husband that our daughter is ....' There is nothing in the successive funereal acts to suggest that the family survivors are unwilling to let the dead go: on the contrary, everyone collaborates to send off the dead with food and fanfare—unless it was a small child.

By the very act of dying, it is needless to repeat, the human body becomes separated from its former social life. After some preparation of the body inside the house, it is moved outside onto the front yard, but still on a cot. Thus it is definitively and visibly separated from the household, for no living person would lie on a cot outdoors. (It would be terribly inauspicious for a resting man to be mistaken for a corpse!) Next the body and cot are taken to one side of the yard in front of the Great House. That house was the first one to be built in the village, and

The Funeral: A Conceptual Model

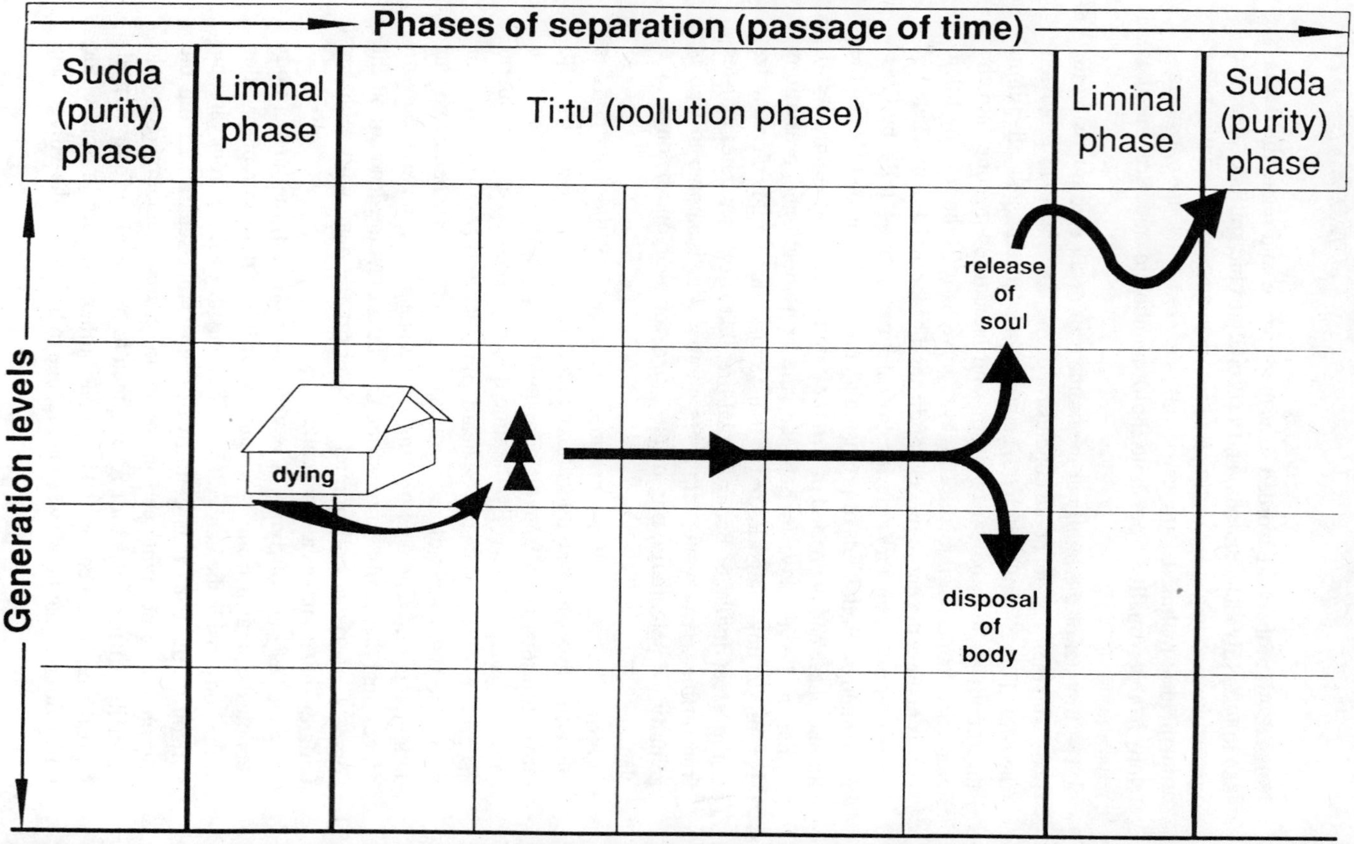

hence symbolizes both the founding ancestral couple and the entire village community that is descended from them. Here as the body lies insensible, dancing, music, wailing, greeting, and gift-giving go on around it, as the village community prepares to separate itself permanently from a member who is no more. Then the corpse is moved to the village green and the Funeral Grass, where the final offerings of milk, of harvested grain, of mud-for-food, and of grass (i.e., grazing) are made to one who had been a participant in, and dependent on, a mixed farming economy. At the Funeral Grass, the deceased is separated by certain rites from his or her spouse, and by absolution from sinful acts of the past. Finally, the burial or cremation separates the body from the soul, which goes off towards the north. There is nothing here of the orthodox Hindu idea that the cremation represents a sacrifice, as Parry has argued (Bloch and Parry 1982: 77–80). Later on some relatives at the house light the soul on its way, and leave it food and water for the journey. After it is all over, the survivors quickly begin to separate themselves from the pollution which this death has caused, and life goes on.

A final diagram (Figure 5.3) is offered to summarize the major features of this transition.

NOTES

1. See Nanjundayya and Ananthakrishna Iyer (1930: 1–76) for a basic account of south Indian practice, both Catholic and Protestant, by a Hindu anthropologist.

Plate 1. The Ke:ti valley viewed from near Hulla:ḍa, ca. 1949. (Photo: David G. Mandelbaum)

Plate 2. The Ke:ti valley viewed from near Ke:ti Toreke:ri, 1963. (Photo: William A. Noble)

Plate 3. Ke:ti Toreke:ri as seen from Hulla:ḍa

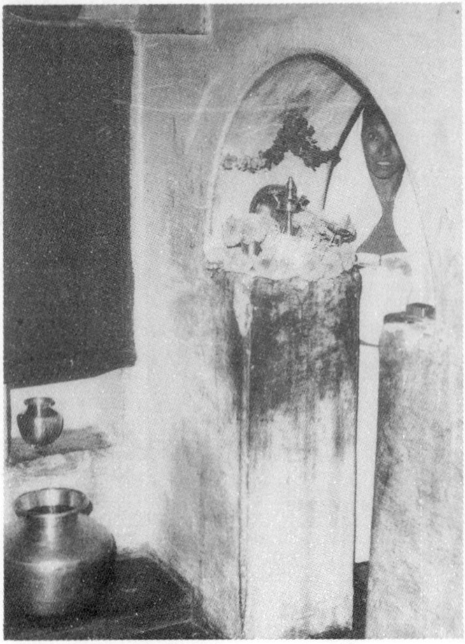

Plate 4. Arched doorway inside a Ke:ti house. (Photo: W. A. Noble)

Plate 5. Hulla:ḍa village, 1963

Plate 6. Fields and eucalyptus plantations near O:rana:yi, 1963

Plate 7. Threshing grain on the yard, O:rana:yi

Plate 8. Grain and vegetables drying on the yard, Ka:ṭe:ri

Plate 9. Winnowing grain, O:rana:yi

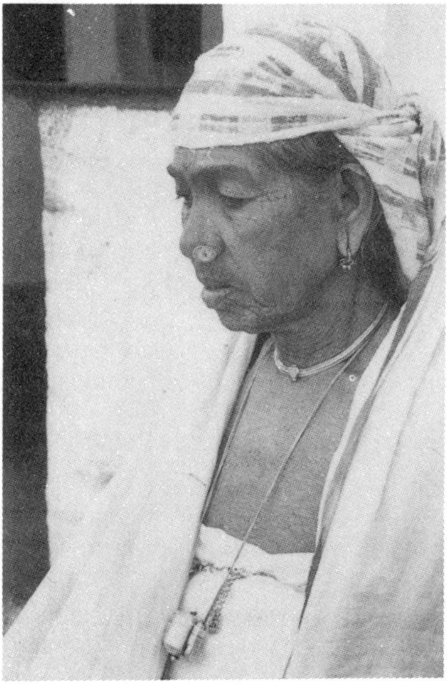

Plate 10. K. Sithamma, mother of M.N. Thesingh

Plate 11. M.N. Thesingh with two of his daughters, 1963

Plate 12. Second and fourth generation members of Guṇḍa Jogi's lineage, Hulla:ḍa, 1990 (see Figure 7.6)

Plate 13. An entrance to Ki:y Oḍeyaraṭṭi village, 1990

Plate 14. Modern and traditional houses, Ki:y Oḍeyaraṭṭi

Plate 15. Ka:ṭe:ri, the only village in the area with a dam

Plate 16. Village water source in Ka:ṭe:ri, 1963

Plate 17. Ke:ti's headman (behind fire) conducts a discussion, 1963

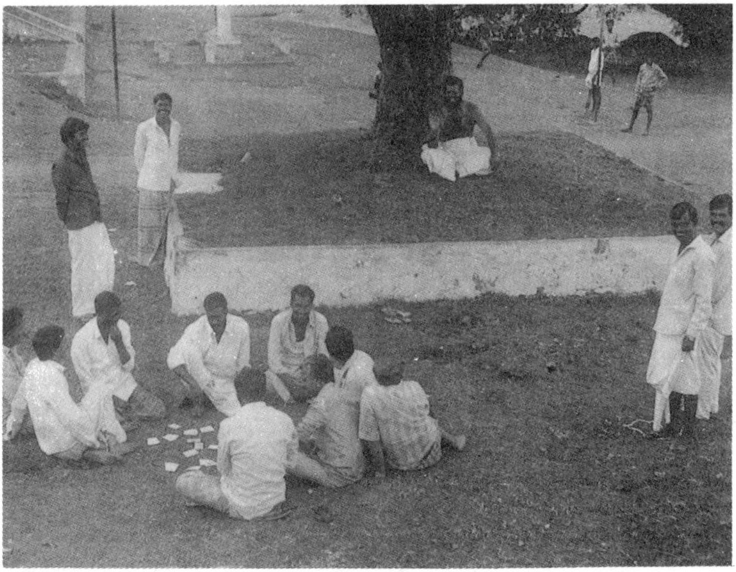

Plate 18. Sunday afternoon on the village green, Eḍappaḷḷi, 1994

Plate 19. Ganga pūja, worshipping the stream in Ke:ti, 1963

Plate 20. Woḍeya priest from Ki:y Oḍeyaraṭṭi being venerated in Ke:ti during the Hiriodea festival, 1963

Plate 21. Linga and *pūja* materials: a temple ornament in O:rana:yi

Plate 22. A Ha:ruva bride from Ha:la:ḍa reaches her new house, 1963

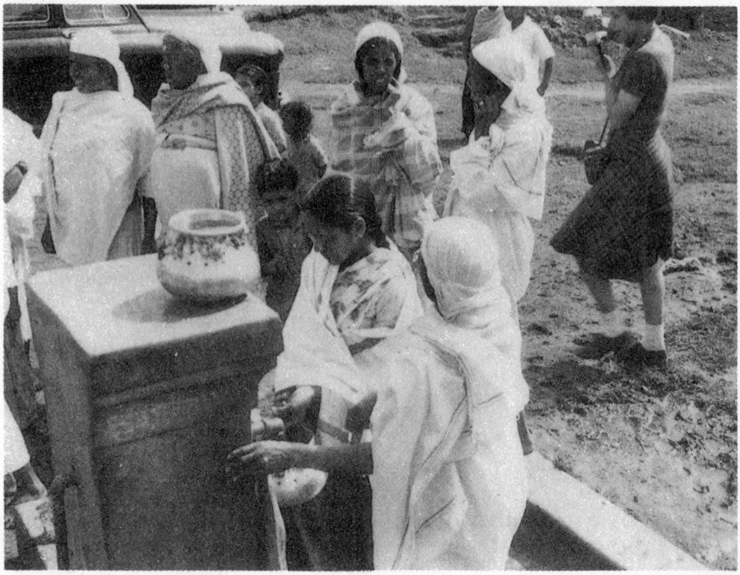

Plate 23. The bride's first task, to fetch water, in Kundesappe, 1963

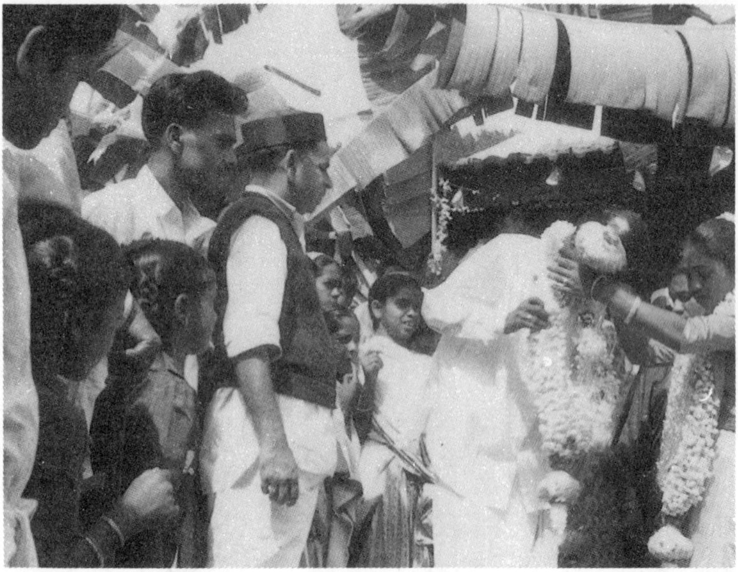

Plate 24. Ha:ruva bride and Gauḍa groom garland each other

Plate 25. Wedding couple, Kundesappe. (Photo: William A. Noble)

Plate 26. Bride and groom bow down to his parents

Plate 27. A wedding feast is prepared for the village

Plate 28. Ke:ti headman (left, without hat) and council of elders, 1963

Plate 29. Badagas create a dance drama at a Coonoor hotel, to promote family planning, 1994.
(Photo: courtesy of Family Planning Association of India)

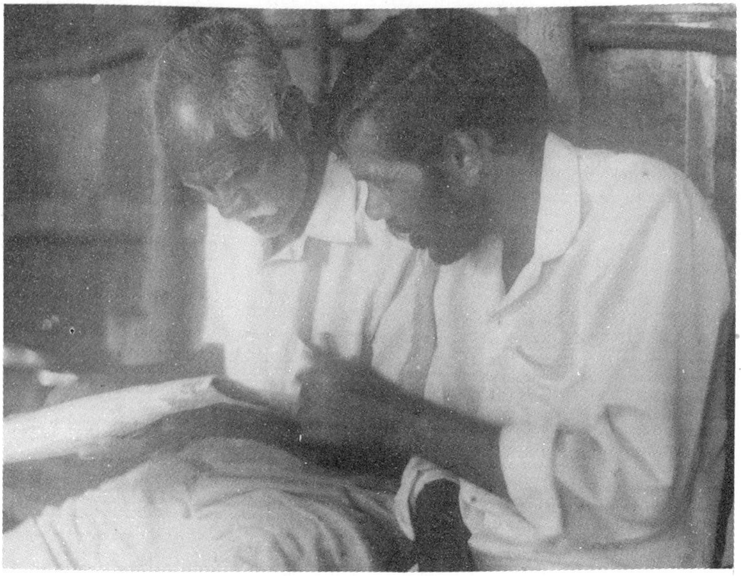

Plate 30. Discussing the news in an Eḍappaḷḷi teashop, 1994

Plate 31. Famous tourists in the Nilgiris:
here the USSR First Secretary Nikita Khrushchev
and Prime Minister Nikolai Bulganin visit a Toda hamlet, 1955

PART III

QUANTITATIVE FINDINGS

Chapter 6

FAMILY AND HOUSEHOLD

Home is home, be it never so homely.
— Charles Dickens

Marriage Networks

Badaga kinship is a Dravidian kinship system, and as the detailed patterning of marriage has been examined earlier (Chapter 3), it need not be repeated here. Overall, the main features of their social system are not dissimilar from what can be found in most of India. This is seen succinctly enough when one notes that the following statement about north and central India could be applied just as well to the Badaga case, by substituting my term 'phratry' for 'caste':

> ... almost every Hindu considers himself a member of a shallow patrilineage ..., and of a patrilineal clan, usually called the *gotra*, as well as of a caste, or *jāti*. The caste is endogamous, but the clan and the lineage are typically strictly exogamous. Among most groups, also excluded as possible marriage partners are persons known to be consanguineally related to ego through females, at least for a certain number of generations. Additionally, throughout most of North India, the village is exogamous, and in some regions even whole groups of villages are exogamous. In Central India, while marriages within the same village occur, marriages linking residents of different villages are preferred. The bride is usually expected to make her official residence with her husband and his parents — usually strangers to her — in a village which may be many miles distant from her natal home (Jacobson 1977: 265).

But since the normal Badaga form of marriage recognizes a rule of village exogamy except in Woḍeya villages like Ki:y Oḍeyaraṭṭi, where only clan exogamy is demanded, certain consequences follow on the decision to marry a MBD, on the one hand, or a FZD on the other. MBD marriage, a slightly less common choice than that with FZD, precisely replicates the movement of a bride in the previous generation: i.e., the young man's own parents' marriage. Thus, to cite a concrete instance, if the groom lives in Hulla:ḍa and his mother originally came there from Tu:ne:ri at the time of her own marriage, then one generation later his bride would come from Tu:ne:ri too, since that is where all of his mother's brothers would be living. (Such a pattern, if too popular in one family, might hypothetically be draining marriageable women away from Tu:ne:ri while sending fewer back there, since a youth in Tu:ne:ri could only marry a cross-cousin in Hulla:ḍa if he could find a FZD.) The alternative of FZD marriage, on the other hand, is reciprocal in many cases, though by no means all: an exchange of marriageable women occurs in alternating generations. Ego's father 'gives' a FZ to a family of another clan, and one generation later the FZD is 'given' to Ego himself as bride. Reciprocity between two villages is not assured when FZD marriage occurs, however, for it may happen that a man who took his wife from village B will give his daughter to village C.

It is possible to tabulate the known marriages in recent decades that involved my four villages, to see precisely what amount of reciprocity is exhibited and thus how important it is as a factor in marriage arran-

Table 6.1

MARRIAGE NETWORKS OF HULLA:ḌA GAUḌAS, UP TO 1990

Village	Known girls sent to:		Known girls coming from:	
Tumanaṭṭi	32	18%	51	23%
Mainele	27	15%	27	12%
Kundesappe	28	16%	20	9%
Tu:ne:ri	19	11%	26	12%
Kappacci	15	8%	13	6%
Kekkaṭṭi	12	7%	15	7%
Bikkaṭṭi	3	2%	11	5%
Pa:la:ḍa Hosaṭṭi	3	2%	8	4%
Maḍitore	11	6%	8	4%
Total of 38 other villages	28	15%	43	18%
Total of known wives:	178	100%	222	100%

gements. For example, the case of Hulla:ḍa is documented in Table 6.1.

It will readily be seen that some villages in Table 6.1 are 'popular' and others not. What might the reasons be for this? In the first place, those villages showing a higher degree of reciprocity—in that the number of girls known to have been sent is close to the number known to have been received—also show the highest amount of intermarriage. This in turn can be explained by friendship and kinship networks that the women themselves have promoted. It is not uncommon for two sisters to marry two brothers, or occasionally as co-wives to marry the same husband. It is certainly very common for several sisters to go in marriage to families living in the same village that their own mother came from. These brides will already be familiar with that village from previous visits to their mother's natal family, and indeed are quite likely to marry into her particular family, to a MBS. On the other hand, some villages which show only a small number of marriages within recent memory also may be showing a certain imbalance in reciprocity patterns. Here it is worth mentioning that villages are regularly conceived as 'good' or 'bad' places to live in, depending on whether the people are deemed friendly and economic conditions are attractive or otherwise; and it is no doubt such subjective categorizations that lie behind the variable popularity of different villages for marriage purposes.

There are even *blasons populaires* (Hockings 1988: 32–33, etc.) that reinforce these stereotypes. One of them does no credit to the people of Hulla:ḍa, though it is not true even as an exaggeration in the 20th century: *Hulla:ḍavaka kalla:de keṭṭaru / Karimoravaka kappa:gi keṭṭaru*— 'The people of Hulla:ḍa have failed because of no education; the people of Karimora have failed because they are black.' The implication about Karimora people may not be that in the past they were descended from dark-skinned people, but in all probability is more a play on the etymology—*Karimora* is said to mean 'burnt tree'. (In recent decades Karimora has had no marriages with Hulla:ḍa.)

It might be objected that my data on marriage reciprocity are skewed or invalidated because of the process of forgetting. It is true that a woman from Hulla:ḍa who married into Tu:ne:ri half-a-century ago and who subsequently died may now be forgotten about in her native village, even though her family in Hulla:ḍa were questioned by me during the censuses. On the other hand, women who came into Hulla:ḍa from Tu:ne:ri are more likely to be remembered by my respondents even after their death. The response to this objection is that what is important *is* which women are remembered; and this is why 222 women are remembered as having come into Hulla:ḍa, but only 178 (80 per cent of that figure) remembered as having gone away from it. Thus my numerical data include women who went to another village perhaps 40 years ago but are still remembered to have done so—probably because they were alive at the time of some censuses and sometimes came back on visits to their relatives. They still figure therefore in reciprocity estimations. These figures, however, are in stark contrast with the data on marriage networks in the other three sample villages, each of which showed a greater number of girls marrying out than marrying in.

In Hulla:ḍa, 65 per cent of the 400 marriages about which I had some locational information were with just five other villages: Tumanaṭṭi (32 girls going there, 51 coming), Mainele (perfect reciprocity with 27 girls going there, another 27 coming back), Kundesappe (28 girls going there, 20 coming), Tu:ne:ri (19 girls going there, 26 coming), and Kappacci (15 girls going there, 13 coming). A few other villages had a sizeable number of intermarriages with Hulla:ḍa: Bikkaṭṭi sent 11 girls in marriage and received three; Kekkaṭṭi sent 15 and received 12; Maḍitore sent eight and received 11; Pa:la:ḍa Hosaṭṭi sent eight and received three. And Hulla:ḍa itself was the scene of six village-endogamous marriages. All of the other marriages were with villages that had only a tiny handful of remembered cases—but there were 38 such villages, one of them in Kerala.

One certainly cannot explain the aforementioned five most 'popular' villages in terms of propinquity. To reach each required two bus journeys, with a change in Ootacamund. Other villages that were within a mile or so of Hulla:ḍa—and were mostly agnatic—accounted for almost *no* cases of marriage: Ke:ti, the next Gauḍa village, had just one; Accanakal had two. The great majority of Gauḍas in these neighbouring villages belong to the same maximal lineage as the Hulla:ḍa people, so that for them intermarriage is out of the question. The popularity of the above-mentioned five villages is rather to be understood in terms of long-standing affinal networks that had linked them with Hulla:ḍa over a century or more. Girls marrying into Hulla:ḍa were already quite familiar with its inhabitants, and had many friends there; and *vice versa*.

Village Exogamy

A general rule of Badaga marriage is that the village (unless Woḍeya) will be exogamous. This follows from the presumed fact that most village populations are descended from one founding male ancestor, and hence all villagers living in one place consider themselves related 'by blood' unless they have married into it. Marriage with a fellow villager would usually be within one's clan, and so would be conceived as incestuous and impermissible.

Two of my four villages illustrate this rule in action. Ke:ti Toreke:ri had 98 per cent exogamous marriages (*N* = 49). The single case of endogamy there is easily explained by the fact that the woman's father had come to Ke:ti from elsewhere. Hulla:ḍa, though five times as large, presented an identical situation: 97.9 per cent exogamous marriages, 2.1 per cent endogamous (*N* = 237). In this village there was one case of a native woman residing there while her husband had come from elsewhere. Another marriage was in the exceptional instance of a Ha:r-uva priestly family—the only one in Hulla:ḍa—one of whose daughters could and did marry with a Hulla:ḍa Gauḍa. There were also two Adikari women who stayed on as the wives of two local Gauḍas after their father left Hulla:ḍa with his family: this too was acceptable because they were of different clans. In short, the apparent exceptions do not offend against the prohibition on incestuous marriages within the clan.

These two villages were non-vegetarian, and their occupants held low and middle rank respectively in the traditional Badaga hierarchy. The other two villages of my sample were vegetarian, Lingayat, and high-status; and as it happened their practice of exogamy was very different. O:rana:yi, an Adikari village, certainly looks statistically very much like the two cases just discussed: it had 99.2 per cent exogamous marriages (the single case of endogamy being where a local woman's husband had originally come there from another village; *N* = 122). What is somewhat unusual about O:rana:yi, however, is that 66.8 per cent of all marriages known to me were with women from the one neighbouring village of Ka:ṭe:ri, scarcely a kilometre away (Figure 7.3). It in turn has had a very high rate of intermarriage with O:rana:yi. Taken together this pair of Lingayat villages have been relatively self-sufficient in the supply of marriage partners to each other.

This certainly contrasts with the situation in Ke:ti, where the Toreyas have intermarriage with 11 other villages; or in Hulla:ḍa, where the Gauḍas have intermarriage with 48 villages. Instead, the pattern at

O:rana:yi foreshadows that found in my fourth sample village, Ki:y Oḍeyaraṭṭi (also Lingayat), where 42.9 per cent of all known marriages were endogamous and only 57.1 per cent exogamous. This remarkably high incidence of village endogamy is explained by a general Woḍeya pattern of clan exogamy; for in the other sample villages virtually all village members belong to one clan, which is rigidly exogamous, whereas Ki:y Oḍeyaraṭṭi villagers belong to several distinct septs, also exogamous; but this explains why the village itself is not. One might speculate that the unusually high incidence of spinsterhood among the young women of Ki:y Odeyaraṭṭi, referred to elsewhere (p. 176), should be explained in part by the lack of extensive networks of affinal kin in other Woḍeya villages—at least as compared with the other three sample villages which are 98 or 99 per cent exogamous. Extensive networks are needed when marriages are being arranged by the family, or loans have to be sought, as is regularly the case in Badaga society.

Structural Types of the Household

Following the categories which were developed for the Indian family in general by Kolenda (1987: 11–12; see pp. 60–61 earlier), we can tabulate the kinds of household structure in the four Badaga villages, which indeed showed a great variety of forms. In fact *all* of her categories occur here (leaving aside the ill-defined 'Other'). Polygynous households, though very rare, also showed considerable variety, and hardly any two of them were alike in their structure. Monogamous households made up 97.5 per cent of the total sample of 283 households studied, so polygynous ones accounted for only 2.5 per cent. The households where monogamy had been practised can be further divided into the two broad and common analytic categories, nuclear and joint. Of these, the various nuclear forms (according to Kolenda 1987) were by far the most numerous, (except for her type no. 5, 'Supplemented subnuclear', which only showed one example).

The number of *types* of household organization increased somewhat with the actual number of households in any one village. Thus Ke:ti, with only 26 Toreya households at its greatest extent, showed 12 forms of household. Ki:y Oḍeyaraṭṭi, with more than twice that number of households (65), showed 18 types. O:rana:yi, with an identical number (65), had 23 household types. Hulla:ḍa, twice as large as the preceding two villages (127 households), had 27 types of household.

In compiling these figures I was able to use more refined categories than Kolenda, since the depth of time in my study, one generation, allowed me to talk about the *direction* of structural change. Thus I can identify households that changed during the course of the study from type no. 1 (after 1963) to type no. 8 (by 1990) a change that was particularly common in the O:rana:yi data, where I counted eight cases. Hence I have found it useful to treat type 1, type 8, and type 1 changing to type 8 as three distinct categories. This latter village, however, had no case of type 8 changing to type 1. Ki:y Oḍeyaraṭṭi (the same-sized village), by way of contrast, had three households that changed from

Table 6.2
FREQUENCY OF OCCURRENCE OF 50 HOUSEHOLD TYPES, 1963–1990

MONOGAMOUS	*N*		*N*		*N*
1 throughout	116	**4** throughout	5	8 —› 10	4
1 —› 2*	17	4 —› 2	1	8 —› subpolyg.	1
1 —› 3	11				
1 —› 4	4	**5** throughout	–	**9** throughout	–
1 —› 5	1	5 —› 4	1	9 —› 1	1
1 —› 7	2	Nuclear subtotal: 231		9 —› 2	2
1 —› 8	17				
1 —› 10	2	**6** throughout	–	**10** throughout	–
		6 —› 2	1	10 —› 2	1
2 throughout	11	6 —› 3	1	10 —› 3	1
2 —› 1	15	6 —› 7	1	10 —› 8	1
2 —› 3	2	6 —› 11	1	*Joint subtotal:*	*36*
2 —› 6	1				
2 —› 8	7	**7** throughout	1	POLYGYNOUS	
2 —› 10	2	7 —› 1	1	Simple polygynous	3
				Simple polygynous —› sub-polyg.	1
3 throughout	8	**8** throughout	4		
3 —› 1	2	8 —› 1	4	Supplementary polyg. —› 2	1
3 —› 2	4	8 —› 2	6		
3 —› 5	1	8 —› 3	3	Sub-polyg. —› 6	1
3 —› 6	1	8 —› 7	1	Polyg. collat. —› 9	1
		8 —› 9	1	*Polyg. subtotal:*	*7*

*The units 1–11 refer to household types in Kolenda's list; see pp. 60–61.

type 1 to type 8, and two more that changed from type 8 to type 1. In every village the nuclear family was most popular or convenient throughout the 27-year period of my study, a fact that is borne out by figures from each village:

Ki:y Oḍeyaraṭṭi, total of 65 households; 45 nuclear throughout, and eight changed to nuclear;
O:rana:yi, total of 65 households; 42 nuclear throughout, and one changed to nuclear;
Hulla:ḍa, total of 127 households; 96 nuclear throughout, and eight changed to nuclear;
Ke:ti, total of 26 Toreya households; 20 nuclear throughout, and three changed to nuclear.

In general we can say that each village contained 66–88 per cent nuclear households by the end of the study in 1990.

(1) *Household cycles*: What Table 6.2 suggests is that, given a century or more, any type of household structure can pass through several stages and end up as it began: e.g.,

1 —› 2 —› 8 —› 1
1 —› 4 —› 2 —› 1
8 —› 2 —› 3 —› 1 —› 8
8 —› sub-polygynous —› 6 —› 2 —› 8, etc.

It is not uncommon for people in India to plan for their old age. In no states, however, is there an adequately funded old-age pension scheme, and even keeping some savings for use during old age can become supremely difficult in the face of demands from children and the current realities of marriage payments. One thing that is certain is that one among an ageing couple will die first, and among Badagas it is usually the husband because he is the older one. Aware of this likelihood, many couples seem to give quiet encouragement to their children to continue living with them in adulthood. One typical pattern is to encourage the youngest son to stay on in the household of his ageing parents, and ultimately to inherit the house (i.e., ultimogeniture). But meanwhile he will almost certainly marry. What was a nuclear family (types 1–2) will thus become a stem family (types 8–11); and then as soon as one of the parents dies it will be converted to a supplemented nuclear family (type

2). In short, there is an inevitable revolution of types 1 —› 8 —› 1 (and other variations). Or perhaps several sons stay with their parents, living space permitting. Then the evolution is from a nuclear to an extended family (1 —› 8), which is likely to break up into several nuclear families again once both parents have died, hence 1 —› 8 —› 1.

(2) *Joint households*: Against this finding we should set the fact that not only was there a minority of joint families and polygynous ones of various sorts, but interestingly in 32 cases there were shifts whereby a nuclear household had become joint by the end of the study period. The high figure at O:rana:yi (12 cases) included eight cases where a simple nuclear family (type 1) had become a lineal joint family (type 8). In the other villages this was a rare occurrence. Hulla:ḍa yielded the largest example of a joint family. In 1963, this contained 12 persons in a collateral joint family (type 6) headed by two brothers. By 1990 this had grown to 19 persons, now organized as a supplemented lineal–collateral joint family (type 11, the only instance of that I encountered) headed by a remarried widower, and also containing two married sons with their wives and children, plus two married sons of his long-dead brother, with their families; altogether five married couples under one roof! (Figure 7.6).

During the study period a total of 20 (in 1963) joint families became nuclear. On the other hand there were 32 nuclear families that became joint. The conclusion to be drawn from these data is that by 1990 that form of the joint family called a stem family was seen as a desirable residential arrangement, and it was to be found in all four villages, viz.:

Ki:y Oḍeyaraṭṭi, total of 65 households; three joint, five joint-stem (12 per cent altogether);
O:rana:yi, total of 65 households; three joint, 14 joint-stem (26 per cent altogether);
Hulla:ḍa, total of 127 households; nine joint, 12 joint-stem (17 per cent altogether);
Ke:ti, total of 26 Toreya households; two joint-stem (8 per cent).

All four villages show higher percentages of joint families than was the case in the study done in Karnataka during 1979–1984, which concluded that only 'Five percent of families are joint-stem and 1 percent joint' (Caldwell *et al.* 1988: 230). However, the proportions of joint-stem to joint are similar in both cases. The distinction made here by the

Caldwells and Reddy is an important one, for stem families are those joint families in which only one married son is living together with his own family and parents. Such an arrangement (also typical of rural Japan) avoids the bickering which can arise between wives of brothers, and can lead to an uncontested inheritance of the house by the one resident son after his father dies. Structurally, the stem family is thus quite different from extended families embracing several married sons.

The situation among Badaga joint families is one in which these families break up early, typically as soon as the patriarch has died. It accords well with the all-India picture that Kolenda (1967: 172–80) has offered, wherein joint families that break up quickly are a phenomenon that is correlated with a high incidence of divorce and the custom of paying bridewealth: both are characteristic of Badaga society. Younger Badaga men now prefer to live in nuclear units, and to develop their careers or farming pursuits independently of their father and brothers. In that way income differentials and the sharing of a common household kitty will not have the potential for generating quarrels within the joint family that they did. The family that pays together, stays together—unwillingly, though. Stem families have however proved to be a useful compromise between the 'classic' Hindu joint family of Sir Henry Maine and the modern, urbanizing nuclear family.

(3) *Polygynous Households*: Polygyny and the levirate have been practised in all of the villages, but they never account for more than a very small percentage of all marriages. A typical case of polygyny (if there is such a thing) occurred in O:rana:yi where an elder sister had been married into Maṇihaṭṭi (a nearby Ha:ruva village) for half-a-dozen years. When her husband concluded that she was not going to produce any offspring he proposed returning her to her father's house. The father, who was blessed with several more daughters still waiting to be married, succeeded instead in getting the son-in-law also to accept one of his wife's younger sisters as a co-wife, and there the matter concluded. A pair of sisters normally make the most congenial co-wives: in a small Badaga house there is hardly room for constant inter-personal friction (Figures 1.1, 1.2 and 1.3).

O:rana:yi was somewhat unusual in having three households that we should designate as polygynous. One actually consisted of three elderly wives and their husband; (the second and third wives were thought to be barren). Another household became polygynous when the eldest son took a second wife shortly before his father died; but it was not also joint, as the two younger sons, each with his one wife and children, moved away at or shortly after marriage to form two separate nuclear households. Another polygynous household became sub-polygynous for a time when one of the two elderly wives moved out (somewhat), to live with her adult son in a separate part of the same house—a situation that I would treat as constituting a separate household, as too would the Census of India. A final case in that village was one of a sub-polygynous household. The old man had had three wives, but before 1963 he had died, leaving a household headed by his two widows and also including the daughter of a third wife—who herself had disappeared, probably at the time the husband died.

In Hulla:ḍa the one case of a polygynous collateral household contained a man with two wives and their children, plus a married son with his wife and children. By the end of the study period what had been a family of 10 persons in 1963 had become one of 17, and (the head having died in 1983) they had split up into one supplemented lineal joint family (type 9), and another nuclear family of four people (type 1).

(4) *Female-headed Households*: One problem that often arose during the census-taking concerned who was really the 'head of household'. A patriarch is certainly seen as one, even if he is weak and chronically ill. But after his death it is his oldest adult son, rather than his widow, who is viewed as being head of the household. This lady may be 'taken care of' there, even if she is in point of fact a forceful and even domineering member of the household.

Nonetheless, there were some female heads of household too, who were of course widows. If a widow is the mother of sons under the age of 20, it seemed legitimate to identify her as head of the household. The small number of female-headed households remained steady during 1963–1990, at 5 or 6 per cent of the total, with no village in either year having more than five of them.

Size of Household

It is possible to survey a lifetime of growth in the number of households in each village. This is because in 1932 (i.e., roughly one generation prior to my first enumeration) the only other listing of all Badaga households was made. It was done by M.K. Belli Gowder, a Badaga antiquarian and local government official (and was locally published;

Table 6.3
NUMBER OF HOUSEHOLDS IN FOUR VILLAGES, 1932–1990

Year	Ki:y Oḍeyaraṭṭi	O:rana:yi	Hulla:ḍa	Ke:ti Toreke:ri	Av. size
1932	21	22	55	[45]*	[4.62]§
1963	28	47	73	16	5.37
1990	65	65	127	26	4.59
%ge increase, 1932–1990	210	196	131	–	–

* The figure for 1932 includes both Toreya and Gauḍa households in Ke:ti, whereas mine for 1963 and 1990 only include Toreyas.
§ Average based on the overall figures discussed below.

Jogi Gowder 1934: 6 *ff.*). In a manuscript which Belli Gowder left behind, he mentions the reason for this work: 'Soon after the Govt. Census of 1931, a census of Badagas houses was taken by me personally since I had the unique privilege of visiting almost every household in connection with organising Panchayats' (Belli Gowder 1923–41: 58). Belli Gowder lived in Accanakal, the village lying immediately to the west of Ke:ti, and hence I have every reason to believe that his enumeration was based on an accurate knowledge of the locality. His counts have been incorporated into Table 6.3.

From my censuses it is possible to calculate the average size of a household (right column of Table 6.3). However, no population figures are available for 1932, although the 1931 Census of India (Yeatts 1932: 2) has yielded a figure of 4.29 inhabitants per house in the rural parts of the Nilgiris district. This rural population was, I estimate, about 37 per cent Badaga in that year. That they were only a large minority implies that the 4.29 figure would not be an accurate estimate of the number of persons per rural *Badaga* household. Rather more accurate, I feel, after correcting for the difference of one year, is to take the 1932 Badaga total as 44,370 and divide it by the total number of 9,695 households in Belli Gowder's district-wide survey: this gives a mean Badaga household size of 4.62 in 1932.[1]

Household size was perhaps depressed in 1932 as a continuing effect of the great influenza epidemic of 1917–1919. As the official District Gazetteer was later to note, 'Influenza broke out in a severe form in the district during 1917–1918 and there were an unusual number of deaths, and the whole district suffered very badly from this disease. It was prevalent in many places in 1925 and many of the victims were children under 10 years' (Madras 1928: 63). In Ketti Pastorate the death register recorded 15 deaths attributable to it (only 3 of them non-Badaga Christians) during the period January 1918 to March 1920. One can only presume some hundreds of deaths among the much larger Badaga Hindu population living in the area. Table 9.1 reflects the same depression in health and fertility: the decade 1911–1921 saw the lowest rate of population growth of any decade since 1821, one of 5.6 per cent, and this rate barely advanced to 6.8 per cent in the following decade, 1921–1931. The data in Table 6.3 suggest that subsequently the mean household size rose somewhat in the next generation (1932–1963)—if my four-village sample is representative—but then fell again by one person in the last generation (1963–1990), for important reasons which will be discussed in Chapter 9.

For comparative purposes it may be mentioned here that at a point midway between my 1963 and 1990 censuses, namely in 1976, Gough recorded household size in two multicaste agricultural villages of Thanjavur district, Tamil Nadu, as follows: Kirippūr had 4.5 persons per household (N = 236), while Kumbapeṭṭai had 4.0 per household (N = 233; Gough 1989: 242, 367). There had been little change in these figures since her earlier survey in 1952. It must be remembered, however, that both villages were multicaste, and dependent on an economy of irrigated rice cultivation. Their cultural similarities with a Badaga village did not therefore extend much beyond the realms of Hindu worship and Dravidian kinship practices. Nonetheless, mean household size is quite close to my 1990 figure.

Badaga Endogamy and the Levirate

The Badagas generally believe they are an endogamous community. Part of the reason for their long-term rejection of the Badaga Christian community as being true Badagas is their correct observation that some Badaga Christians, of either sex, have married Christians from other parts of south India — although it is an uncommon practice. Yet this same argument for rejecting a segment of the Baḋaga population could also be applied to those Lingayat clans which occasionally intermarry with Lingayats from Karnataka; yet it seldom is, perhaps because Lingayats rank high socially but Christians rank low.

My data do throw a slight quantitative light on this question. There were virtually no cases of out-marriage in Ke:ti or in Hulla:ḍa (except that one Toreya man had married a Badaga Christian from neighbouring Santu:r, 1 km away, and one Gauḍa woman had married a Malayali in Kerala); but Ki:y Oḍeyaraṭṭi and O:rana:yi both provided a few instances of out-marriage. In O:rana:yi this was quite reciprocal, in the sense that during the period 1963–1990 three Lingayat girls from the Mysore area married into the village, while three girls from O:rana:yi married into Mysore families (one of these, however, had done so some years prior to 1963). Ki:y Oḍeyaraṭṭi did not show quite such a fine balance: two girls from Mysore Lingayat families (hence non-Badagas) had married into the village, while four Woḍeya girls from this village had married into Mysore families and another had married someone in Madras.

These same two Lingayat villages also provided neat examples of the levirate, a rare but acceptable form of marriage among Badagas. In O:rana:yi a woman was married to a man who died at the early age of 23. She then married his elder brother, aged 30. In Ki:y Oḍeyaraṭṭi there was a more complicated arrangement that combined the levirate with polygyny. Here a man decided that his wife was barren, and so took a second wife too (the same age as his first) who was at that point the widow of his elder brother.

Length of the Generation

Since textbooks offer varying ideas as to just how long one generation is, if they mention the matter, I decided to use as a measure the mean derived from a sum of all observations of women who had produced living children and completed their reproductive lives. These women's ages at the midpoint between their oldest and their youngest child provided me with the approximation I needed. For example, if a woman's oldest child was born when she was 18 and her youngest when she was 32, the mean fell when she was 25, and so 25 can be taken as the length of a generation in her family. Such a calculation may suffer, however, from the occurrence of contraception, and in any event will vary from one woman to another. To avoid any effects of contraception on these calculations, I have mainly used 1963 data, as these were collected at least a decade before family planning became of interest to some Badaga women. In some families it was nonetheless necessary to look at the 1972 census if the mother had not completed her reproductive history by 1963.

Each woman's birth history is unique, and this would affect generation length as calculated by this method. In Ke:ti Toreke:ri it was possible to identify 17 women who had completed their reproductive histories by the 1960s or early 1970s: they yielded a mean generation length of 27.4 years for that village. In the other villages, it was significantly shorter: O:rana:yi averaged 26.7 (N = 53); Ki:y Odeyaraṭṭi averaged 26.0 years (N = 45); while Hulla:ḍa averaged 24.5 years (N = 65). Taken together, all these cases yielded a mean generation length of 25.8 years (N = 180), which we will round off to 26.

NOTES

1. I have slightly amended the published total of households in the light of additional information given in Belli Gowder's manuscript.

Chapter 7

THE FOUR VILLAGES

A village is a hive of glass
Where nothing unobserved can pass.

— C.H. Spurgeon

Basic Findings from the Four Villages

Without exception all households in the four villages were found to be made up of Badaga people who were related to each other, whether by 'blood' or by marriage; thus supporting one common view of the household as 'the living arrangements of a family'. In other words, no household at any period of the study was recorded as including unrelated servants, nor were 'institutional households' (a Census of India term) found where only unrelated persons lived together. No case of intermarriage *between* these four villages was discovered, either, for reasons of phratry endogamy.

The Badaga *household* can be viewed as a mechanism whereby a family, of variable size, arranges on a daily basis for the accommodation, sustenance, care, and sexual reproduction of its members. The *family* is the smallest Badaga social unit, a grouping of close relatives which has the functions of (1) assuring its biological continuity by arranging marriages for its younger male members, (2) usually operating a common economic enterprise, and (3) transmitting the material property to male members following the death of a family's male head. A family is concerned as a consequence with its continuity and reputation.

The preceding chapters may serve as a general introduction to the more specific findings outlined later here. In this chapter some of the more distinctive demographic characteristics of the sample villages are further described and tabulated. The very important structural feature of lineage organization—which links families—is explored in some detail, using an example from Hulla:ḍa.

(1) *Ki:y Oḍeyaraṭṭi*: Ki:y Oḍeyaraṭṭi, a Woḍeya (*Lingakaṭṭi*) village 6 km WNW of Coonoor, dates back at least two centuries, and is marked on a local map made in 1812. It was not the most cut-off of the four sample villages: that was certainly true of O:rana:yi, which until a road (and even a daily bus) went there in 1978 could only be reached by walking two or more kilometres along footpaths. But in most other respects Ki:y Oḍeyaraṭṭi was about equally remote from urban influences (Figure 7.1). It had a bus service to town only from 1985 to 1993, yet even this came no closer than about 0.5 km for the road does not actually enter the village; for most people this had been no great inconvenience because the junction village of Pa:la:ḍa, only 1 km away, has had a regular bus service to town since about 1960. An elementary school was opened in Ki:y Oḍeyaraṭṭi in 1970. By the time of my visit in 1990 the village had two television sets (but 14 in 1994!). At the same period, 1990, Hulla:ḍa (twice as large) had 10 sets—whereas in 1963 it only had had three radios. The Woḍeyas who inhabit the village are by several criteria more conservative and less urbanized than people in the other three villages, and this was reflected for example in my earlier censuses where several cases were encountered of girls being married seemingly in their early to mid-teens. That was extremely rare in the censuses of the other three villages. Ki:y Oḍeyaraṭṭi was also the only Badaga village in the Nilgiris where, in 1963, I was still able to see one small house, little more than a hut, that had the thatched-roof style of the 17th–19th centuries and was made of branches and mud (cf. Jagor 1914: 38, Figure 56).

Alone of the four sample villages, Ki:y Oḍeyaraṭṭi showed a very high rate of endogamy, a marriage arrangement which as we have seen is in general quite unusual in Badaga villages. Among families of the small Woḍeya phratry, however, it is common to practise endogamous marriage provided the partner is drawn from another sept (*kola*) and clan in one's village. Thus in Ki:y Oḍeyaraṭṭi, out of a total of 36 families that were identified (living in distinctly more households, however), village endogamy was seen to have occurred at least once and often more frequently in 28 of these families, or 78 per cent of them. Of all known married women, 33 per cent found husbands within the village. Thus the rule in this village was one of clan or sept exogamy, but not of village exogamy. Within recent memory there have been cases

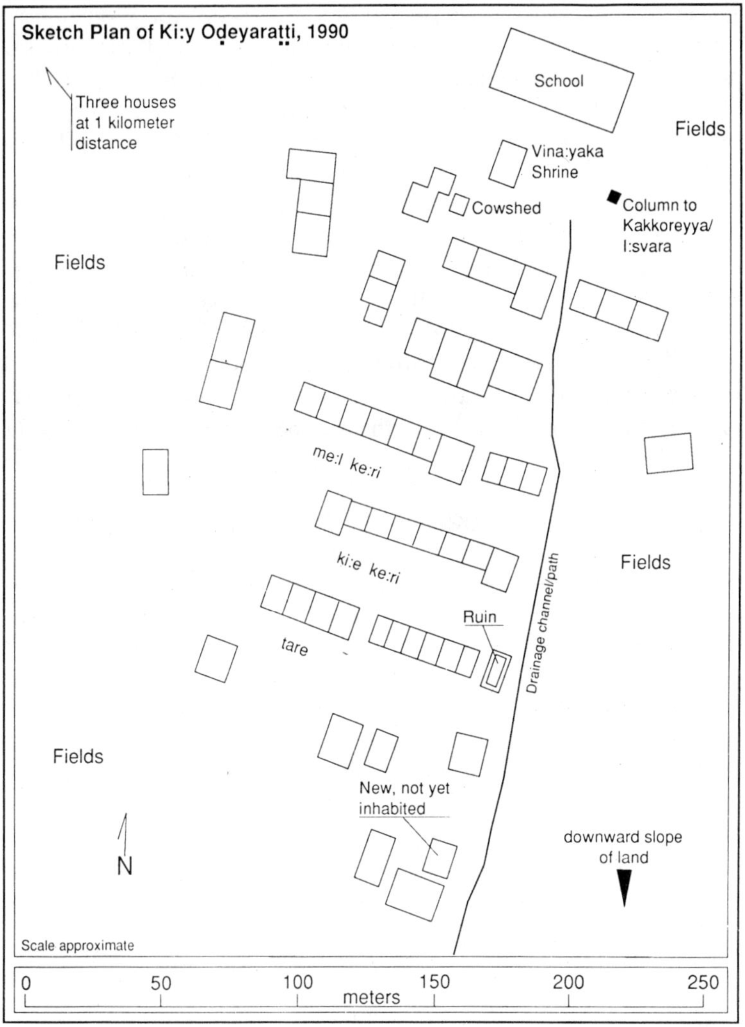

Figure 7.1. SKETCH PLAN OF KI:Y OḌEYARAṬṬI 1990

just within this one village of all possible combinations between the three or four septs: Oḍeya/Ma:ntu with Selandi, Beḷḷi and Ko:ve:ru; Selandi with Ko:ve:ru and Beḷḷi; and Beḷḷi with Ko:ve:ru. Women pass reciprocally on marriage in either direction between these groups. According to my earlier analysis of the Woḍeya septs (Hockings 1980a: 84–85), pairs of septs make up each of the three clans of the Woḍeyas, and all three of these unnamed clans are represented in the population of Ki:y Oḍeyaraṭṭi, viz.: Clan I–Selandi sept, eight households; Clan II–Ko:ve:ru and Beḷḷi septs, 33 households; Clan III–Oḍeya/Ma:ntu sept, 20 households. (There is considerable variation in the different Woḍeya villages in the exact names of these septs.) The fact that a single marriage occurred between Beḷḷi and Ko:ve:ri, however, might call for a revision of the structure I had postulated: there could be four clans, if this is not to be treated as an aberrant case.[1]

The fact that the Woḍeya villages are not exogamous in the way that all other Badaga villages are is perhaps to be explained historically. In

Table 7.1

MARRIAGE NETWORKS OF KI:Y ODEYARAṬṬI WOḌEYAS, UP TO 1990

Village	Known girls sent to:		Known girls coming from:	
Ki:y Oḍeyaraṭṭi	37	33%	37	43%
Ha:ḍaṭṭi	14	12%	13	15%
Kilkotagiri Tu:ne:ri	15	13%	10	11%
Suḷḷigu:ḍu	13	12%	10	11%
Me:l Oḍeyaraṭṭi	6	6%	12	13%
De:na:ḍu	6	6%	2	2%
Hiṭṭegallu	4	4%	1	1%
Iḍukore	4	4%		
Todana:ḍu Oḍeyaraṭṭi	3	3%		
Kilkotagiri Me:lu:r	1	1%	1	1%
Koṇakore			1	1%
Neḍuguve	1	1%		
Total of 6 other places beyond the Nilgiri Hills	5	5%	2	2%
Total of known wives	109	100%	89	100%

Suḷḷigu:ḍu, another Woḍeya village far from the Ke:ti Valley area, I noted four septs named Suḷḷugu, Iḍukore, Oḍe:ru and Ko:vuru. (Variants on the latter two occur in Ki:y Oḍeyaraṭṭi, namely Oḍeya and Ko:ve:ri.) Three of those four septs could intermarry within Suḷḷigu:ḍu, but Iḍukore and Oḍe:ru could not as they were originally agnates. I suspect they split apart into two septs long ago when some men (Oḍe:ru) became accepted as priests and others (Iḍukore) did not. Ko:vuru definitely came to the village later than the other three groups and so, as 'strangers' albeit Lingayats, they were treated as affines. The same kind of later advent explains one or two marriages within Hulla:ḍa between Gauḍas and Adikaris.

We may note here that the lineages which A.M. Shah analyzed in Radhvanaj, Gujarat (1977; and see Appendix II), continue to be strictly exogamous groups. In this respect—and despite the multicaste situation —they offer a parallel to the lineages of any Badaga village. Where, however, they are not comparable is in the ritual supports of these lineages. In Radhvanaj there were and are many lineages which maintain small shrines for a separate cult of their own divinity (*kula devi* or sometimes *kula devata*—most are female). While this worship may legitimize the position of such lineages in the village, it has a fractionizing effect on village life too. Among Badagas (other than Kongaru), in contrast, there are no such lineage cults. The closest thing to this practice—and it is exceptional—is the cult of several different divinities supported by the several clans of Woḍeyas. Since the distinctive Woḍeya settlement pattern places members of different, intermarrying clans in the same village (e.g., Ki:y Oḍeyaraṭṭi), this fractionizing tendency may be present there. Otherwise all worship of village divinities is conducted by a priest on behalf of the village population as a whole, even on behalf of participating non-Badaga residents who are occasionally present. Thus Badaga village worship is in no sense divisive.

(2) *O:rana:yi*: This Adikari village, 7 km. south of Ootacamund, came into existence at the beginning of the last century, and is marked on a local map made in 1812. It was started as a colony of Adigaraṭṭi, and for most of its existence was a constituent hamlet of Adigaraṭṭi commune. Recently though it became part of So:gatore commune; (the other three sample villages belong to Ke:ti commune). The founder was the great-great-grandfather of my chief informant and assistant there, the late M.N. Thesingh (see Chapter 4). This founder, Nanjayya, simply built a house on the hillside (now identified as the Great House), not far

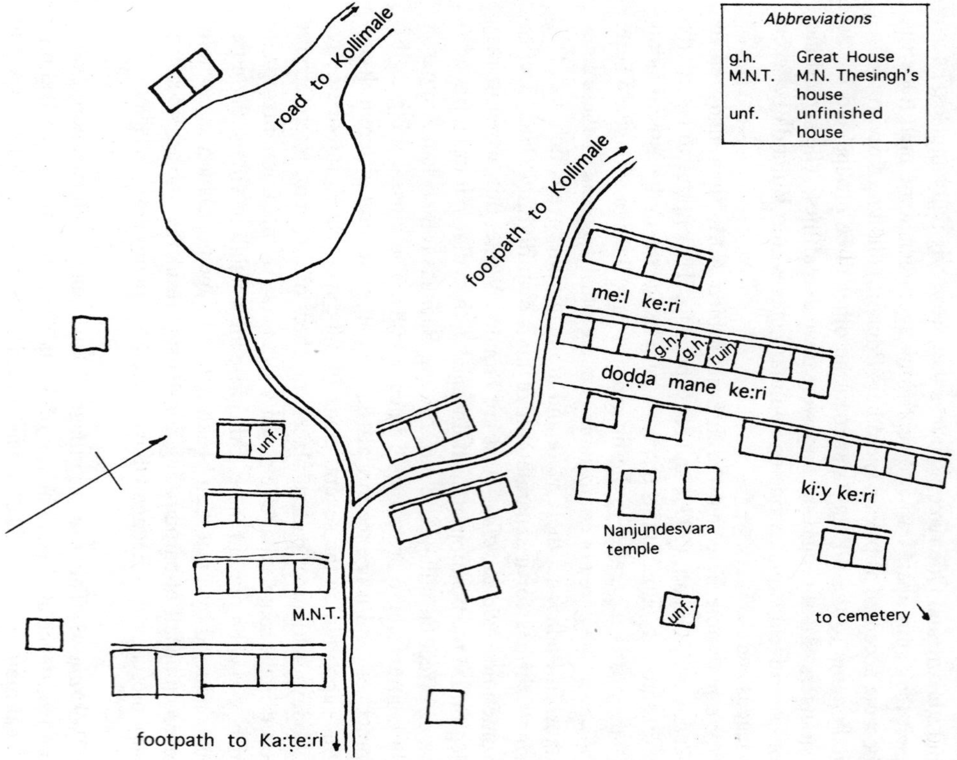

Figure 7.2. SKETCH PLAN OF O:RANA:YI, 1990

from the Kota village of Kollimale (or Kolmel), just before the first British settlers reached the hills. His twin brother (born 'five minutes later') built a house adjacent to it, so that now O:rana:yi has *two* Great Houses (Figure 7.2). Slowly the village expanded by the process of exogamous marriage and patrilineal descent. It did not acquire an elementary school until 1964, or a road and a bus service until 1978.

Table 7.2

MARRIAGE NETWORKS OF O:RANA:YI ADIKARIS, UP TO 1990

Affinal villages	Known girls sent to:		Known girls coming from:	
Ka:ṭe:ri (Kaṇakka)	70	55%	79	66%
Ajju:r (Kaṇakka)	10	8%	3	3%
Naḍuhaṭṭi (Kaṇakka)	6		4	
Tu:raṭṭi (Kaṇakka)	4		3	
So:gatore (Kaṇakka)	2		4	
subtotal, Kaṇakka clan:	92		93	
Maṇihaṭṭi (Ha:ruva)	12	10%	6	5%
Tanga:ḍu (Ha:ruva)	8	6%	6	5%
Me:lu:r Hosaṭṭi (Ha:ruva)	3		1	
Hullaṭṭi (Ha:ruva)	1		3	
Pudugaṭṭi (Ha:ruva)	—		2	
subtotal, Ha:ruva clan:	24		18	
Kekkaṭṭi (Gauḍa)	1		1	
Hulikal (Gauḍa)			1	
Be:lito: (Gauḍa)	1			
Kenduva (Gauḍa)	—		1	
subtotal, Gauḍa phratry:	2		3	
Ha:ḍaṭṭi (Kaggusi)	2		2	
Di:naṭṭi (Kaggusi)	1			
Mysore Dist. (Lingayats)	2		3	
Aruvanga:ḍu (mixed popn.)	3			
Ellena:yi (mixed popn.)	1		—	
subtotal, Kaggusi clan, Mysore Lingayats, and mixed:	9		5	
Grand total	*127*		*119*	

The traditional agriculture was mixed farming of millets and other crops, along with cattle; but during the past two decades people have been switching over to tea cultivation. Today the average tea holding is one hectare. Figure 7.3 contrasts the long strip fields running down-slope near O:rana:yi and neighbouring Ka:ṭe:ri with the smaller, more compact fields of the Kotas near Kollimale. In 1963 there had only been one radio, Thesingh's; but by 1990 O:rana:yi had three television sets, and by 1994 the number was up to 18.

The most salient feature of the marriage pattern of this village is its unusual reliance on one neighbouring village, Ka:ṭe:ri, for over half of its marriage arrangements. During the period of the study I learnt of 70 girls who had gone in marriage to Ka:ṭe:ri—which is a Kaṇakka village, the closest of all Badaga ones to O:rana:yi—and 79 girls who had come from there. These figures mean that it supplied 66 per cent of all known brides in O:rana:yi, while receiving more than half of its in-marrying girls from that village. None of the other three sample villages was nearly so reliant on a single village for its marriage ties.

Adikari exogamy is somewhat unusual (Hockings 1980a: 87–88), but only in the sense that they are a named clan, not a phratry, so all marriages, without exception, have to be with other named clans in other villages. These may be, and commonly are, with the equal-status Lingayat Kaṇakka clan; or they may be with the higher-status Ha:ruva clan, a priestly clan which is also vegetarian but not Lingayat; or they may even be with lower-status Gauḍa men or women, who are not Lingayat and furthermore are generally meat-eaters. Adikaris never marry the Lingayat Woḍeyas. Table 7.2 gives all of the data on 246 marriages within recent memory.

It is clear from these data that marriage with Kaṇakkas is by far the most popular arrangement. Marriage with Ha:ruvas stands as a very distant second choice; while marriages with Gauḍas, Kaggusis, or Mysore Lingayats, though permissible, are of slight frequency.

(3) *Ke:ti Toreke:ri*: This small Toreya sector is a portion, part of Lower Ke:ti in effect, of the larger village of Ke:ti, and traditionally held the lowest ranking of the four sample villages. Ke:ti, 4.5 km southeast of Ootacamund, dates back several centuries, and is marked on the first local map, made in 1809 a decade before the first European settlement. Most of the population of Ke:ti (usually spelt *Ketti*, or formerly *Kaity*) like that of Hulla:ḍa 0.5 km away, is of the Badaga Gauḍa phratry, but it was only that section of the Ke:ti population

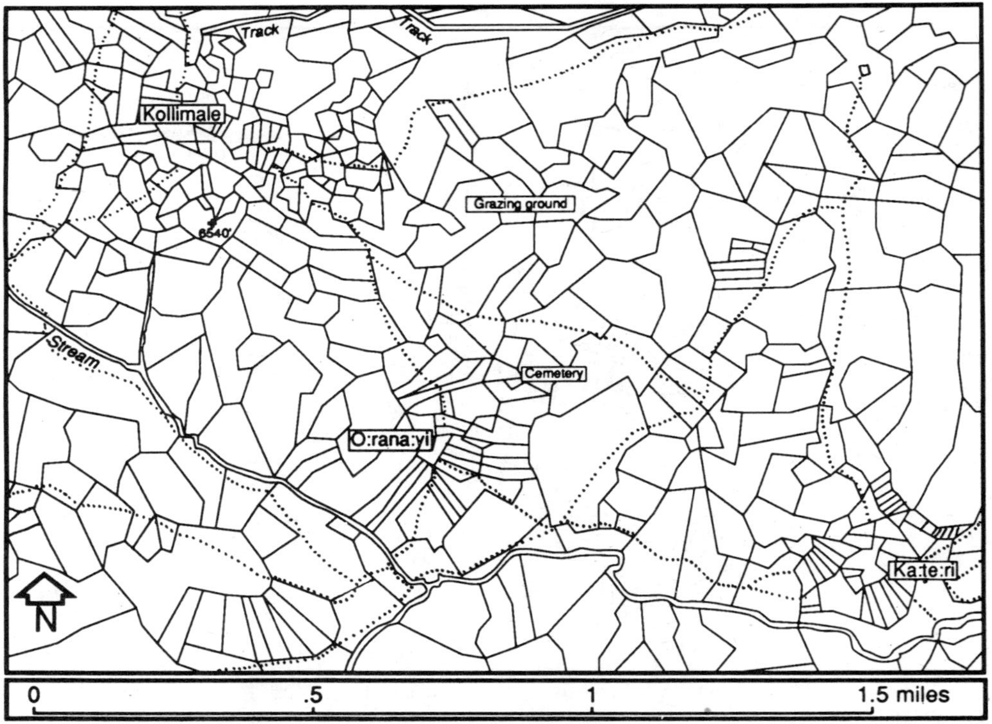

Solid lines represent field boundaries; dotted lines, footpaths

Figure 7.3. FIELD PATTERN AROUND O:RANA:YI AND NEARBY VILLAGES, MID-20th CENTURY

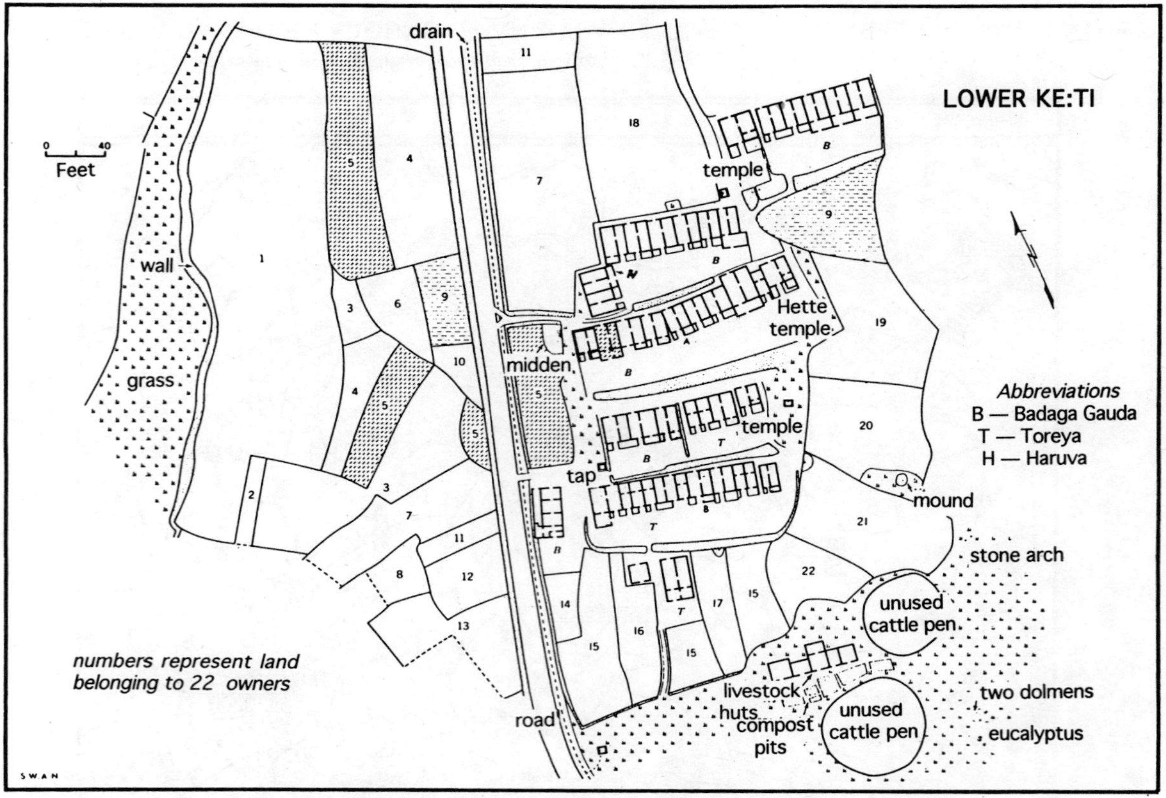

Figure 7.4. PLAN OF LOWER KE:TI VILLAGE, 1963

which was Toreya that concerned me; and conveniently it consisted of a well-defined subhamlet, Toreke:ri, only about 215 x 300 ft and somewhat set off by a small field from the main Gauḍa village lying uphill to the north (Figure 7.4). Thus the Gauḍas of Ke:ti do not enter into this study, although they are much more numerous. Their social superiority to the Toreyas was paralleled topographically, as it happened, by their living at a slightly higher elevation (5–50 metres) than their Toreya neighbours to the south.

Ke:ti is both the traditional and the modern administrative headquarters for the Ke:ti Valley area (Ketti Panchayat). It became home to missionaries of the Basel Evangelical Mission in 1846, and half a century later to those of the Roman Catholic Société des Missions Étrangères. That historic fact accounts for the sizeable number of Christians in the area today, most of them living in the relatively new village of Santu:r which is about 0.5 km west of Ke:ti, and which contains two churches, a Catholic school, and a convent of nuns. But perhaps the greatest significance of this evangelization was that some of the earliest schools in this part of the country were opened in the Ke:ti neighbourhood. Today the village has elementary, middle, high, and higher secondary schools. There are also about six preparatory schools teaching in the English medium. These latter are small private schools established since 1978 and running from junior kindergarten to fifth standard. And as this book goes to press the Church of South India, the local successor to the Basel Evangelical Mission, intends to open an engineering college on its property in Ke:ti. The Toreyas have taken advantage of these varied educational opportunities and have also been lucky with their agriculture, so that today they have much developed since about 1981. Some have second jobs, such as tailors, but many have simply started tea cultivation on their lands. This gives a steady income, and their hard work has helped them move into a position that is economically comparable with the Gauḍas'. Among these Toreyas there were two television sets in 1990.

The total number of Toreyas in this village went through slight changes during the course of my censuses, vi.z: 78 in 1963, 91 in 1972, 98 in 1981, and still 98 in 1990. Yet although the total number of households did increase over the census period, viz.: 16 in 1963, 18 in 1972, 22 in 1981, and 26 in 1990, it is clear that household size has been declining in this village over much of the period, as it averaged 4.9 in 1963, 5.1 in 1972, 4.5 in 1981 and 3.8 in 1990. A crude expression of this is the fact that the *mean* age of each household increased in

18 out of 23 households; in other words, the Toreya population in Ke:ti has generally been ageing, as it has in the other villages.

The Toreya population is divided unevenly between three lineages about four generations deep (*kuḍumba*; for various reasons five households could not be assigned to any of them). In general, knowledge of one's lineage membership was much less in 1990 than what I had recorded in 1963: by 1990 people commonly no longer knew what I knew about their family's lineage affiliation. The three lineages, named from their male founders, are Kakki Me:stri (with 14 households), Jo:gi Me:stri (with six), and Sevana Me:stri (with just one). Jo:gi Me:stri's was described to me in 1990 as the most important, since Jo:gi had been an influential person in Ke:ti.

Among the total of 52 Toreya hamlets in the Nilgiris, Toreyas of Ke:ti intermarried with only 11: so 40 other villages which have some Toreya population are not linked affinally with Ke:ti and are thought to be agnates. Since there are only two clans of Toreyas, this implies a large and puzzling imbalance in their sizes, probably to be explained by

Table 7.3

MARRIAGE NETWORKS OF KE:TI TOREYAS, UP TO 1990

Village	Known girls sent to:		Known girls coming from:	
Malligore	14	26%	9	19%
Me:lu:r Hosaṭṭi (Bra:ma)	7	13%	12	25%
Bebbe:ṇu (Maduve/Haṭṭara)	7	13%	9	19%
Bella:ḍa (Kasturi)	8	15%	6	13%
Happuko:ḍu	6	11%	5	10%
A:regacci (Kasturi)	3	6%	3	7%
Kallaṭṭi (Maduve/Haṭṭara)	4	8%	–	–
Ki:yu:r	3	6%	–	–
Jakkaṅa:ri (Mad./Haṭṭara, Ma:ri)	–	–	2	5%
Arave:nu (Maduve/Haṭṭara)	1	2%	–	–
Śantu:r (Christian)*	–	–	1	2%
Total	53	100%	47	100%

* Names in parentheses are those of exogamous septs—except the last.

differences in the sizes of the hamlets themselves. Table 7.3 ranks the affinal villages in order of 'marriage popularity'.

(4) *Hulla:ḍa*: This Gauḍa village, 4.5 km southeast of Ootacamund, dates back several centuries, and is marked on a local map made in 1812. It has had a primary school since before my field study began (Figure 7.5). While Hulla:ḍa is not physically closer than are the other villages to Ootacamund, the district headquarters, it has more direct transportation connections with that town as well as with the Wellington–Coonoor conurbation. This is because the village is right beside (i.e., 100 metres from) the Ketti railway station which services those towns and connects with Madras via Coimbatore; and the village is scarcely 300 metres from the only direct road linking Ootacamund with Wellington and Coonoor (Map 2.1). Bus service is more frequent on that road than any other in the district. Each town is therefore barely half-an-hour away by bus.

This convenient feature of modern life in Hulla:ḍa does not make the village more urbanized. Agriculture, plus a couple of small shops—a tea stall and a co-operative store—account for the only economic activity within the village itself. But a greater number of people in this village have urban jobs, and a greater number of children attend a school in town, than is true of the other three villages in the survey. Many too have converted former potato fields into small tea plantations, which give a steadier income.

One day in 1981 an idler's dream came true. Since some labourers were needed to work on the nearby metre-gauge track, a railway official went into Hulla:ḍa and found 23 men there who were not currently busy. For three years they were temporary manual labour on daily wages, and then their positions with the Indian Railways became permanent. These men and their families thereby became eligible for a variety of valuable facilities, including accommodation in railway quarters, education and medical benefits for family members (including the workers' parents), lifetime employment and a pension, and even the possibility of the job descending to a son. Of the 10 households that had moved away from the village by 1990, several had moved because of railway employment. Two of these men moved out of Hulla:ḍa with their families, and two more moved by themselves to railway quarters in Ootacamund, Coonoor or Meṭṭupāḷaiyam. One man was transferred to the coastal city of Mangalore. The end result of this windfall and other factory employment was that, by 1990, most households were not

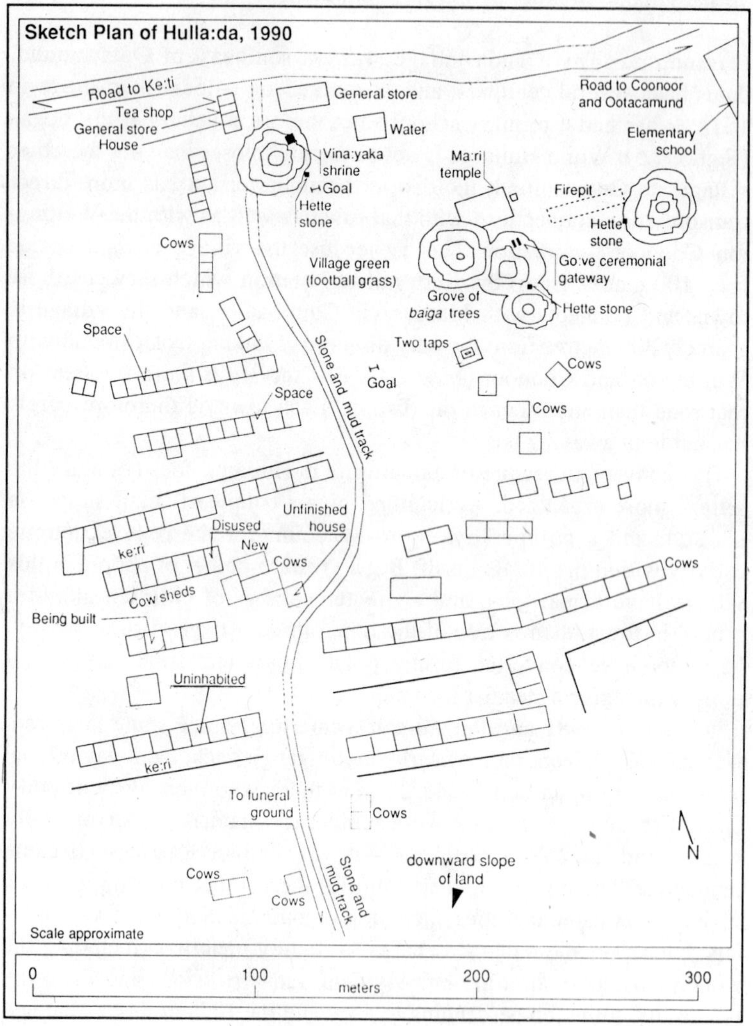

Figure 7.5. **SKETCH PLAN OF HULLA:ḌA, 1990**

just relying on their cultivation but included one or more salaried workers.

Hulla:ḍa differs from the other three villages in another important respect: it is much larger. By 1990 it had a total of 127 households, twice as many as the 65 found in Ki:y Oḍeyaraṭṭi or O:rana:yi, and five times as many as were in Ke:ti Toreke:ri. Socially too Hulla:ḍa is different, in that it is home to members of the numerically dominant Gauḍa phratry, who make up perhaps 85 per cent of the entire Badaga population and occupy a medial rank but a dominant position in the society.

> Hulla:ḍa in 1963 had a powerful headman and well-defined communication networks based most importantly on the cross-cutting linkages of (a) age-grades, and (b) lineages. Information can thus flow quickly *across* any of the six age-grades and *up and down* any of the five lineages. (Hockings 1977: 480)

It was possible to gain information on 400 marriages there, a comfortably large sample for statistical analysis. The marriage networks of Hulla:ḍa have already been tabulated (Table 6.1, on p. 132), and some further details about the social structure of Hulla:ḍa are presented in the following section.

Lineages

A lineage is a corporate group made up of families sharing a common male ancestor. Eventually after the passage of some generations one major lineage segments into several minor ones, each descended from one of a set of brothers.

> Progressive orders of inclusiveness are formulated as a succession of generations; and the actual process of segmentation is seen as the equivalent of the division between siblings in the parental family. With this goes the use of kinship terminology and the application of kinship norms in the regulation of intra-lineage affairs. As a corporate group, a lineage exhibits a structure of authority (Fortes 1970: 86).

> ... the internal segmentation of a lineage is quite rigorous and the process of further segmentation has an almost mechanical precision. The general rule is that every segment is, in form, a replica of every other segment and of the whole lineage. But the segments are, as a rule, hierarchically organized by fixed steps of greater and greater inclusiveness, each step being defined by genealogical reference (Fortes 1970: 85).

*

> Thus lineage segmentation as a process in time links the lineage with the parental family; for it is through the family that the lineage (and the society) is replenished by successive generations... (Fortes 1970: 87).

Each of the four Badaga village populations consisted of a number of households divided amongst four or five major lineages quite similar to the African ones Fortes was familiar with. These lineages were usually named after the founding male ancestor, but only in Ke:ti and O:rana:yi. In Hulla:ḍa they were named after the locality in the village where their houses were, and in Ki:y Oḍeyaraṭṭi these groupings were seemingly Nilgiri-wide septs of the Woḍeyas rather than village-specific lineages. By 1990, the following was the distribution of households in each of the major lineages.

I will examine the third of these villages for further detail on the internal structure of a lineage (Table 7.4).

Some three centuries ago the area generally known as Ke:ti valley, which includes the sites of Ke:ti and Hulla:ḍa (and is overlooked by my other two villages on nearby hills), was settled by a man named Bijja-

Table 7.4

NUMBER OF HOUSEHOLDS IN EACH MAJOR LINEAGE

Ki:y Oḍeyaraṭṭi	Oḍeyar/Ma:ntu	Ko:ve:ri	Selandi	Beḷḷi	
	20	4	8	29	
O:rana:yi	Nanjayya/ Doḍḍayya	Kakkayya/ Kunnayya	Bijjayya	Adikari Ayya	
	28	7	7	18	
Hulla:ḍa	Hosamane	Naḍumane	Doḍḍamane	Me:l ke:ri	Undetermined
	17	21	18	25	32
Ke:ti Toreke:ri	Jo:gi Me:stri	Kakki Me:stri	Sevana Me:stri		Undetermined
	6	14	1		4

ṇarasu (one of three brothers from Kongalli, in Mysore state), said to be a ritually high Kasturi. His Gauḍa descendants together form a maximal lineage spread through 20 hamlets, and so all belonging to Kasturi *kula* or clan. He had three sons, Konga, Kore and Moraṭṭuva (?), who built houses in various parts of the valley and became the founders of the three major lineages which are named after them. The oldest son, Konga Hettappa ('ancestor Konga'), remained in Ke:ti, though some of his descendants founded Kereha:ḍa and Hulla:ḍa nearby. This major lineage in these three villages (to which some later arrivals of 'undetermined' lineage do not belong) is further divided into four minor lineages, which as we have just seen (Table 7.4) are named Hosamane ('new houses'), Naḍumane ('middle houses'), Doḍḍamane ('great house') and Me:l Ke:ri ('upper sector'). All four are represented in Hulla:ḍa's population; but the other two major lineages are not. Households of the four minor lineages are intermingled within a village, and reflect where land was once available for building; but the land of these four lineages is not dispersed, instead forming a single block. Each lineage has its own Great House, that of its founder, to be used for certain lineage rituals. The minor lineages are in turn made up of, and constantly being supplemented by, minimal lineages such as the one I will now examine in detail.

At the time of my initial inquiries in Hulla:ḍa in 1963, four brothers belonging to Doḍḍamane lineage were living in three separate houses, of which one, the original family residence, contained one brother and his family, as well as K. Guṇḍa Jo:gi, the widowed father of the four. His wife De:viammal was from a Hulla:ḍa 'outsider' family, and had died in the 1950s. By the time I had completed my inquiries in 1990 it was clear that this cluster of households, which had by now grown from three to seven, constituted a nice example of a minimal lineage (*guppu*).

Jo:gi's minimal lineage—since he must be considered its founder—compares in structure with another one in O:rana:yi that I have already published details on in a more cursory fashion (Hockings 1980a: 73–74). Those readers familiar with Meyer Fortes' books on the Tallensi of West Africa (1949) will notice a great similarity with his examples there too. In either case we are examining a segmentary patrilineal descent system.

The kinship diagram presented (Figure 7.6, somewhat shorn of detail by leaving out personal names) locates Guṇḍa Jo:gi and all of his descendants who were living at some point during the study period

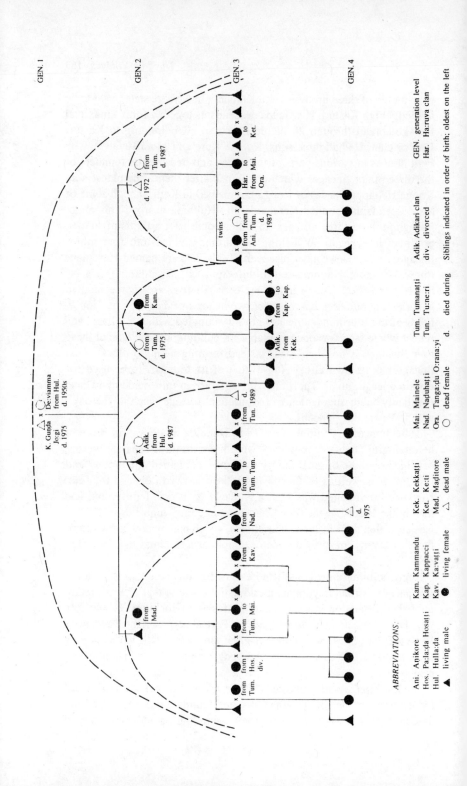

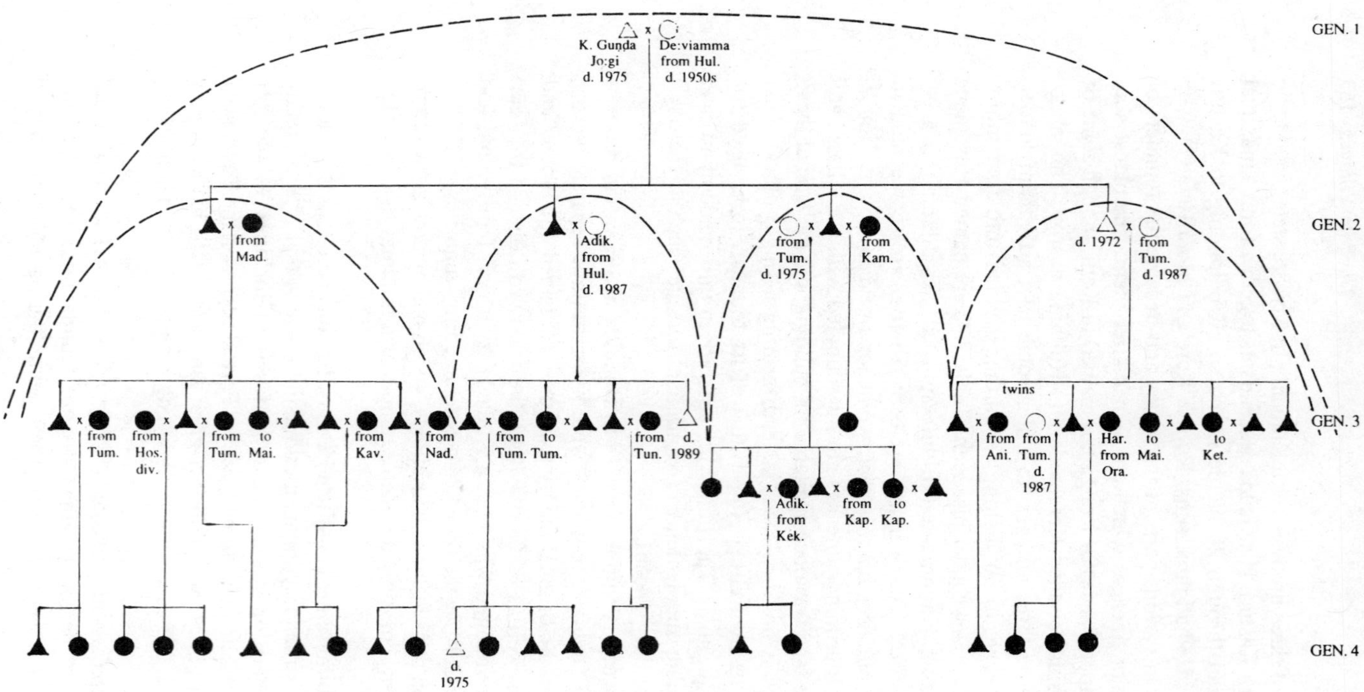

ABBREVIATIONS:

Ani. Aṇikore	Kam. Kammandu	Kek. Kekkaṭṭi	Mai. Mainele	Tum. Tumanaṭṭi	Adik. Adikari clan	GEN. generation level
Hos. Pa:la:ḍa Hosaṭṭi	Kap. Kappacci	Ket. Ke:ti	Nad. Naḍuhaṭṭi	Tun. Tu:ne:ri	div. divorced	Har. Ha:ruva clan
Hul. Hulla:ḍa	Kav. Ka:vaṭṭi	Mad. Maḍitore	Ora. Tanga:ḍu O:rana:yi			
▲ living male	● living female	△ dead male	○ dead female	d. died during	Siblings indicated in order of birth; oldest on the left	

1963–1990, essentially the span of one generation. Daughters are included in the diagram, but it must be emphasized again that once they marry they leave the natal family and lineage in most senses, take up residence in their husbands' villages, and do not raise up children as their brothers do to become descendants of Guṇḍa Jo:gi. This is the essence of any patrilineal descent system.

Given that the founder of this minimal lineage had four sons (Plate 12) and no daughters, it might seem that the particular group chosen for analysis is top-heavy with males; but as a matter of fact there is an almost even balance between the sexes among his descendants (if we disregard for a moment the wives who had been brought in from elsewhere). By 1990 Guṇḍa Jo:gi had acquired 25 male and 20 female descendants, of whom three males and no females had died: thus 22 males and 20 females, very close to the 'natural' proportion of the sexes (to judge from the 1981 *taluk*-wide figures of 102 males per 100 females of all rural Nilgiri communities).

However, because the great majority of these females are very young and not yet married, there is no perceptible balance in the marriage arrangements that Jo:gi's lineage has made. In brief, his male descendants have taken brides from 12 different villages, whereas girls have been sent in marriage to only four villages. The greatest imbalance in this reciprocity relates to the village of Tumanaṭṭi, which has sent six girls in marriage to the Jo:gi lineage over the past generation but has received only one bride from them. Perhaps when more of the girls are old enough to marry some of these apparent imbalances may be righted.

One trend that the diagram certainly reflects is the reduction in the numbers of children in each family. For Generation 2 ('Gen. 2'), that of Jo:gi's sons, his wife had produced four offspring. In Generation 3 the mean number of children per couple was 3.8. In Generation 4 this mean was further reduced to 1.8. While this last low figure may reflect the adoption of family planning practices, and probably does, it is not a realistic average to draw any conclusions from, because (aside from one mother who died and another who was divorced) the 10 remaining wives in Generation 3 are still young enough to produce more offspring in the future. The oldest of these women was 44 in 1990, barely approaching menopause, but most were in their middle child-bearing years, the mean age of the 10 wives being 31. Only one of the 10 was childless in 1990, when she was aged 22.

Generation 2, as we have seen, contained no daughters, but Generation 3 produced seven daughters. Of these it is worth noting that one remained unmarried in 1990, when she was aged 35. (Another too was unmarried, but was only 15 then.) Such spinsters are not too uncommon in these villages: some may have had marriages that did not last, others perhaps fell for an already married man, but others are waiting for their fathers or brothers to put together the necessary financial inducements. At the time of writing this book (1994), 50,000 rupees might be considered a normal monetary settlement for the marriage of a fairly ordinary village girl with no high educational accomplishments.

Without being able to delve into the psychological history of each household, it would still be interesting to discover what factors have prompted one household to split into two or three, something that has occurred several times during the past quarter-century of Guṇḍa Jo:gi's lineage. Badaga houses are not especially spacious (Figures 1.1, 1.2 and 1.3), consisting typically of no more than three rooms, with only the loft as a possible direction for the expansion of living quarters. It might therefore seem that there would be a critical number of occupants beyond which a household would become too small to contain them all. My evidence from this particular lineage, however, does not really support such a hypothesis; and indeed people are building second storeys on their houses. The largest size of three of the constituent households was four members (in 1990). Three more had six, seven and nine members at their largest. Yet the largest household of all in 1990—the same kind of house—contained 19 members, all descendants of two couples (one living and one then dead). The newer households established in Generation 3 can hardly be attributed to population pressure within the house, but rather reflect a desire of young married couples today to have a home of their own, as their fathers had. At some point in the 1940s or 1950s, the four brothers were still living together with Guṇḍa Jo:gi and his wife as a joint family; but by the time I began my study in 1963 they had already split up into three separate households. For Generation 3 the nuclear family was an attractive proposition too, and the cash income that was coming to professional men in Generation 3 made it possible to build or rent another dwelling and thus move away from the parental abode. Of the 11 living sons in Generation 3 by 1990, four had opted for their own nuclear family households.

On the other hand, it cannot be denied that the seven remaining sons of that generation (of whom six are married) have not yet found reason to break up their joint family. They may not in the future, either, although studies from all over India suggest that once the elder couple from Generation 2 are no more, their sons and nephews *will* tend to move apart emotionally and probably spatially too.

Perhaps a more useful index distinguishing nuclear households from joint ones is the number of adult males in each, rather than the total number of occupants. For the period after 1981 (and after three adult males had died in this lineage), we find that every nuclear household contained either one or two adult males, never more, whereas the one joint household contained six adult males in that period.

One has a strong sense that the splitting up of joint families into several nuclear households during the period of study was not only a necessary effect of the family population increasing beyond the point where the building could continue to house them. Equally relevant is the fact that while nearly every household was primarily dependent on agriculture in 1963, quite a number of them were not in 1990. The household is obviously not just a reproductive unit but an economic unit too: the joint family was an organization that distributed among its members the various tasks of ploughing, seeding, weeding, guarding crops, harvesting, processing and cooking food, and child and animal care, all of which activities had to be interrelated and performed at the appropriate times, places and frequencies. After segments of any such joint family become dependent instead on factory, office, school or hospital employment, their interests and timetables differ so much from the rest of the family that a physical splitting normally becomes desirable, at least to the parties who are bringing in a regular cash income. It has been noted elsewhere in India that the wife of a salary earner, often an educated or urbanized woman herself, is a major stimulus for this splitting away from the joint family, as she reasons with her husband that their earnings could more effectively be spent just on their children and themselves rather than be shared with all the other members of the joint family. I have heard the same argument repeatedly in Badaga villages too.

One remarkable feature about this particular lineage is the apparent failure of the men in it to make the classic Dravidian marriage choice of a cross-cousin, either a FZD or a MBD. The reason, however, is clear. In Generation 2 there were no girls, so the men of Generation 3 *have* no father's sisters from whom to seek a daughter; while Generation 4 are still too young to be married. MBD ought to be a possibility, on the other hand, for men in Generation 3. And yet only one man out of the 10 who married appears to have chosen a MBD. He was one of the twins, who took his bride from Tumanaṭṭi, his mother's home village. (Tragically for him, both his mother and his wife died in 1987.) The

MBD is never the preferred match, as marriage with the daughter of one's *guru* brings some ambiguity. Two marriages in Generation 3 follow another pattern of considerable theoretical interest: brother-sister exchange, a situation in which a young man marries the sister of his sister's husband. This happened once in connection to Tumanaṭṭi, once to Kappacci; (11 per cent of all marriages in the lineage).

The 17 wives of the 14 men in Generations 2 and 3 came from a total of 14 different villages. This broad network is a stark contrast with O:rana:yi, where the entire village had much more restricted marriage alliances, and commonly just with one village, neighbouring Ka:ṭe:ri. The wide network which this minor lineage has created in the past two generations (Generations 2 and 3 in the Figure 7.6) probably reflects the fact that parents were increasingly thinking about the monetary gifts a bride would bring with her: this may have been more important than the traditional consideration of marriage with a cross-cousin. Perhaps the closeness of relationship in a cross-cousin marriage implied that a small monetary settlement would be acceptable. By going to the other extreme of arranging marriages with girls from villages that this particular lineage had hardly had previous contact with (at least recently) it was perhaps easier to argue for a substantial gift to accompany in-coming brides. And Hulla:ḍa is after all a pleasant village to live in, with good farm land and excellent rail and road transportation to the nearby towns.

As the Caldwells and Reddy observed, 'Over a quarter of a century, the circumstances of rural marriage have been changed by two major transitions: that from bridewealth to dowry, which has been rapid and traumatic, and that toward marriage with nonrelatives, which has been slower and caused much less concern' (Caldwell *et al.* 1988: 88); as they point out, 'both have implications for age at marriage' (ibid.: 84). Village respondents in Karnataka told the Caldwells that 'The marriage market has changed ... from a surplus of potential husbands to a surplus of potential wives' (ibid.: 85–86). These words could equally well apply to Hulla:ḍa.

A final point of some interest that the diagram (Figure 7.6) illustrates is one I have discussed at greater length elsewhere (Hockings 1980a: 86–92). It is the matter of intermarriage between Gauḍas and members of the higher phratry that is made up of the Ha:ruva, Adikari and Kaṇakka clans (and which is unique in not bearing a phratry name). Of the 23 marriages recorded on this diagram, two were with Adikari women and one with a Ha:ruva woman. This proportion of 20:3 is not particularly remarkable, but on the contrary would be a fairly typical one in the Gauḍa community. What is of more interest, however, is that all of these 'outside' marriages (the term is mine, not theirs) are hypogamous in nature. Throughout India and Sri Lanka, hypergamy occurs as an acceptable if unusual marriage pattern in many castes, and it does amongst the Badagas too; hypogamy, on the other hand, can only be described as an extraordinarily rare alternative anywhere outside the Badaga community.

NOTES

1. The wife died around 1972, aged about 40.

Chapter 8

AGE AND SEX, BIRTH AND ITS CONTROL

Every generation needs regeneration.
— C.H. Spurgeon

Population Structure by Age and Sex

The age and sex structure of the population is an important tool for getting an overview of vital data. It can be expressed in a pyramid-shaped graph (Figure 8.1). In order to clarify and indeed simplify the picture as much as is feasible, I have here combined results from all four villages to yield two superimposed age–sex pyramids, one at the beginning of the study and one at the end; that is to say, at two points one generation apart. In general, the shape of the solid-lined pyramid is one that is usual today in less-developed countries (Handwerker 1990: 325–27). The greater width at the base than at any other age level of the 1963 histogram reflects a high level of fertility—as compared with industrialized countries like England or Japan. In 1963 the village population was a very 'young' one, as was impressionistically apparent to a casual visitor at that time. By 1990, in contrast, the histogram was much more like that of the U.S.A., with a 'middle-aged' population that was visibly more numerous than that of the children. An important shift had occurred in the interim.

The Malthusian cycle is one in which the population is expected to grow at a faster rate than the food supply will, with dire results. A recent idea, the demographic transition (Caldwell 1976) is a general model of population changes which in a sense represent an escape from this. Initially there is a stage where both birth and death rates are high, yet total population remains low. Then there is an early expanding phase with a continuing high birth rate but steadily declining death rate.

In this phase life expectancy increases, but so does population. There follows a later expanding phase, a period in which the death rate stabilizes and the birth rate declines; thus the rate of population expansion slows down. At the end of the cycle is a low stationary phase, when both the birth and death rates have stabilized at a low level and population is again stationary, though at a higher level. The demographic

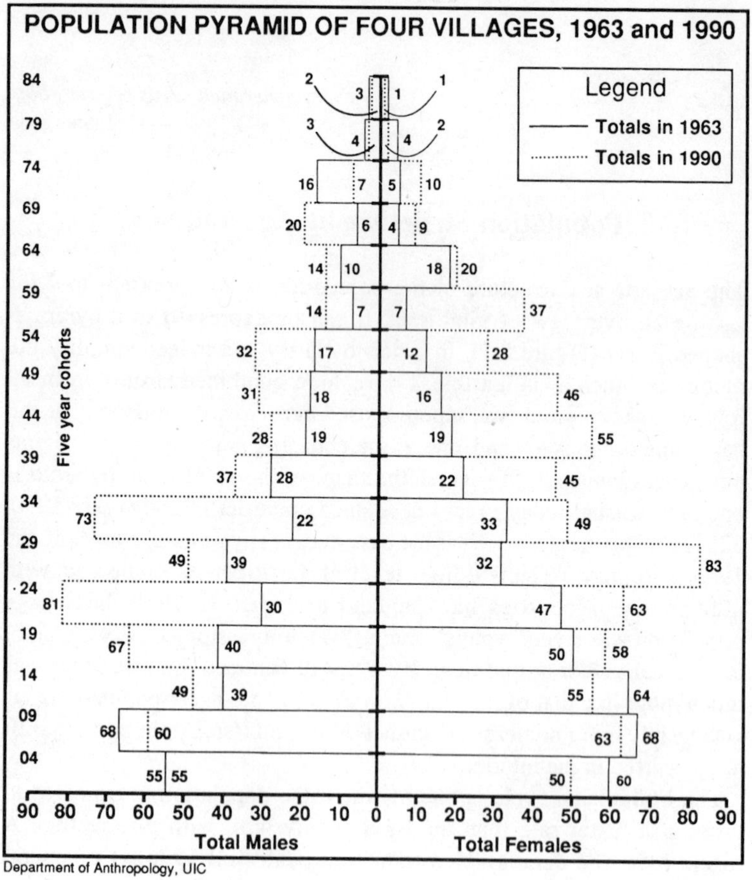

Figure 8.1. POPULATION PYRAMID OF FOUR VILLAGES, 1963 AND 1990

transition seems to be an effect of rising income. Maybe the very poor want many children as they see their income increasing; but after a while the numbers of their children begin to decline while income continues to increase. This point seems to have been reached in the Badaga villages in the 1970s, during the course of my field study.

This particular pyramid is designed to show what has changed demographically in one generation. Because there are reasonable grounds for doubt about the precise age of any individual in the survey, as I have already pointed out, I here follow the common practice of presenting the age data in five-year increments which have the effect of minimizing these small discrepancies and inaccuracies. The relatively large number of young people and the relatively few old people implies that a large body of Badaga youth are demanding educational and public health facilities from the state government while contributing virtually nothing to that government in the form of taxes. The taxable part of the adult population, essentially male farmers, are fewer relative to the number of youth in their community. The elderly are at present still a small minority, who place very few demands on the state and local government facilities.

The age–sex pyramid combining data from all four villages (which never intermarry with each other) contains several surprises. First and most significant is the clear indication that from the mid-1970s family planning had caught on with this community—or more specifically with the women of this community, as I discovered through further questioning (see later). There is hardly any other explanation for the fact that the total numbers of girls and boys in the 0–14 age range were slightly lower in 1990 than they had been in 1963, that in fact the population is distinctly less 'young' now than it was a generation ago.

On the other hand there was a surprisingly large increase in both men and women in their middle years, a clear sign of demographic transition. Men aged 20–34 jumped from 91 in 1963 to 203 in 1990; while women of that age bracket jumped from 112 in 1963 to 195 in 1990. At higher ages, the increases in number over one generation were more modest. (Overall population increase for the sample was 47 per cent.) It is also of interest to note that in the adolescent group aged 10–19 there were nearly identical numbers of the two sexes in 1990 (116 M, 113 F). This was in marked contrast with the situation a generation earlier, when the four villages contained 79 boys but 114 girls.

Table 8.1
JURAL POPULATION TOTALS AND MASCULINITY RATIOS IN FOUR VILLAGES

	Ki:y Oḍeyaraṭṭi	O:rana:yi	Hulla:ḍa	Ke:ti Toreke:ri	Totals
1963 M	81	90	229	34	430 M
F	100	122	186	44	449 F
ratio	0.8	0.7	1.2	0.8	1.0
Total 1963	181	212	415	78	886
1990 M	144	160	276	39	603 M
F	173	150	297	59	655 F
ratio	0.8	1.1	0.9	0.7	0.9
Total 1990	317	310	573	98	1,298

Table 8.1 gives jural population totals and masculinity ratios for each of the four villages.

The proportion of the sexes fluctuates considerably from 1963 to 1990, in two of the four villages; and in no single case approximates the 'natural' figure of 105 males per 100 females. Yet on the average the four villages showed a ratio of 1.0 in 1963 and 0.9 in 1990. These are not of course 'natural' proportions, since they have undoubtedly been skewed in some cases by a greater number of males than females having left a village for studies or for employment. We may speculate that these fluctuating figures reflect varying employment opportunities. In 1963, just after the Chinese army attacked India, the biggest steady employment facility in the neighbourhood was the government's cordite factory at Aravanga:ḍu, which is only about 5 km from Hulla:ḍa and 12 km from O:rana:yi, (the furthest away of the four sample villages). One inhabitant of O:rana:yi, M.N. Thesingh (Chapter 4), who was related to well over half the people in the village, could name 12 men among his male relatives there in 1963 who worked at this munitions factory, as well as a further 17 affinal relatives in neighbouring villages who also worked there. (Women were not doing factory work, except perhaps for several at the local needle industries.) A few of the munitions factory workers in each village except Hulla:ḍa maintained a semi-permanent residence somewhere at Aravanga:ḍu so as to be able to get to work conveniently on time; workers living in Hulla:ḍa, however, could always get there quickly by bus, bicycle or on foot because for them the distance was quite short and was downhill. By 1990 there were wider employment opportunities open to the village men and women; and in 1991 the overall town population of Aravanga:ḍu did not go up like those of all other Nilgiri towns, but actually had dropped by 58 from its 1981 figure of 5,620, a small sign of the reduced importance of its only industry.

Of course, employment opportunities elsewhere would have had only a limited effect on the proportions in Table 8.1. In some cases the attraction of employment at some greater distance took not just one man but his entire nuclear family away from the village, thereby having a minimal effect on the proportion of the sexes there.

Another factor that removes males from their village is the need for school or college study elsewhere. Since this mainly affects children in the age range 5–19, I will isolate those figures for the four villages. Table 8.2 shows that in most cases the proportion of the sexes of these children differs from that for the village population as a whole; and that in most instances girls are more numerous than boys in each village. It will be noticed that the proportions of females to males are higher in this age group than they are in the population at large. (This is also true if one looks at a slightly older cohort, those aged 15–29 who include nearly all unmarried people looking for a spouse.) The table reflects the common practice of sending boys away to live elsewhere with a relative where they will have better opportunity for schooling; or to a city for a

Table 8.2

JURAL POPULATION TOTALS AND MASCULINITY RATIOS OF CHILDREN AGED 5–19 IN FOUR VILLAGES

		Ki:y Oḍeyaraṭṭi	O:rana:yi	Hulla:ḍa	Ke:ti Toreke:ri	Totals
1963	M	24	37	79	10	150 M
	F	42	46	73	16	177 F
	ratio	0.6	0.8	1.1	0.6	0.8
Total	1963	66	83	152	26	327
1990	M	48	42	75	6	171 M
	F	71	34	68	8	181 F
	ratio	0.7	1.2	1.1	0.7	1.0
Total	1990	119	76	143	14	352

career education. Such opportunities are sometimes accorded to girls too, but less often. The practice became quite prominent in Hulla:ḍa, where a general masculinity ratio of 1.2 in 1963 dropped to 0.9 in 1990.

The excess of young women in two out of our four villages, in 1990, is not only to be explained by a tendency for larger numbers of young men than young women to go off to urban situations. Before 1981 there was a nationwide surplus of females over males; and in this, therefore, our villages serve as a microcosm. In the rural Nilgiris district in 1981, the total number of never-married females of *all* communities in the cohort 10–19 (which contains most potential brides) was 45,135 — 247 per cent of the number of men in the cohort 20–29 (which contains most potential grooms; cf. Caldwell *et al.* 1988: 95). In the Badaga community the change is evident when we look at my five-year cohorts. In 1990 the largest female cohort in three of the villages was aged 25–29, whereas in Ki:y Oḍeyaraṭṭi the largest was 10–14. This surplus of women in that age bracket in the first three villages is a reflection of its make-up: young wives plus unmarried daughters. (In my 1963 census, before this shift became apparent, the largest cohorts of females were found among teenaged girls; by 1990 this remained true only in the more conservative village of Ki:y Oḍeyaraṭṭi.) If nationwide men are marrying women who on the average are (let us say) seven years younger than they, they are marrying from a cohort of women whose numbers reflect the proportionate increase in births in the national population over the seven years following their own births. Under such circumstances it is no wonder that women are marrying much later now, and that dowry demands have been sky-rocketing throughout the country: 'desperate' is hardly too strong a word to describe the predicament of millions of Indian parents with unmarried adult daughters today.

Among Badagas, to be precise, dowry is not a usual requirement. The tradition was to pay bridewealth, which in 1963 ranged from Rs 100 to 300, with Rs 200 usual. Since then it has remained around Rs 200. The bridewealth (*honnu*) was originally intended to purchase gold jewelry for the bride, and was an assurance that the groom could look after the bride. As early as 1963, however, the girl's father sometimes gave gifts to the groom worth some thousands of rupees, while still receiving the bridewealth from his family. After 1970 a monetary settlement had still not been formalized, but a car, house or land might be given by the girl's father, if wealthy enough, and after the wedding he might secretly hand over a substantial amount of cash too. By 1990 Rs 50,000 was not an unusual sum to ask for, even if it was still not formally called a dowry. Ke:ti provided a fairly typical example in 1992 of a Gauḍa bride's father who spent altogether Rs 152,000 (then about U.S. $5,000) on his daughter's wedding. First of all, he gave his daughter 25 gold sovereigns, worth Rs 80,000, which were not a dowry and had not been demanded. The clothes he gave her cost a further Rs 25,000. Feeding villagers and affines at a hotel on the day before the wedding amounted to Rs 35,000. Transport between Ootacamund, Ke:ti and Kotagiri the next morning totalled Rs 12,000. The main reason for the gift of gold was so that the young woman would have some financial security, and even be in a position later to make gifts to her own daughter. Badagas living near Kotagiri, however, recommend giving just three sovereigns and two measures of rice; but this, it is felt, will deprive the bride's father of prestige.

Even if these payments have not yet been institutionalized as a dowry requirement, we find that, in summary, 'Two major changes are under way throughout most of south India. One is from a bridewealth to a dowry system, and the other is reduction in the proportion of all marriages between close relatives. Both have implications for age at marriage' (Caldwell *et al.* 1988: 84). 'In the study area the first dowry paid by a Vokkaliga (the major peasant caste) was in 1965' (ibid.: 85). There, village respondents told the Caldwells, 'the marriage market has changed over a few decades from a surplus of potential husbands to a surplus of potential wives' (ibid.: 85–86). If this is true for the Badagas too, then it had become a fact of life by the time of my first census, for in 1963 just as in 1990 I found in the critical cohort aged 15–29 an excess of females over males (whether married or not) in all villages; the exceptions being that by 1990 this situation had shifted in Ki:y Oḍeyaraṭṭi and O:rana:yi, where there was now a slight excess of males over females in this age category. This general tendency helps explain the surge in dowries, at least in my study villages.

Natality

We cannot estimate the total birth rate because of a lack of any systematic information about neonate deaths: that would depend on some kind of registration, which does not occur. Births normally occur at home, so hospital records are of no help. Nor can we estimate accurately the birth rate in intercensal years, because of the likelihood that a certain number of children were both born and died without their existence being reflected in my census records. We could perhaps attempt to calculate the crude birth rate: this is the number of live births per 1,000 per annum. Here the main problem is again a lack of birth registration. I can only work from the approximation that children I was told were 'one year old' or only a few months old were surviving infants in roughly their first year of life. With this proviso I have calculated the crude birth rate in the four villages for both 1963 and 1990, as well as an overall rate of 36 in 1963 and 35 in 1990. There is however considerable fluctuation between the four villages in birth rates: three of them appear to have remained virtually unchanged from 1963 to 1990, while Ki:y Oḍeyaraṭṭi appears to have dropped from 39 to 26. I distrust these results, however, as the general reliability of the data is highly questionable, simply because of the uncertainty over the *exact* ages of the infants.

For comparative purposes it does seem possible to reconstruct the growth rate of Christians in the latter part of the 19th century, since for each year the Basel Mission published totals of the number of Badaga Christians in Ketti Pastorate.

For those same years we can check in the Death Register of that Pastorate and find the number of neonate burials; also in the Baptismal Register, which gives information on the number of live births surviving to baptism. By 1890, when there were 101 Christian Badagas, there had apparently been a total of 16 infant deaths over the preceding years 1863–1890. Since about 52 Badagas were born over that period we may assume an infant mortality rate of 308. This presumes that newly converted Christian parents would indeed get all their living babies baptized and dead ones buried; but it is a safe assumption, given the assiduousness of the German and Swiss pastors. By 1994 in the Hindu community of the same area, the infant mortality rate was 218.

The general fertility rate and the rate of reproduction should also be calculated, by giving the number of live births and the number of females, respectively, born per 1,000 women aged 15–49. Because of the nature of my census data, however, these ratios proved difficult to produce, since (as mentioned earlier) I cannot tell how many live births occurred, of either sex, in intercensal years when infant death followed soon afterwards.

In short, the statistics presented in this study actually veil and distort the realities of both natality and mortality. The passage of time no doubt masks the memory of some of the miscarriages and infant deaths

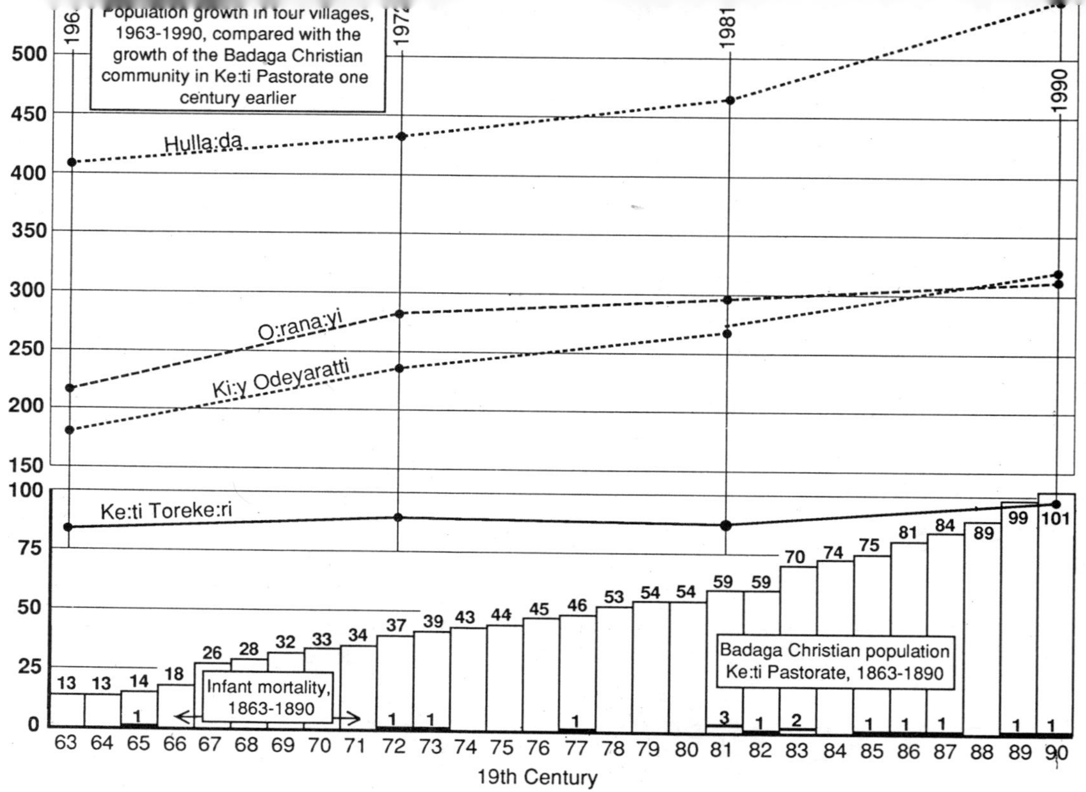

Figure 8.2. POPULATION GROWTH IN FOUR VILLAGES, AND AMONG EARLY CHRISTIANS

which mark the childbirth history of many mothers; for it is a history that my procedure of nine-yearly village surveys does little to reveal. Questions were not asked about the full picture of natality among respondents, and would in any case have quickly raised suspicions about my true interests and still yielded faulty data.

Fertility Reduction

A traditional rationalization for having many children in peasant households has been that (a) some, perhaps most, will die young (thus during 1860–1914, 60 per cent of all recorded Christian deaths here were of children under 12 years); while (b) the remaining sons should be in a position to support their ageing parents; further, (c) the labour of children could be relied on to add something to the household budget, even, in an extreme situation, by their ability to beg or steal. Today, hardly any of these considerations still applies, at least among Badagas, since (a) infant mortality has declined markedly; (b) even if there is only one son, he can still be relied upon to care for his elderly parents, as Table 9.7 (on p. 206) makes clear; and (c), child labour is now a thing of the past. Virtually all Badaga children attend school, so that in the first two decades of life they are, in economic terms, always an expense factor, hardly ever contributors to the household budget. In addition to the food they eat, they regularly require books, stationery, school uniforms, fees, and often bus fares too. Declining infant mortality actually leads to declining fertility, because breast-feeding is less often cut short by a child's death. Since that period of lactation correlates with very low fertility in the mother, an effect of suppressed ovulation, this means that the longer she is breast-feeding, the lower are her chances of becoming pregnant again.

With a total of 765 recorded live births in the four villages during the study period, there was a mean birth rate of 28 per annum: this ranged from 32/1,000 in 1963 to 22/1,000 in 1990. This drop was paralleled throughout southern India, if with somewhat lower figures here than elsewhere. 'There is ample evidence in demographic literature ... that fertility in India has indeed been consistently falling at least since [the] early 1950s' (Shariff 1989: 3).

To what extent do the parents look forward to a time when their sons are grown and able to support *them*? The question is not easy to frame.

but in 1963 I was able to ask my sample of 101 Badagas how they felt about delayed gratification. The question used was: 'If you could be given ten rupees now or a hundred rupees a year from now, which would you choose?' Of this sample, 93 per cent of men and 62 per cent of women said 'today', the rest said 'a year from now'; except that two wary women said they would accept neither, and one other woman was undecided. Perhaps because the question was framed in monetary terms it was a poor way of measuring gratification, since it must have been apparent to many respondents that (a) I might not be there a year later, and (b) Rs 100 would not purchase so much after a year. (In those days Rs 100 was quite a substantial sum; today it is worth less than three dollars!)

The high cost of bringing up children was stated or implied as a reason for limiting their numbers. Hardly any other reason is called for to explain the sterilizations recently sought by mothers in their late twenties. Many people, the aforementioned figures suggest, are not willing to delay their gratification 20–30 years in the expectation that more children will make their senior years more comfortable. Where subsistence farming is prevalent, as in central Karnataka, periodic household crises are occasioned by drought and crop failure (Caldwell *et al.* 1988: 196–205). The Nilgiri hills, though quite close, are very different in this respect. For one thing, rainfall is rather more certain; but, in addition, the Badagas have adopted a mixed farming economy with tea. Some people have small farm plots, some have cattle, and some grow tea on small plantations for the world market. A failure in one farmer's area of activity is thus not likely to affect everybody among his kindred. Tea, in particular, is not a seasonal crop, but is plucked every 15 days. It was the failure of several seasons of the potato crop in the 1960s that prompted much conversion to tea in the 1970s. Parents no longer need many children when the farm tasks have been reduced along with the size of holdings, and coolies can be hired for plucking the tea.

Again, the Caldwell–Reddy study reported much the same finding:

> Their chief, all-pervasive worry was the instability of rural incomes, both their seasonality and their longer-term cycles from relative plenty to widespread scarcity. They discussed desired marriages largely in these terms, much preferring daughters' husbands to have urban jobs with guaranteed continuing incomes than to be farmers of even substantial size. For the same reasons, they preferred some of the family to work off the farm, at least part-time, and felt safer if a son had a job in Bangalore, especially a permanent position with the government or in a bank, necessarily requiring education (Caldwell *et al.* 1988: 216).

And further, 'labor has moved out of farming not only because of the duress of population pressure but because diversification is safer' (ibid.: 217). 'There is an almost desperate realization that it takes more and more education for children to maintain a constant chance of securing a town job or a government position' (ibid.: 218). All of this is equally true of contemporary Badaga households.

In view of the rapidly expanding population of South Asia in general and the relative failure of family planning programmes to control this in rural areas, one finding of the present longitudinal study is of especial importance. At the time I began this study many villagers must have been aware of contraception but in all probability no one was practising it. About halfway through the study, in the early 1970s, many women were discussing among themselves the need to limit the size of their families because of the high cost of bringing up children. Thus the year 1976 (or the mid-1970s) is roughly the time when family planning practices first began to be adopted by some of the villagers in the study area.[1] I spent the year 1976–77 among the Badagas, and there were somewhat clearer though informal indications of this trend than during my previous visit in 1972. By the time of my last census, in 1990, there had been at least a decade of contraceptive practice in these particular villages; (see later, on Family Planning Programmes, pp. 187-93).

For purposes of analysis it is useful to divide the female population into those who had reached the age of 46 by 1976, in other words those born before 1930, and those who were still in their fertile years in 1976 and later.[2] This heuristic division allows me to contrast the possible contraceptive practices of older women (OW) in my sample with those of younger women (YW), in order to see if there is any apparent trend towards earlier restriction of births (Table 8.3). It also shows us which were the more 'progressive' villages in this regard.

Crude as this tabulation may be, it suggests a quite dramatic reduction in the number of fertile years between the older and the younger cohorts of women in my sample who have given birth. (Other data on younger women were excluded from consideration in those many cases where it was likely a woman would have additional children after my 1990 census.) It may be mentioned for comparative purposes that in the Delhi village of Shanti Nagar women interviewed in 1958/59 (and corresponding to my 'OW' cohort who on average had their first birth at 20.8 years) experienced *their* first childbirth two years earlier, on the average, at age 18.98; whereas the Shanti Nagar women who were interviewed in 1977/78 averaged a first birth at 19.66 (as compared

Table 8.3

AVERAGE AGES AT CHILDBIRTH IN FOUR VILLAGES

Woman's age	Ki:y Oḍeyaraṭṭi OW	Ki:y Oḍeyaraṭṭi YW	O:rana:yi OW	O:rana:yi YW	Hulla:ḍa OW	Hulla:ḍa YW	Ke:ti Toreke:ri OW	Ke:ti Toreke:ri YW	All sites OW	All sites YW
average age at first live childbirth	19.3	20.5	21.2	20.9	20.6	17.7	22.2	22.6	20.8	20.4
average age at last live childbirth	32.8	32.0	36.3	29.1	33.0	27.9	34.8	32.5	34.2	30.4
average number of fertile years	13.5	11.5	15.1	8.2	12.4	10.2	12.6	9.9	13.4	10.8

with my 'YW' cohort, at 20.4; Freed and Freed 1985: 271–73).

Another technique for analyzing the reduction in fertility is to calculate the child–woman ratio in 1963 and 1990. This is a ratio that relates the total number of children aged 0–4 in a unit per 1,000 women aged 15–49.

By these calculations fertility has on the average been halved, with Ki:y Oḍeyaraṭṭi and Hulla:ḍa showing the most marked declines—a remarkable achievement in a single generation. But not only was the child–woman ratio dramatically lower in 1990: even in 1963 it was remarkably low if we compare my data with the one set from Shanti Nagar, near Delhi, which is in a format that invites comparison. The Freeds' Table 3 (1985: 242) compares fertility in that one, multicaste village in 1958/59 and again 19 years later. Although the span of time is slightly shorter than one (Badaga) generation, it is close enough to

Table 8.4

CHILD–WOMAN RATIO IN FOUR VILLAGES

	Ki:y Oḍeyaraṭṭi	O:rana:yi	Hulla:ḍa	Ke:ti Toreke:ri	All sites
1963	604	509	505	556	532
1990	204	407	204	355	262
%ge reduction	66	20	60	36	51

Table 8.5
COMPARISON OF CHILD–WOMAN RATIOS IN SHANTI NAGAR AND FOUR BADAGA VILLAGES

Number of:	1958/59	1977/78	Badaga *estimate* for 1976, all sites
Children (0–4)	152	189	ca. 143
Women (15–49)	166	216	ca. 301
Child–woman ratio	916	875	475

(*Source*: Based on Freed and Freed 1985: 242, Table 3).

invite comparison. However, the Freeds have given figures for women aged 15–45, instead of 15–49;[3] but with the help of their Tables 1 and 2 (Freed and Freed 1985: 238–39) it is possible to estimate there were about 8 women aged 46–49 in 1958/59 and about 27 in 1977/78 in that village. Adding these to the Freeds' published data, one arrives at Table 8.5.

One has to conclude that in Shanti Nagar—which is right beside the national capital—little progress was made on fertility reduction over this period. It is known that, from 1959 to 1977, 32 women in that village had been sterilized—scarcely 15 per cent of the adult women in 1977—and that (by coincidence) a further 32 men, probably not the husbands of these women, had also been sterilized. The impact on fertility, it must be concluded, was meagre, however; whereas the Badagas have halved their child–woman ratio in the course of a single generation.

The earlier Table 8.4 of child–woman ratios in the Badaga villages shows that, of the four villages, the greatest reduction, by two-thirds, occurred in Ki:y Oḍeyaraṭṭi, rather surprising in a village which on various grounds I have identified as being the most conservative among the four. In 1990, it had only one TV set per 159 inhabitants. It also happens to be the only one of the four villages which still lies away from any road, though it is less than 0.5 km uphill from a poor side-road. These two factors must somehow be related to its rating on the question of fertility reduction, for here we find the paradox that the reduction between our older and younger groups of Woḍeya women (Table 8.3) was only two years. The low-status Toreyas of Ke:ti showed a similar decline of two years. This slight reduction is partly attributable to the effects of school attendance raising the mean age at first surviving birth by 1.2 years in Ki:y Oḍeyaraṭṭi, and only 0.4 years in Ke:ti, between my older and younger categories of women. Other incidental indicators of the conservative attitude towards reproduction in Ki:y Oḍeyaraṭṭi are that in my data the youngest woman to give birth there was reportedly then 13 among the older group, while two gave birth at 13, it was said, among the younger group (but as was pointed out in Chapter 2, one may be skeptical about precise ages). The oldest recorded age of a mother giving birth in this village was 49 among the older group and 43 among the younger. In short, we can infer—and the villagers here agree—that the fertile period remains long for married women. And yet this particular village has the best record for reducing its child–woman ratio, which obviously has to be credited in part to the chaste behaviour of the unmarried young women still living here with their parents; for the truth is that the number of unmarried women aged 15–49 here was increasing from 1963 to 1990.

The end result of this tabulation, rough as it is (Table 8.3), is the positive finding that on the average women in the four villages *have* reduced their fertile years by 3.4, from the older cohort born before 1930 to the younger cohort born after that date. The results are interesting in that they show neither cohort of women was reproducing at a particularly young age despite adolescent marriages, and this situation did not change. What did change was the mean age of women at their *last* live birth, prompting the average number of fertile years to show a marked decline of nearly four years. This has to be attributed to some slight use of condoms and, much more commonly, sterilization as methods of birth control that were adopted after two or three births. The pattern accords closely with what we know about this subject from the Caldwell–Reddy study, where 86 per cent of all couples known to practise family planning had a sterilization (usually a tubectomy), while only 6 per cent used condoms—and these mainly the Muslim minority (Caldwell *et al.* 1988: 72).

Menopause, the 'change of life' when hormonal changes cause a woman to lose her fertility, is a gradual process, and so one cannot assert that it would occur precisely at, let us say, age 46. But it is certainly not unusual for Indian women to give birth up to that age. Table 8.3 records data on women who have passed this threshold in their lives, but my dividing point of 46 years is obviously an approximation. In determining the age at last childbirth I cannot be certain that some later case of a stillbirth or infant death did not pass unrecorded by me. 'Births' as analyzed by demographers are normally live births, however.

In the national Census of 1981, it was calculated that for *all* rural women in the Nilgiris who were then in the 45–49 cohort and had thus completed their reproductive years, the number of children ever born to them averaged 5.02. This is supported by another study done in 1980, which found that a sample of rural Nilgiri women aged 40–44 had a mean of 4.91 children ever born to them (Khan and Gupta 1985: 16, Table 2.5). There are not many women in the 45–49 cohort among the Badagas in my four villages, although five is probably a reasonable estimate of the number of their children. However, a cautionary anecdote is in order here.

In one of my sample villages, a well-to-do farmer in the mid-19th century had four wives. They produced altogether 22 children, which may sound like a true population explosion until one learns that all but two daughters died in childhood; and those two, following tradition, left the natal village upon their marriages. The man left no patrilineal descendants. A more recent case history from the same village and lineage, in the first half of the 20th century, has one man taking only one wife (born five years after her husband). During her reproductive life she had a total of 11 births, as follows:

1. a son, now married;
2. a daughter, who died after 52 days;
3. a son, who died after 54 days (after this, no coitus took place for six months);
4. a daughter, now married;
5. a daughter, now married to the same husband as 4;
6. a daughter, who died after 3 years;
7. a daughter, now married;
8. a daughter, who died after 4 years;
9. a daughter, now married;
10. a daughter, now married;
11. male foetus spontaneously aborted after five months.

In total, one son and five daughters have survived from a reproductive career of 21 years. In this instance, the first birth occurred when the mother was aged about 19, although she had married some six years before.[4] The miscarriage listed here occurred when this woman was just over 40. Coitus continued once or twice a month at least until the age of 52, according to the husband, and she was still menstruating at that age.

Only 55 per cent of her progeny survived to adulthood, and are all still living. Less precise informants—or investigation done under more exiguous circumstances—would no doubt have recorded this as a family with six children, nothing more. In this particular case the oldest daughter (no. 4) seemed to be infertile, and so her next younger sister (no. 5) joined her as a co-wife in a polygynous marriage; but still no children were produced. Indian peasants rarely conceive of the possibility that a male might be infertile: they habitually blame the wife, as though it is her intentional fault.

One can only speak definitively of infertility in such women who are aged 46 or more, and have thus completed their fertile years. E.D. Driver (1963), in a book dealing with fertility in central India, found that the incidence of infertility in his study group was 3.9 per cent. In my own study the incidence was estimated at 6.7 per cent in the Ki:y Oḍeyaraṭṭi Woḍeyas (N = 45), 4.9 per cent in the O:rana:yi Lingayats (N = 61), 8.4 per cent in the Hulla:ḍa Gauḍa women (N = 95), and 3.3 per cent in Ke:ti Toreya women (N = 30). The average incidence for the four villages was 5.8 per cent (and as it happened the incidence was higher, the higher the social status of the phratry). These figures, however, probably over-represent the incidence of infertility in every village, since I am not in a position to tell which of these women may have had a child who died very young at times not close to any of my four censuses and was hence unrecorded by me. Being unlucky is hardly the same thing as being infertile.[5]

Family Planning Programmes

For a background to the data presented in the foregoing pages, it may be useful to review the formal institutions which have been responsible for promoting family planning in the Nilgiris district. There are two: one is the District Medical Board, an arm of the Department of Medicine of the state government; the other is one of 41 localized programmes run by the Family Planning Association of India. Both have been active in the Ke:ti valley area where our four sample villages are located, for about a quarter of a century. (In another *taluk* of the district, this association maintains a women's development and family planning project too.)

The government's programme got off to a shaky start here in the early 1960s when police constables were pressured to set an example by getting vasectomies, and other members of the public were offered transistor radios and a small amount of money if they would have the operation. Unfortunately, in about 1963, one police constable suffered a terrible infection from a badly performed operation at the District Hospital, and word of this near-disaster spread quickly. At about the same period posters extolling family planning were sent to the panchayat offices of many villages (including Ke:ti), where typically they remained undisplayed. Condoms were nowhere in evidence; and anyway would have been too costly for regular users at that period. In general, the official approach was that influential men should be talked to about the need for family planning; never the women!

The picture began to change for the Ke:ti valley area when, in 1965, the District Medical Board opened a Primary Health Centre (in the exact centre of Map 2.1, p. 55) on land near Ke:ti which had once been a Boer War prison camp. This institution, which is still in operation, is midway between the four sample villages, so that geographically they all have equal access to it. Its staff is headed by a trained doctor, and one of its main functions over the past two decades has been to perform sterilizations on women, but usually field labourers and not Badagas.

The Family Planning Association of India, based in Bombay, chose the Nilgiri hills as one of 41 areas in India where it would concentrate its efforts at population control. Here it began as an educational programme around 1965, and a Family Planning Centre was started in the town of Coonoor in 1969. In that year four vasectomies were performed, but since then it is mainly women who have been coming for sterilization after one to three children. The government has pressed for female sterilization rather than vasectomies in recent years in part because women will more readily present themselves for the operation, but mainly because it takes a mere twentieth of the time that a vasectomy does, and hence is 'cost effective'. Many women suggest that they want sterilization because they would not want their husbands to suffer pain (although the vasectomy is not in fact a painful operation when done under local anaesthetic). When vasectomy is broached to men, they tend to say 'My wife won't let me!' Family planning fieldworkers routinely approach both husband and wife before getting agreement on a sterilization of the latter. Only three or four fieldworkers are Badagas, but they and others have over the years worked in selected Badaga villages of the Ke:ti valley (primarily Kammandu) and elsewhere on the plateau. Over the past two decades fieldworkers have found that the contraceptive pill and the intra-uterine device (I.U.D.) are sometimes sought by women, but condoms are still not popular, perhaps because of their thickness. Some old ladies in the villages are asked to hold a supply of them for those women who are relying on condoms. Tubectomies after a couple of births are still the most popular contraceptive procedure. Abortions have not been tabulated by the Family Planning Association. It is very rare for women to seek a reversal of their sterilization, and if it is required this may involve a trip to specialists in Bombay.

In recent years no great effort has been made by fieldworkers to reach the Badagas, because their women are coming forward voluntarily for treatment. I found that from the early 1970s the attitude of women towards birth control was changing because illiterate old ladies were pointing out to them how wearying were the high costs in health and money of producing unlimited numbers of children. But in general, incentives have always been offered. The Family Planning Association does not offer radios or blankets as the government programme has done, but both programmes offer money as an incentive. In 1969 when the Coonoor centre began its work, Rs 50 or 60 was offered. By 1994 (with much inflation), men were being offered Rs 130 (U.S. $4.00) for a vasectomy, and women Rs 160 (U.S. $5.00) for a tubectomy. The Primary Health Centre near Ke:ti (state government) offers Rs 250 and performs the operation in a Coonoor or Ootacamund hospital. In the past government fieldworkers would get Rs 50 as a reward for initiating a sterilization, but this is no longer done. Early on, propaganda commonly involved posters and large notices painted on walls. While these advertisements continue in use, today one finds—for example, in the Ke:ti valley at Kammandu—songs and dances specially composed in Badaga to include propaganda about family planning (Plate 16). Government fieldworkers show propaganda films in some of the villages too.

In the Nilgiris district by 1994, 52 per cent of sterilizations were done by the state government's facilities and 48 per cent by the Family Planning Association. The operation and recuperation occur in their clinics, taking altogether five days and four nights. It is normal to get the husband's agreement unless he chances to be incapable; for instance, a chronic alcoholic. No complaints have been voiced about the loss of the woman's work during these five days, and indeed the operation is sufficiently accepted that many relatives and friends commonly visit a women during her recuperation.

The Family Planning Association maintains one male and one female doctor on a part-time basis to perform the operations. It is interesting that no one comes for sterilization on Tuesdays or Thursdays because these are inauspicious days. At the Coonoor clinic nowadays Monday, aholy day, is not very popular, and sees only 6–7 new cases. Thus the clinic experiences a rush of 16–20 new cases each Wednesday and Friday. The woman comes with a family group, but only one relative may stay with her at the clinic. Others come and go, most bearing gifts. Follow-up visits are required one, two and four weeks after the operation, and if the women fail to come a fieldworker has to go after them. Most of the women initially approach the clinic for an abortion, which is done if within the first 12 weeks, or after delivery of a child; sterilization is then suggested. It is very rare for unmarried women to come because of a pregnancy. In recent years laparoscopy has become widespread, as it is thought to have less side-effects than tubectomy:

> Carbon dioxide is infused into the abdomen so that the Fallopian tubes may be isolated. An endoscope, a small tube with lights and mirrors, is inserted through a small incision below the navel, the Fallopian tubes are located, cauterized or tied, and the incision is closed with sutures ... it is done in a minute and costs only $US 10.00. (Freed and Freed 1985: 247–48)

Table 8.6

PRIMARY HEALTH CENTRE STATISTICS, KE:TI, TO 1994

Sterilizations	5,374
I.U.D.	335
Condom use	106
Oral pill	186
Birth rate	13.51
Death rate	5.25
Infant mortality rate	21.77
Maternal mortality rate	0
Average birth weight	2.5 kg
Mean age at marriage:	
Males	26
Females	21
Number of local midwives	25
Trained midwives	11

Current statistics from the Primary Health Centre near Ke:ti are impressive (Table 8.6), and reflect the acceptance of family planning among poorer Badaga and immigrant Tamil or Kanarese labouring women. These figures relate to early 1994, but again no data on abortions are provided. In June, 1992, it was calculated that the 'catchment' population for this particular Centre consisted of 8,047 eligible couples, i.e., some 16,100 people out of a total local population of over 26,130 males and 24,873 females (1991 Census figures). Of these eligible couples, 73.71 per cent (i.e., 6,001) were protected.

Annual reports from the local branch of the Family Planning Association made it possible to see how contraception has increased in popularity. I have no record for 1972, when Badagas were probably not yet involved in family planning. But for 1975, when I suspect their attitudes were beginning to change, and for the two census years 1981 and 1990, basic data for the Association's target population, which included Badaga villagers, can be given (Table 8.7). The decline in the popularity of vasectomies and condoms (which require male responsibility) is quite eclipsed by the rapid rise in the use of I.U.Ds. and of tubectomies.

The data for the Ke:ti area villages have been paralleled by a broader study which compared family planning practices in the Nilgiris and in Salem, a nearby district of Tamil Nadu. Artifical protection was higher in the Nilgiri sample: 39 per cent of couples were protected in 1980, as compared with 34 per cent in Salem and 28 per cent in Tamil Nadu as a

Table 8.7

CONTRACEPTION ACCEPTANCE AMONG VILLAGERS, 1975–1990

Types of contraception	1975	1981	1990
Target population	20,000	20,000	?
Oral pill users	15	21	34
I.U.D. "	2	152	894
Condom "	119	51	107
Vasectomy	90	34	–
Tubectomy	460	971	2,026
Laparoscopy	–	–	78
Percentage protected	14.5	32.5	› 60 ?

whole. As part of the same comparison, it was found that the Nilgiris district had a consistently higher rate of acceptance from 1973–1974 onwards, except that during 1977–1978 there was a slight decline, part of the nationwide reaction after Mrs Gandhi's 'Emergency' and the forced sterilizations which it permitted (Khan and Gupta 1985: 3). The Nilgiri sample was by no means predominantly Badaga, but was drawn from the towns of Ootacamund and Coonoor and their two surrounding *taluks*. Random sampling yielded 200 households in the urban areas and a further 125 in villages and 75 on tea estates. Of the five villages included in the Nilgiri sample, four were mainly Badaga in population, and one of them was actually Ke:ti (spelt *Ketty*, and no doubt sampling more Gauḍa than Toreya households). But of the total number of rural households in this survey, only a fifth (22.7 per cent) were Badaga (Khan and Gupta 1985: 24, 127). Achieving a 99 per cent response rate, the interviewers were able to accumulate some impressive data on techniques of contraception. Six of these were modern techniques that family planning workers have been promoting in India (see Table 8.7); but it is very interesting to note that 28 per cent of the rural sample and 29 per cent of the urban were protected by more 'traditional' methods, including 'rhythm', certain (unspecified) herbs, and simple absence of the marriage partner (Khan and Gupta 1985: 13–14).[6]

The conclusions drawn by this particular study are very positive and hopeful:

> A comparison of the socio-economic situations ... shows that the Nilgiris was better than Salem so far as literacy, particularly literacy among women was concerned. It was better also in respect of accessibility to modern amenities, such as electricity, toilet facilities, tap water, etc. The most crucial point ... was that, in the Nilgiris, there was...significantly less disparity between the rural and urban population in respect of education, accessibility to modern amenities and exposure to mass media. The disparity was wider in Salem .... This was also true of the monthly household income. (Khan and Gupta 1985: 119–20)

At the end of their study Khan and Gupta concluded, in summary:

> ...as to what has caused this high acceptance of family planning in the Nilgiris, the findings ... indicate that the "success story"... may be attributed to the individual and the mutually reinforcing effects of the following five broad factors:

(i) *A relatively more equitable distribution of benefits of socio-economic development in rural and urban population ....*
(ii) *A better organised health and family welfare programme....*
(iii) *Extensive efforts put in by voluntary organisations in promoting MCH* [mother-and-child health] *care, including family planning ....*
(iv) *The status of women in the Nilgiris was relatively better than in Salem....*
(v) *Benefits* ... as many as 95–98 per cent [of] users replied that they were financially better off than they were 5 years before .... A higher percentage of females in the labour force emerged as one of the benefits of the higher acceptance of family planning. (Khan and Gupta 1985: 123–25; italics in the original)

NOTES

1. This is not to suggest that ordinary villagers were totally unaware of family planning before that period. In 1963 a local official told me that villagers often came to him for advice on planning: he was an animal husbandry officer.
2. Coincidentally, 1930 was the year in which the Sarada Act, passed in 1929, came into force: it aimed at preventing marriage of girls below 14, although paradoxically it had the effect of creating a rush of child marriages just before the Act came into effect.
3. While the Freeds' Table 3 (1985: 242) labels the infant cohort as (1–5), their text states that they mean 'up to 5', hence (1–4).
4. In Tamil Nadu state, it has been estimated that, ca. 1971, menarche occurred on average at 14.6 years (Chakravartti and Renuka 1970). Another more recent study in Chittoor district of Andhra Pradesh among unmarried Hindu girls found a mean age of 13.46 (Murthy 1993: 51).
5. Another study, by G.B. Saxena (1965), based on work in three villages in Uttar Pradesh, identified a total of about 19 per cent of wives who had had no pregnancy; but this would certainly have included young wives and perhaps others too who simply had not yet conceived as of the time of the study, and it is therefore not comparable with my own figures. The Freeds estimated sterility in Shanti Nagar, U.P., at about 2 per cent in 1958/59 (Freed and Freed 1985: 257).
6. See Table 8.6. A demographic examination of fertility in south India was done in the middle of my study period, in 1972–1974, by K. Mahadevan and associates. Their interviewed sample consisted of 1,912 currently married women living in a Development Block of Madurai District, on the border with Coimbatore district. There were three social strata in Mahadevan's multicaste sample: the dominant Gaundans (mainly Kongu Vellalas); Nayakas, Chettiars and some other intermediate-status castes; and Harijans. An interview schedule was designed that focused on fertility and contraceptive practices, and was administered by six women interviewers. The results of the study were published in 1979.

Chapter 9

MORBIDITY AND MORTALITY

Time does not become sacred to us until we have lived it.
— John Burroughs

Masculinity Ratio and Infant Mortality

Although several quite remarkable social customs were practised by the various Nilgiri tribes, only the Todas became infamous for the practice of female infanticide. Yet by the 1950s at the latest this practice had stopped amongst them, and the imbalance between the sexes has been seen to decrease further at each subsequent census of that tribe. Do we have any evidence that the same custom prevailed in recent times among the Badagas? Seemingly not, because the many official and semi-official censuses show little disproportion between the sexes for this community at all ages.[1]

For each census the total of Badagas and the masculinity ratio were as shown in Table 9.1. (This ratio has been obtained simply by dividing the total number of males by the total number of females.)

In 1981, the year in which my censuses occurred within several months of the national Census of India, it was found by that organization that the national masculinity ratio was 1.07; that for Tamil Nadu state was 1.02; that for the Nilgiris district was 1.04, but in rural areas was 1.02; and that for the rural parts of the subdivision called Coonoor *taluk,* where my four sample villages are located, was 1.01. In those villages I myself then recorded a *Badaga* masculinity ratio of 0.97. This is extremely close to the official figure: the national Census recorded a Nilgiri-wide ratio of 0.98 for all rural 'Kannada' speakers—a figure that in fact referred primarily to Badagas! In summary, all Badaga ratios between 1812 and 1971 range within 0.94–1.21, most being very close to the mean of 1.00. This finding is in sharp contrast to

Table 9.1
TOTAL POPULATION OF BADAGAS, AND MASCULINITY RATIO, AT ALL CENSUSES UP TO 1971

Census	Madras intercensal interval	Males	Females	Ratio	Total	Decennial increase
1812	–	–	–	–.–	2,207	–
1821	–	1,977	1,780	1.11	3,757	–
1825	–	2,819	2,328	1.21	5,147	–
1847	–	3,346	3,223	1.04	6,569	–
1856	–	6,574	6,778	0.97	13,352	–
1867	–	–	–	–.–	17,778	–
1871	9.26	9,775	9,701	1.01	19,476	[*ca.* 19.3%]
1881	10.02	12,253	12,145	1.01	24,398	25.3%
1891	10.01	14,892	14,721	1.01	29,613	21.4%
1901	10.03	16,561	17,617	0.94	34,178	15.4%
1911	10.02	18,898	19,282	0.98	38,180	11.7%
1921	9.94	20,097	20,232	0.99	40,329	5.6%
1931	10.00	21,819	21,256	1.03	43,075	6.8%
1941	10.00	27,971	28,076	1.00	56,047	30.1%
1951	10.00	33,436	33,822	0.99	67,251	20.0%
1961	10.09	43,055	42,408	1.02	85,463	27.1%
1971	9.92	52,070	52,322	1.00	104,392[2]	22.1%

other parts of the country over the past half-century. In her study of Karimpur village, in Uttar Pradesh, over the period 1925–1984, Wadley repeats an all-too-common account of the north Indian sex ratio. She finds:

> … a shift in the sex ratio, from 866 adult females per thousand males in 1925 to 814 in 1984. The shift in the juvenile sex ratio (under age fifteen) has been even more dramatic, dropping from 900 females per thousand males in 1925 to 790 in 1984. Deaths of female children often come about from those illnesses that are most attributable to neglect, particularly forms of malnutrition, including kwashiorkor and pellagra. More girls than boys also die of fever, diarrhea, and chicken pox (and formerly smallpox), suggesting a lack of medical attention for sick daughters. (Wadley 1994: 14)

Similarly, in the Caldwell–Reddy study in central Karnataka:

> Indian sex ratios are high, being 105 males per 100 females in the study area in 1981, compared with 104 in Karnataka and 107 in India as a whole. The explanation is relatively high female mortality, probably arising from sex differentials in nutrition and other treatment. (Caldwell *et al.* 1988: 236–37).

It may well be objected that the Badaga masculinity ratio within our four villages in recent years has been affected by out-migration of a disproportionate number of males. This may to some extent be true; yet the argument does not, in my judgement, affect the national ratio, since a similar number of females to males have migrated overseas because of families going together. Nor has it affected the state figures, for when Tamilian (and Badaga) men have moved out of the state they too have often taken their nuclear families with them. The Nilgiris is not a district with a pattern of much out-migration, rather the reverse; and those few Badaga males who are not students but have gone elsewhere for employment opportunities have usually taken their nuclear families with them too. There remains the one area in which migration *has* affected the masculinity ratio, and that is immigration into the Nilgiris district, and Coonoor *taluk*, by Tamil and Malayali males who came looking for labouring positions, primarily in plantations. For Ketti Panchayat, the 'administrative village' or commune which encompasses three of my four villages, the 1981 official census ratio for all persons (Badaga and immigrant) was 1.06. The immigrants in that 'administrative village' area were several thousand Tamilian or Malayali labourers and a few petty officials, transport workers and shopkeepers. It had a total population of 21,336, including of course the non-Badagas. In this population there were altogether 10,978 males and 10,358 females, which yields a ratio of 1.06; the excess of males undoubtedly reflecting differential migration patterns.

On average the censuses over the years have yielded a Badaga ratio of 1.00; so, to repeat, there is neither statistical nor indeed anecdotal evidence that would lend any support to any former systematic infanticide among the Badagas, unless perhaps it had occurred prior to 1856. From my own data it is possible to lay to rest the matter of possible neglect of female infants, as I can look for an imbalance in the sexes in the 0–4 year cohort. Any imbalance in this cohort cannot have been offset by the importation of brides from another village, since the Badagas have not practised child marriage. Nor can it reflect the importation

Table 9.2
MASCULINITY RATIO IN THE 0–4 YEARS COHORT

Census	Ki:y Oḍeyaraṭṭi	O:rana:yi	Hulla:ḍa	Ke:ti Toreke:ri
1963	0.81	0.38	1.82	0.43
1990	0.58	2.08	1.11	0.57

of boy relatives from other villages who have come temporarily for the convenience of better schooling opportunities, since at 0–4 they are not yet of school age. The data speak however with different tongues, doubtless because the numbers were too small to mean much (Table 9.2).

A natural masculinity ratio in this cohort would be about 1.05, so there are indeed strong grounds for concluding that females were under-represented in the cohort in some villages, but at the same time over-represented in others. I would certainly not suggest, however, that female infanticide was being selectively practised here (and amniocentesis was unknown when I began this work), for I have no corroborating evidence whatever of any such practice from informal interviewing. There are no clear indications that female infants in 1963 were not so well cared for, not so well fed, or poorly treated when ill, in a sufficient number of cases that this imbalance in the sexes would result in *one* village alone. In 1981 (by my census) the over-all masculinity ratio for the entire Hulla:ḍa population was 1.16—the highest of the four sample villages in that census year. By 1990, we can see that the masculinity ratio for the 0–4 cohort is again within the historical Badaga range in Hulla:ḍa, 1.11. By 1990, grown daughters were often expected to bring a large dowry with them at marriage, something that had not been a traditional Badaga practice at all, and could not have affected the female survival rate as far back as 1963. Clearly education may have had something to do with an alteration in ideas about the worth of baby girls.

Imbalance in the sexes among infants is more characteristic of demography in northwestern India. The Badaga data, in contrast, accord well with the pattern in southern India.

> ...in both rural and urban Tamilnadu—as also in Kerala—the infant mortality rate for females is generally lower than the rate for males, whereas for the

> country as a whole—in both rural and urban areas—the situation is the exact reverse. This does not mean that there is no discrimination against female infants in Tamilnadu and Kerala. The lower mortality rate for female infants —in comparison with male infants—in the two states may be in spite of such discrimination, because of the well known fact 'that the female infants are biologically better fitted than male infants for survival'. (Nagaraj 1992: 116, 118)

Most cases of infant death in rural India occur during the first 12 months of life. The matter is still a serious health problem, for in 1994 a mortality rate of 65 per cent in the first month of life was calculated for Tamil Nadu as a whole (which has an infant mortality rate of 57 per 1,000, the second lowest figure of any Indian state; *The Hindu*: May 10, 1994: 4). The death registers for Christians of Kaity Parish (as it was then called) record that, during the years 1860–1914, 153 Badaga Christians died and were buried. These converts and their children lived in two of my sample villages, Ke:ti and Hulla:ḍa, and in eight other villages close by. They included former Gauḍas, Adikaris, Kaṇakkas, Ha:ruvas and Toreyas, and genetically were closely comparable with my own sample in the same area. Those who died while in their first year of life accounted for 29 per cent of all Badaga Christian deaths in the Pastorate; those who died aged 0–4 years were 52 per cent of all Badaga Christian deaths. But there is no sex difference at all in the death rates of these Badaga youngsters: 40 boys and 40 girls died between 1860 and 1914. For the childhood deaths, as we have already seen, the most common contributory factors — according to the German pastors — were respiratory diseases, then 'convulsions' (probably whooping-cough or tetanus; Birch 1902: 369-74), fever, and some other childhood diseases. Years which saw particularly heavy rates of death (e.g., a total of nine of *all* ages in 1900, 1902 and 1906; 10 in 1907; and 11 in 1911 and 1913) were usually occasions of epidemic disease. While these pathetic figures and the burial registers yield no suggestion whatever of female infanticide even in the 19th century, one would hardly expect it to occur at all in a newly Christian community who had been repeatedly told about the worth of each individual soul and how God loves all children, boys and girls. If it is suspected that the practice had occurred among some Hindu Badagas of that period, I have no evidence of it, either quantitative or anecdotal, and the census figures lend no support whatever for such a practice.

Table 9.3
NUMBER OF INFANT AND OTHER DEATHS IN FOUR VILLAGES

Deaths	K. Oḍeyaraṭṭi	O:rana:yi	Hulla:ḍa	Ke:ti T.	All sites	1863–1890
Number of boys aged 0–4 years	2	–	2	2	6	6
Number of girls aged 0–4 years	2	2	1	2	7	6
All other deaths 5–93 years	30	47	90	24	191	7

It is also possible to state from this archival material that, precisely one century before my own study, in 1863–1890, there was a total of six Badaga boys and six girls who died during the first five years of life. We can thus compare these figures with the number of recorded deaths in my own data over 27 years.

These figures suggest therefore that only 7 per cent of all deaths were in the 0–4 cohort in my sample, as compared with 63 per cent among the earlier Christians in that cohort. But my figures are not in fact reliable, as they must represent an under-enumeration. I was only working in these villages once every nine years, and hence could only take note of those deaths that had occurred in the intervening years if someone told me about them. In some cases a baby may have died as long as eight or nine years prior to my census enquiries, and its family members had by that time simply forgotten about it. Or a child's existence may never have come to my attention because it had both been born and died at points intermediate between two of my censuses. On one or two occasions family members in 1990 were incredulous when I assured them that they had had a small baby in the family in 1963 or 1972. It had of course soon died and been forgotten about by all save, we may suppose, its mother. In contrast, people would easily remember the year of death of an elderly relative. No death records were kept anywhere except at the Christian church. The missionaries, who lived a mere 50 metres from Ke:ti Toreke:ri, were obliged to complete an official register of all Christian deaths.

Morbidity

Morbidity is the demographer's word for illness episodes or lack of good physical care, even for lack of mental care. It is a concept that has proven to be easily measureable in Western countries through counting such data as number of days lost from work, number of days in bed or in a hospital, etc. Village conditions in traditional cultures like the Badaga one make it very difficult to establish similar data systematically from the families of cultivators. There are obviously going to be slack periods in the annual farming cycle when older people may spend a lot of time lying around the house, either on a bed or in a sunny spot on the veranda. A spate of coughing perhaps interspersed with cigarette smoking would give the observer every ground for asking questions about the poor man's prognosis. Yet a month or two later at harvest-time, if not actually 'cured' of his ailment, he might perhaps be seen working energetically in a field.

Some indications of prevalent diseases in the 19th century population

Table 9.4
PRESUMED CAUSES OF DEATH AMONG CHRISTIANS, BY PERCENTAGE, 1860–1914

Diseases	Age				
	under 1 yr.	1 – 12	12 – 25	25 – 55	› 55
Respiratory	7.3%	8.9%	4.4%	5.7%	2.5%
Fever	3.5	8.6	3.5	3.2	2.5
Gastro-intestinal	1.0	5.7	1.0	0.6	2.5
Communicable	1.3	4.8	1.3	1.9	0.6
'Convulsions'	4.1	1.6	–	–	0.3
'Childhood illness'	2.5	1.3	–	0.3	–
Heart failure	0.3	1.9	1.0	0.6	1.6
Maternity	–	–	0.3	1.0	–
Genito-urinary	–	0.3	0.3	–	–
Other	2.8	4.4	1.6	1.8	1.2
Total, by age	22.8	37.5	13.4	15.1	11.2

(Total, 100%; $N = 314$)

may be gathered from a statistical analysis of the presumed cause of death among 314 Christians of all ages and communities who died in Ke:ti Pastorate between 1860 and 1914. (Diagnosis was normally by a doctor or missionary; again, the data have been drawn from burial registers of that Pastorate.) In Table 9.4 the fatal diseases are listed roughly in order of severity/frequency. The age categories have been designed to discriminate between infants, children and adults.

That 60 per cent of all Christian deaths during that half-century were of children under 12 years, and 23 per cent were of infants under 1 year, explains why fertility remained depressed for so long. The worst season for childhood deaths was, according to the registers, May–June, a period when the weather usually changes from hot and quite dry to cold and very wet. 'Convulsions', a dangerous killer of infants, could be brought on by whooping cough, birth injuries or tetanus (Birch 1902: 369-74): it peaked around June, as did fevers. Respiratory infections were dangerous in May and June too, though they proved to be equally fatal in most other months of the year.

My own study did not seek systematic data on morbidity; whereas mortality is documented better. Consequently my observation on the rates of mortality can be discussed at some length, whereas not much is offered here on morbidity. I have however devoted an earlier book (Hockings 1980b) to the traditional system of health care among Badagas, which surveys their herbal medicine and related curing procedures. The pressure of other obligations and lack of a full-time research team made it impossible for me to mount a sustained study of morbidity throughout the sample population in the way that the Caldwells and associates were able to do in Karnataka, beginning in 1979 (Caldwell *et al.* 1988: 135–60). What I did find out about the subject indicates a close similarity with the findings in Karnataka, however, and two of their very general conclusions are applicable to the Badaga situation:

> First, any new injection of modern medical technology or services will not have its full impact at once, but may take many years to achieve its full potential as the interpretation of sickness changes. This change is largely the product of a broad social transformation secularizing many aspects of social life and tending to remove medical explanations and cures from the area of theology. The latter process is probably accelerated by some of the successes of the new technology. Secondly, even if medical technology were to stagnate at its present level, mortality levels would almost certainly decline for many years to come. (Caldwell *et al.* 1988: 160)

Actually, the health care facilities improved in both my sample villages and in those of the Caldwells' team around 1930. In their case, 'Modern (or allopathic) medicines arrived in the large village in 1929 when the Maharajah of Mysore ordered that a health center be provided' (Caldwell *et al.* 1988: 132). In the Badaga case a clinic was maintained in Ke:ti from 1921, to be replaced by another that the Ketti Medical Mission established in 1930 about 0.5 km south of Ke:ti Toreke:ri (thus centrally located among the four sample villages; at the exact centre of Map 2.1). This clinic was run from 1933 until its closing in 1955 by Dr K. I. Simon, a medical missionary from Kerala, with a compounder, nurse and other staff. Its clientele were largely Hindu Badagas. The number of patients treated ranged from 8,602 in 1933/34 to 7,134 in 1953, but at its highest point in 1943 there were 13,043 patients. In that same year, however, only eight of these were maternity cases; and this was nothing exceptional, for in the previous year when there had been 12,848 patients only 10 maternity cases were handled. Clearly the role of modern medicine in Badaga childbirth has been absolutely negligible, even in the final years of the clinic's operation. In the late 1960s, a Dispensary and Primary Health Centre were opened in Ke:ti at the same place. There was also a Maternity and Child Welfare Centre there with two medical practitioners by 1971. By 1980, when the comparative study of Khan and Gupta, already quoted, was carried out, the earlier situation must have shown substantial improvement:

> An analysis of the ... health services indicated that these were more extensively utilized in the Nilgiris than in Salem. A majority (64 percent) of the deliveries in the Nilgiris were conducted in hospitals ....
>
> ... the accessibility to health and family planning services was more satisfactory.... The provision of follow-up services was also better organised in the Nilgiris, and special attention was given to rural areas. Rural-urban disparities in the accessibility... in the Nilgiris were almost non-existent. (Khan and Gupta 1985: 120–22).

In 1963, some years after this clinic closed following Dr Simon's retirement, I asked a sample of 101 adults drawn from the populations of Hulla:ḍa and O:rana:yi who they turned to for medical help or information. The responses, given in Table 9.5, break down rather sharply into two categories, modernizing and traditional. (The mention of the visiting nurse by only one man probably means that she was only available at the Cordite Factory.) What is really remarkable about this table

Table 9.5
PERSONS CONSULTED FOR MEDICAL ADVICE, 1963

Information source	Men	Women
Doctor or clinic	25.3%	80.9%
Visiting nurse	1.3%	0%
Herbal therapist	10.7%	0%
Old people	36.1%	3.8%
Close relatives	16.0%	11.5%
Friends	9.3%	0%
No one (or 'never sick')	1.3%	3.8%
	(*N* = 75)	(*N* = 26)

is not so much the fact that only a quarter of the men were going to a modern doctor or clinic: it is that 80 per cent of the women (in an admittedly small sample) were doing this in 1963. One can argue that, with such a positive attitude towards scientific medicine, it is not too surprising that a decade later the women began to adopt family planning measures. And lest any reader feel that, with such a small sample, the findings should be dismissed as relatively meaningless, I might add that we shall later find (Table 11.17) that an even larger proportion of these poorly educated women in 1963 opted for a national future of industrialization whereas their menfolk were equally solidly in favour of India continuing as just an agricultural country. Here too, therefore, the women appear to be more progressive than the men.

One aspect of the age–sex pyramid (Figure 8.1) that is ambiguous is the health status of the elderly. Longevity can be taken anywhere as one good indicator of a healthy diet and care of the body; and one would expect that as culture modernizes longevity would increase somewhat. In point of fact this is not altogether the case in my data. Although several cases of men in their nineties were recorded, including one O:rana:yi man who died at 93, there were no such extremely advanced ages noted in either of the two censuses of 1963 and 1990 on which the pyramid was based. It may be worth noting that among the elderly in 1963 there was a total of 39 men aged 60 or over; 3 men were over 80. By 1990 there were 46 such men. On the female side the numbers are 32 aged 60 or over in 1963, 43 in 1990, (one of the latter being over 85).

Table 9.6
OLDEST INHABITANTS OF FOUR VILLAGES

	Highest age bracket in			
Census	Ki:y Oḍeyaraṭṭi	O:rana:yi	Hulla:ḍa	Ke:ti Toreke:ri
1963	70–74: 3 M	75–79: 1 M	80–84: 3 M	65–69: 2 M
	60–64: 1 F	75–79: 3 F	80–84: 1 F	60–64: 2 F
1990	70–74: 3 M	80–84: 2 M	75–79: 1 M	75–79: 1 M
	85–89: 1 F	80–84: 1 F	70–74: 2 F	70–74: 2 F

What is perhaps more telling than these statistics is the breakdown by village (Table 9.6, where M = male, F = female). In all villages except Hulla:ḍa (where it was already high but showed some decline) longevity increased perceptibly between these two censuses. It is worth noting that in both Ki:y Oḍeyaraṭṭi and in O:rana:yi the populations were entirely vegetarian in their diet, and furthermore (at least till the mid-1970s) both of these villages had a resident traditional herbal therapist (Hockings 1980b:182–208). Ke:ti and Hulla:ḍa, by contrast, were meat-eating and tended to rely more on modern scientific medicines, and for nearly a lifetime they had been very close to the clinic of the Ketti Medical Mission and its successor clinics.

There is considerable evidence that family elders are adequately cared for, and hardly ever are they abandoned to their own devices. Table 9.7 indicates that in the sample villages only about 4.4 per cent were living alone. A slightly larger percentage were living with one (in one case two) spouses. Very similar percentages of people, who no longer had a spouse, were now living with one or more of their unmarried children. In most cases these were widows living with an adult daughter. Taken together, such arrangements accounted for less than 20 per cent of the elderly: the preponderant arrangement was as it had long been—a man living with his wife and children in a nuclear or a joint family. The percentage of elderly living in this manner increased from 44.3 in 1963 to 56.2 per cent in 1990, a reflection of increased longevity in the community. After this, and following from it logically, the next most common residential arrangement was one in which a surviving spouse was now living with a married child or children, together with their own families. About 28 per cent of the elderly were in such families. A rather similar picture has been portrayed for central Karna-

Table 9.7
RESIDENTIAL STATUS OF ELDERLY PERSONS

Residence	1963	1990
Solitary	4.3%	4.5%
With spouse	7.1%	5.6%
With spouse and children	44.3%	56.2%
With unmarried children	7.1%	3.4%
With married child and family	27.2%	28.1%
Other arrangements	10.0%	2.2%
	(*N* = 70)	(*N* = 89)

taka (Caldwell *et al.* 1988: 188–90).

While the tiny number of solitary people was essentially three widows who lived in poverty, it will be seen from Table 9.7 that for the most part the elderly are housed and taken care of by their younger relatives. No doubt they were often appreciated for their contributions to the housework and to child care. Even elderly couples living by themselves normally had sons or other agnates in nearby houses who would provide for them. Sometimes a widow or widower would ease this burden by periodically moving from the house of one son to another's.

Adult Mortality

It would be possible to calculate the crude death rate per 1,000 for my census years, or for the late 19th century using the Christian death registers; but the Christian population was constantly being augmented by conversions, albeit at an uneven rate; while again, one cannot make accurate estimates for years between my four censuses. This is primarily because a woman's death (mainly a widow's) has not always been recorded by me at the time of the next census, not because I failed to ask but because neighbours were sometimes uncertain what exactly had happened to her. An old lady might indeed have died, but she might equally well have retired to the home of a relative in her natal village where she was still living quietly at the time of my next census; and thus, in either case, would not have been enumerated.

Table 9.8

AGE-SPECIFIC MORTALITY RATES, 1963–1990, IN FOUR VILLAGES

Age bracket	Proporn. of males dying in interval	Death rate	Proporn. of females dying in interval	Death rate
0–4 yrs.	.028	.028	.037	.037
5–14 yrs.	.035	.063	.028	.065
15–49 yrs.	.260	.323	.222	.287
› 49 yrs.	.676	1.000	.713	1.000

Based on 250 recorded deaths in the four villages, Table 9.8 quickly dispels certain prevalent ideas in the literature dealing with mortality in South Asia. In the first place, there is again no statistical evidence for any neglect or a higher death-rate among infant girls: in point of fact four boys and four girls aged 0–4 died during the study period. (At least, that is according to my records. People, it must be admitted, were not sufficiently precise about age at death to allow for the isolation here of the few cases of death within the first 12 months, though my data-gathering techniques have possibly led to an under-enumeration of this cohort.)

A second common supposition, that the death-rate among peasant women of child-bearing age will be higher than that for men in the same age cohort, is emphatically not borne out by this table. (It was however noticed that four girls had died at about the age of 15.) The fact that the total number of female deaths during the years 1963–1990 represented only 76 per cent of the number of male deaths reflects the higher life-expectancy of women in that period, and improvements in women's health. This is underlined by the column showing the proportion dying in each age interval: of all persons who died (total = 1.000), 0.713 of the women were aged over 49 years, whereas only 0.676 of the men were over that age.

To take another view of the same data, Figure 9.1 plots the age at death of these same people. Again, the statistics on which the table are based are probably marred by some under-enumeration of infant death. Widows were occasionally lost track of between censuses, so that in a few cases it is unclear whether they had died or just moved away to another village between censuses. The graph makes clear the unusually

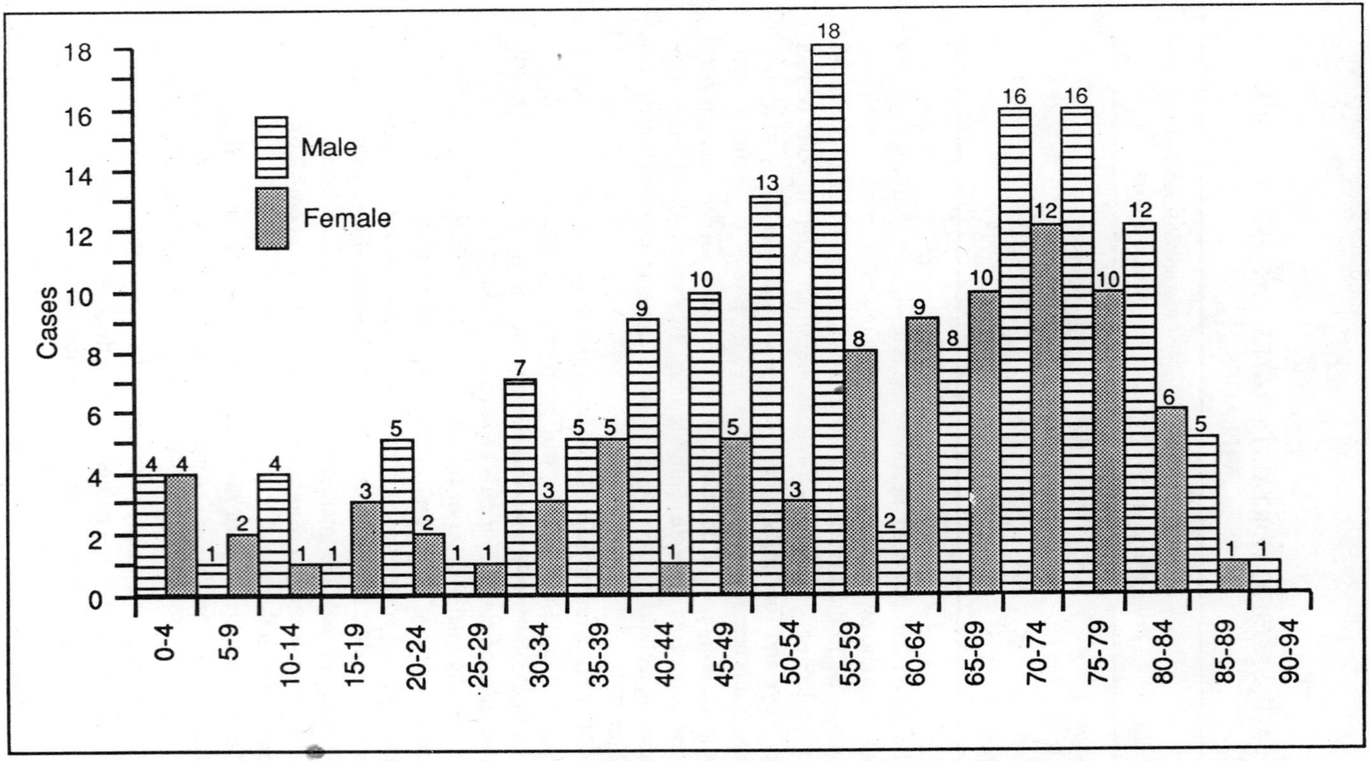

Figure 9.1 AGE AT DEATH IN FOUR VILLAGES, 1963–1990

high death-rate among middle-aged men. In total there were 44 men who died between 30 and 54 years, as compared with only 17 women in the same cohort. Possibly hepatitis B has increased the mortality rate among the middle-aged men. The median age at death for men comes in the years 55–59, whereas for women it comes at 60–64.

Since precisely 250 persons died in the four villages during the course of the study, this would yield an artificial death-rate of 9.25 per annum. Phrased otherwise, we can say that 250 persons had died between 1963 and 1990, leaving behind in that latter year a population of 1,298.

Since most men in modern times have taken brides 5–10 years younger than themselves, and since average female longevity is certainly as high as male for this district, it is no surprise that a number of widows were documented in every village at each one of my censuses. The fate of these old ladies varies, no doubt. Some live on in the family home with one or more sons, and can play a valuable role in socializing and caring for the small grandchildren or great-grandchildren (see Table 9.7). Others return to their place of origin, normally another village from which they had come in marriage half-a-century or so back. This is seemingly reflected in the data on age at death, for in each village the number of women who died over the 27-year period was no more than half to two-thirds the number of men: women often went elsewhere to die. Yet others have no welcoming relatives to return to in the natal village, and so end their days almost alone in their husband's house, sometimes with just an unmarried or a divorced daughter for company.[3] There they can still play with the children and gossip with the neighbours even if they become somewhat incapacitated. And as my book *Sex and Disease in a Mountain Community* (1980b) made clear, an old lady (Plate 10) is occasionally the living repository of a rich store of valuable ethnomedical knowledge, though nowadays this is increasingly seen as anachronistic.

NOTES

1. For further data on the early Nilgiri censuses, 1812–1871, cf. Grigg (1880: 27–30, etc). I am not in a position to assess the relative reliability of the various Presidency/State censuses; (cf. Guilmoto 1992).
2. '... the Revenue Authorities of the Nilgiris district gave us 1,25,821 as the present population .... In the absence of separate Census enumeration it is difficult to estimate the population accurately' (Backward Classes Commission

1975: 8).

3. There is little point in comparing the incidence of widowhood in my sample with that in the Christian burial registers for 1863–1890 because of a selection factor: conversion to Christianity has long been a last resort for an old widow who had 'nowhere else to go'. She could expect charity from the mission; and when she died her status as widow was duly recorded in the burial register.

PART IV

MODERN LIFE: WORK AND THE MASS MEDIA

Chapter 10

THE HOUSEHOLD AND MODERN LIFE

We live not as we wish, but as we can.
— Menander

The State of the Nilgiri Economy

The Nilgiris district, though not highly commercialized except in the plantation sector, is quite progressive both educationally and economically as compared with other parts of India that lie beyond the great cities. In November of 1993 the Economic Intelligence Service, which accords a relative index value of development of 100 to India as a whole, gave an index of 135 to Tamil Nadu State and of 173 to the Nilgiris district. These indices were inversely correlated with the annual population growth, which that Service put at 2.14 per cent for all India, 1.40 per cent for Tamil Nadu, and 1.13 per cent for the Nilgiris. Population density for the district was almost exactly the national figure: 278 per sq. km in the Nilgiris, 273 in the Indian nation, but 429 in Tamil Nadu state.

Other unusual statistical features of the Nilgiris stand out in the report of the Economic Intelligence Service. In a total area of 2549 sq. km, it was estimated that in 1993, 56 per cent of the district was nominally forested, 24 per cent was the net sown area, and of this latter only 0.8 per cent was the net irrigated area. The monsoons are still the major source of a farmer's water. Other districts in the same state showed very different proportions indeed: hence 16 per cent, 44 per cent and 48 per cent respectively for Tamil Nadu as a whole.

The district population in the same year was estimated as 353,430 urban and 356,780 rural; a somewhat artificial distinction perhaps, since many village populations had only recently been included within newly created urban boundaries. The literacy rate in 1993 was estimated at 63 per cent, compared with an all-India figure of 52 per cent.

The major economic activity is plantation agriculture. Thus 69 per cent of the total cropped area in 1993 was devoted to tea, 15 per cent to coffee, 6 per cent to potatoes, and 4 per cent (in the lowlands) to rice. Ginger and cardamom were the only other crops to (slightly) exceed 1 per cent of the cropped acreage. Given the dominance of high value plantation crops, it is not surprising to find that in 1993 the value of the output per hectare of the major crops was put at Rs 21,288, as compared with only Rs 6,622 for Tamil Nadu state, and Rs 3,576 for India as a whole: this value in the Nilgiris is just six times the national average. Figures for the value of output *per capita* are proportionately very similar (Rs 1,862 in the Nilgiris district). *Per capita* foodgrain production is consequently very low: just 6 kg per person in the Nilgiris, as compared with 124 kg in Tamil Nadu and 173 kg in India generally.

Another marker of the advanced state of the regional economy is the comparatively great extent of the road network: in 1993 the Nilgiris had 162 km of road per 100 sq. km of land surface, as compared with 128 km for Tamil Nadu state and 60 km for India as a whole. Bank credit per hectare for agriculture was also far higher in this district than in the state or the nation: in 1993 it was estimated at Rs 6,409 in the Nilgiris, Rs 2,985 in Tamil Nadu state, but Rs 1,046 for all of India.

No doubt these summary economic statements mask much of the diversity within this very small district. Bauxite is an important mineral product (32,485 tonnes in 1993), not mentioned in this volume. Commercial production of minor crops for 1993 included 7,170 tonnes of bananas, 5,003 tonnes of tapioca, 1,878 tonnes of sugarcane, 1,692 tonnes of garlic, 781 tonnes of ginger, 489 tonnes of sweet potatoes, 221 tonnes of turmeric, 219 tonnes of *ragi* (a millet), 112 tonnes of pepper, 85 tonnes of cardamom, and 46 tonnes of castor. Besides tapioca, the main grain produced in the district was rice, but in 1993 this only amounted to 3,647 tonnes.[1]

The figures for foodgrain production illustrate a phenomenon that is widespread in developing countries. As more people move into non-food-producing employment, or produce only such export crops as tea and peppers, a majority of the district's population is put in the position of buying its grain from elsewhere. But that 'elsewhere' in our case is the poorer, more backward rural areas of south India that are devoted solely to rice production. For the Nilgiris there are only 12.5 kg of locally grown grain per person per annum; and as the population swells in other rice-growing localities during the coming century, they are likely to have less rice available for export to cities and to the Nilgiris district, unless biotechnology can come to the rescue.

Agriculture and Tea Planting

One can specify the nature of agricultural change during the 20th century for villages like those of the Ke:ti valley by reference to Nanjana:ḍu, a large Badaga village lying some 10 km to the west of Ke:ti; because for this place it was possible to find the acreage of crops both in 1881 and in 1955 (Table 10.1; a hectare is 2.47 acres).

During that period the cultivated area here only increased by 1 per cent, (and obviously there would be slight fluctuations in such figures for any year in which they were available). What is of interest, however, is the big shifts that three-quarters of a century have produced: tea has quadrupled its acreage; white tinay (*tene*) or Italian millet, a former staple grain, has disappeared altogether in favour of little millet (and more importantly bought rice); cinchona is no longer grown because the market for it has disappeared now that other cures than quinine are available for malaria; and potato has become a major marketable commodity. Since 1955 the main trends have been a decline in little millet and potato, but a continuing increase in the area under tea. These post-war trends are illustrated in Ke:ti, where in 1962 the Toreyas and Gauḍas were growing barley, beans (*Phaseolus vulgaris*), cabbage, garlic and potato as the main summer crops, together with small amounts of amaranth, beetroot, carrot, coriander, mustard, peas, pumpkin, tea and some other beans (*Vicia faba* and *Dolichos lablab*). The winter crop crop in early 1963 included, in addition to most of those included in Table 10.1, some maize, onions, tomatoes, turnips and wheat. By 1990, these crops were not all to be found because of a general switch to tea cultivation.

One development theory that has to some extent been espoused by Indian planners, with a view to bringing the poor somewhat closer in living standards to the urban middle classes, is the so-called trickle-down theory (Hirschman 1958; Rostow 1960). It holds that by stimulating growth in formal parts of the economy, urban industrialization and a shift to cash crops in the countryside will begin to put more benefits within the reach of more people. The practical implementation of this theory—and its limitations—are clearly illustrated by recent government agricultural policy in the Nilgiris district, and specifically in the Ke:ti (or Ketty) valley:

As more and more virgin land was cleared of forest and brought under the plough, mainly for growing potatoes which offered tempting money returns, especially during the last War, the fertile top-layer containing humus was lost in the streams and rivers.

Early in 1950, the State Government took steps to popularize contour bunding and contour trenching. Subsequently, the cutting down of trees and cultivating the hill slopes were also regulated.

A subsequent survey... showed that the Ketty valley... was the worst eroded area, requiring immediate attention. Thus, the scheme for soil conservation was put into operation ....

Inquiries indicated that about 50 years ago, farmers used to apply four to six tons of cattle manure per acre. This manure was gradually replaced by chemical fertilizers starting with about 300 pounds and in the course of a few years giving up to 1,600 pounds of it per acre. Today it is about 2,400

Table 10.1

CROPS CULTIVATED IN NANJANA:ḌU VILLAGE, 1881 and 1955

Crops cultivated	1881	1955
Grains		
White tinay (*Setaria pumila*)	607.00 ha	–
Barley (*Hordeum sativum*)	8.90 ha	1.21 ha
Finger millet (*Eleusine coracana*)	–	1.62 ha
Little millet (*Panicum sumatrense*)	–	125.45 ha
Wheat (*Triticum dicoccum*)	–	2.02 ha
Vegetables		
Garlic	–	0.40 ha
Coriander	–	1.01 ha
Legumes	–	3.44 ha
Greens, carrots, etc.	–	2.43 ha
Miscellaneous vegetables	32.37 ha	–
Commercial crops		
Tea	52.62 ha	208.36 ha
Potato	–	437.37 ha
Cinchona	101.20 ha	–
Eucalyptus	–	28.33 ha
TOTAL:	802.09 ha	811.64 ha

(*Source*: Weigt 1970: 339)

pounds. Bad land management and no regard to soil conservation had brought loss and more expenses to farmers.

In 1952 a small area of 19 acres in the valley was taken over to demonstrate to farmers the usefulness of soil conservation measures. Subsequently it was expanded to another 200 acres. Seeing the benefit of soil conservation measures, the farmers of Kammandu voluntarily took up soil conservation work in their village.

Encouraged by the results obtained, the scheme has now been extended to all the other catchment areas in the Nilgiris, covering an area of about 60,000 acres.

The land use classification and the bunding and terracing techniques adopted in the Ketty valley are interesting. For slopes up to 10 per cent, graded bunds at three feet vertical intervals with waste weirs are adopted. For slopes between 10 and 15 per cent, graded trenches at five feet interval[s] are used. For slopes between 16 and 33 per cent, bench terraces with the disposal drains along the inner edge of the terrace and rock pits at the end have been found to be the best. For slopes over 33 per cent, contour trenches and afforestation or grass planting [are] recommended.

Besides bund terracing and graded trenching, [channelling] and gully plugging and agronomic improvements are also carried out. These practices include contour cultivation, rotational cropping and manuring, grass patching and tree planting ....

At present, farmers do not pay attention to rotational crops. If ever they do, they rotate potato with wheat, *samai, ragi* and rye with the green manure crop of lupin. Often, fallowing is resorted to between two crops, but this is done only in steep, unterraced lands. Fallowing would be quite unnecessary if all lands are terraced.

On the slopes, government tractors do the terracing at concessional rates. Local labour is difficult to get and costly, and hence used to a limited extent .... The cost of terracing per acre comes to about Rs. 350 to 400. From the second season onwards, the increase in the yield on such terraced lands equals this cost ....

Farmers are convinced now that they stand to gain by scientific soil conservation measures. With the luxuriant crop cover on the terraced valley dotted with clumps of blue gum, wattle and cypress and patches of orderly tea cultivation thrown in between, the landscape now presents a different picture from what it was five years ago. (Mudaliar 1957: 17–18; see Plate 1)

Since the 1970s, the Crop Diversification Scheme has been intended to encourage local farmers to switch from potatoes, which had become unprofitable because of parasites, to the cash crop of tea. The problem of actually making this switch was seen as a monetary one, since any farmer now planting his land with tea would not see a harvest for the first three years. Clearly he needed to be tided over with the guarantee of an interim income, provided by the government. Similarly all tea needs pruning once every five years. At this time all remaining leaf is sold for low-grade tea and the branches used for firewood. But then there is no further yield for a year, and so the state government also compensates the grower for this shortfall at a rate (1994 figures) of Rs 6000 (U.S. $200) per hectare. Otherwise leaf is never plucked between December and March, and normal plucking rounds are done by the small growers 22–25 times a year (although the United Planters' Association of southern India now recommends 38–45 times, but that requires more fertilizer and careful plucking).

This would appear to be an adequate and fair-minded intervention by government into what is, after all, a private capitalistic venture. The problems for small growers in the Nilgiris, some 90 per cent of whom are Badagas, have come with recent fluctuations of the world tea market and the unwillingness of the Indian Tea Board to set maximum and minimum prices for leaf (which it was empowered to do in 1952). In 1990 a kilo of green leaf (which produces about 0.25 kg of tea) brought the grower Rs 7.50. This price began to drop at the beginning of 1994 because Russian buyers had stopped coming to the Indian tea auctions. By May of that year the price of green leaf was down to Rs 3.00 a kilo (10¢ U.S.) when the cost of producing it was at least Rs 4.50. Fortunately, in 1995, tea prices recovered somewhat (though the Russian economy continued to falter).

This caused a serious problem for all of the Badaga growers, and especially for those in the Ke:ti valley area. A green-leaf buyer in a village near Hulla:ḍa was getting leaf from about 100 acres of land in 1994, all owned by Badagas. It was estimated that a *good* field will yield some 4,000 kg per acre per year—but after application of 700 kg of urea or ammonia-based fertilizer, costing Rs 1,750. The other essential costs of cultivating one acre of tea in the Ke:ti area are (in 1993 figures) Rs 1,000 for weeding and maintenance, Rs 4,000 or more for plucking, and Rs 1,500 for fencing and caretaking. This suggests the cost of producing one kilo of green leaf was little more than two rupees; but it presumes a full production of 4,000 kg on each acre. In point of fact, drought, frost or other disasters can vastly reduce the production. If it is raining, the pluckers who have been hired for the day still have to be paid. In 1993 that meant giving Rs 16 (or Rs 22 in 1994) plus one rupee for coffee to each woman. On a normal day she would pluck about 20 kg of leaf. If one 15-day plucking round is missed, the crop becomes almost useless. This might happen when there is a shortage of female pluckers; and men will not do the job.

One might expect the farmer, when faced with such difficulties, to revert to more traditional crops, but he cannot. In converting his land into a tea plantation he covered the slopes in a close network of ditches and banks; so that only a massive mechanized terracing and up-rooting of tea bushes could ever make the land again look the way it did—and in the process the topsoil would have been lost! In short, conversion to tea is an irreversible process. No one is willing to meet the heavy expenses that would be involved with going back to unprofitable farming.

Landholding

One very important point of similarity between the nine villages of the Caldwell–Reddy study and the Badaga ones is the decline in available land per capita. 'As population has grown, average farm size has fallen to a point where many farming families do not need the labor of young children' (Caldwell *et al.* 1988: 184). This is demonstrably the case in the Nilgiris too, where I was able to make a precise comparison of one village, So:lu:ru, at two points some 80 years apart (Table 10.2). Although a few other communities are found there as labourers, it is predominantly a Badaga commune. The small amount of land deceptively classified in the surveys as 'available for sale' was in fact so steep and rocky that even today it has scarcely any economic use, unless perhaps for common grazing. Table 10.2 shows the typical, much-diminished amount of mean landholdings in this particular Badaga village; (a hectare is 2.47 acres).

It may not be irrelevant to recall that Driver (1963), working in central India, found a direct relationship between family fertility and size of landholdings. Since, as the aforementioned example indicates, in modern Badaga history too the size of landholdings per capita has been steadily declining, it is not surprising to find this paralleled by declining fertility. The smallness of the average farm plot, combined with the repeated failure of potato crops over the past few decades, have certainly been two of the more important factors prompting Badagas to look for prolonged education for their boys and girls, with a view to

Table 10.2
COMPARISON OF DATA FOR SO:LU:RU VILLAGE, 1884 & 1962

Economic feature	1884	1962
Total 'village' area	9,113 hectares	9,111 hectares
Registered *patta* lands	913 ha. (all Badaga-owned)	1,619 ha. (nearly all Badaga)
Number of *pattas* (deeds)	49 single registrations; 63 joint ones (i.e., 112 total)	372 in total
Population (1881, 1961)	1,772 (all communities)	8,518 (all communities)
Houses	384	930
Mean household size	4.61	9.15
Estimate of cropped area	749 ha. (in 1880–1881)	607 ha.
Average cultivated area	0.42 ha. per capita	0.07 ha. per capita (in 1961)

(*Source*: Based on McIver and Stokes 1883; Benson 1884; Arputhanathan 1953: 43; and Subrahmanyam 1962: 3–4).

their future employment in government or other urban contexts. The frequent observation that young men educated in a city college will require sophisticated wives is motivation enough to keep teenaged girls in school, with the hope of ultimately being able to link them to financially sound affines; but it has the unplanned effect of reducing the number of fertile years of these young women. Some, as I have shown, miss the opportunity to marry altogether: one Gauḍa couple, for example, were living with their children in a joint-stem family in 1990 which included two unmarried daughters aged 43 and 39, as well as a married son aged 37.

Most of the landholdings of a family are quite small. In 1963 it was possible to question a sample of 101 Badagas in Hulla:ḍa and O:rana:yi as to what sized holding they had. While one may be sceptical about the answers most women gave, as they were probably citing their husband's or father's holdings, there were definitely cases where women were using what they considered 'their' land, and the acreage was in fact not identical to what another member of the same family told me about his landholding (Table 10.3). It is notable that the median holding reported was 2 acres for men and slightly less than that (1–2 acs.) for women.

Table 10.3
LANDHOLDING IN TWO SAMPLE VILLAGES, 1963

Acreage held	*Men*	*Women*
None	9	6
Less than 1 ac.	14	6
1–2 acs.	14	3
2–3 acs.	12	4
3–4 acs.	8	2
4–5 acs.	7	2
5–7 acs.	8	3
7–11 acs.	2	–
11–25 acs.	1	–
26–70 acs.	–	–
	(*N* = 75)	(*N* = 26)

The Household Economy

It was very usual for the household to operate a joint budget. Thus the male members would pool their earnings from whatever source, mainly from the sale of tea and farm produce. Those who were employed in local government positions, as a schoolteacher or road inspector, for example, once brought home meagre salaries; so that if they had a wife and several children they might still be fairly dependent on the produce of the family's fields. Today their pay-scales are distinctly improved, however.

Most villagers, like farmers everywhere, from time to time find themselves short of cash. I therefore asked a sample of 101 people in two of the villages in 1963 who they turned to for a loan, and got the responses found in Table 10.4. No doubt interest rates had much to do with their choices: friends and relatives might well charge no interest.

I did not gather systematic information about employment for all members of the four villages during the censuses. This calls for some explanation. Perhaps the main point was that my focus of interest was the household rather than the individual, and it must be admitted that when the study began in 1963 there was little variation in any of the four villages from the traditional occupation of farming. Nearly all

Table 10.4
SOURCES OF MONETARY LOANS, 1963

Sources	Men	Women
Badaga friend	28	2
Non-Badaga friend	–	–
Old people	18	1
Close relatives	9	15
Co-operative Bank or Society	–	–
Village moneylender	2	–
Town moneylender	3	–
Various sources	3	–
No one	12	8
	(*N* = 75)	(*N* = 26)

households owned or at least rented some land, though this naturally varied in extent, and perhaps a few of the households consisting of just a widowed person did not have access to land.

By the end of my study period, in 1990, there was definitely more diversity in occupations; yet it could be said that virtually every household in the four villages was still dependent on agriculture to a very considerable extent: in brief, these remained four farming communities with no obvious urbanization. What had commonly changed, to improve their economic lot somewhat, was the crop. In 1963, it seemed that everyone was growing potatoes for sale. By 1972, a series of losses brought on by blight and the golden nematode parasite, already a pest in 1963, had prompted many farmers to switch to cabbage and cauliflower or sometimes other marketable crops like carrots, onions or tea. By 1990, there were quite a few small tea patches in and around O:rana:yi and Ki:y Oḍeyaraṭṭi, although the other two villages were still cultivating vegetables for the most part. But by that year numerous households contained one or more earning members in local business, industry, transportation, teaching or administration.

Many of the households included students, if this may be considered an employment category. So far as I could discover, all of the children over five or six did attend one of the nearby schools until their adolescence: there was in modern times none of the employment of Badaga children in dreary, repetitive occupations that has been so widely reported from other parts of South Asia. Practically every hamlet in the

Ke:ti valley area had its own primary school, and in addition there were around Ke:ti itself a middle school, a high school, a higher secondary school and a small library by 1971, as we shall see (pp. 237–38). College students too were fairly numerous; but a college education more often than not prepared a youth for a life as a more urbane farmer and a girl for a 'better' marriage to one. My main informant in O:rana:yi, M. N. Thesingh, could identify 94 relatives (including himself) who were resident in that village in 1963. Of these 18 were then school or college students; i.e., 19 per cent of his relatives. (Since the total recorded population for that village in 1963 was 212, his kindred amounted to a very substantial sample.) In general there has been under-employment of college graduates, male and especially female, throughout the entire period of the study; in the sense that fathers wanted their sons and daughters to come home right after graduation and settle down to a life of farming in the village. Many rather frustrated young people did what their fathers wanted, and are still there.

The employment situation, then, and my data on it, contrast sharply with those given in, for instance, the Caldwell–Reddy study. But that contrast is itself a product of two quite different forms of social organization in rural India. The Badagas are an agricultural people living in their single-community, single-clan exogamous villages. They have no other traditional pursuit than mixed farming, no artisans other than the neighbouring Kota tribe. But the nine Karnataka villages of the Caldwell–Reddy study were mostly multicaste, or when single-caste they were nonetheless integrated into a local multicaste socio-economic network. In other words, these latter villages were home to a wide range of crafts and occupations, and so it would be surprising if the authors had not devoted space to the division of labour between castes. Yet there too the great majority of households were directly dependent on their agricultural activities, as one should still expect in almost any rural Indian community. Only 27 per cent of the total village population belonged to non-agricultural castes, the so-called 'service or artisan castes', and in fact this figure was largely made up of the 22 per cent who were Muslims and who were viewed as a 'trading caste'. Present-day realities meant that even some members of this minority category were actually working as farm labourers or in some other agricultural capacity. At the same time 30 per cent of the 'elite castes' in these Karnataka villages were professional people in modern, urban-style occupations; and these traditional elite were in fact Brahmins, Jains and

Lingayats, men of three distinct, high-ranking vegetarian religious sects (Caldwell *et al.* 1988: 27–31).

Despite my earlier disclaimers the topic of employment was by no means neglected. In 1963 (but at no later point), while completing the census of these four villages, I also ran a formal social survey with the help of over a dozen college students whom I had trained in interview techniques. So many assistants were necessary because we found that, in order to complete the survey not just with Badagas but also with hundreds of other respondents throughout the Nilgiris district, we had to have command of five languages, a requirement beyond my own abilities; and besides, the questioning had to be completed quickly. I did, however, closely supervise the interviews, did about 15 per cent of them myself, and personally interviewed the heads of most households in Hulla:ḍa—56 persons—as well as 23 men and women haphazardly selected from the Hulla:ḍa population. This latter group, however, included in a number of cases a son, daughter or wife who 'spoke for' the very aged head of household. By my definition Hulla:ḍa contained 72 households in 1963; so I had interviewed 78 per cent of their heads, each interview lasting about three-quarters of an hour, and containing 77 questions. Some people did not want to be interviewed, were not available, or simply 'did not feel up to it' — not altogether surprising, given the length of the questionnaire. In addition to this large body of 79 interviews, I and my student assistants interviewed a small sample of 12 people, male and female, in O:rana:yi, one of the other three villages (not to mention over 500 interviews we did in about 76 communities elsewhere in the district). The interviewed sample in these two villages represented very approximately the proportions of the major religious sects within the Badaga Hindu community: 85.7 per cent of the sample were Saivite Gauḍas, 13.2 per cent were Lingayats, while 1.1 per cent (one man) was Haruva. The mean ages of informants in the two villages were somewhat different: in O:rana:yi it was 35.7 years, whereas in Hulla:ḍa it was 42.3 years.

I refer to this study here, and will again later in Chapter 11, because that is how I collected my main body of data on occupations and educational level, especially those of the men living in Hulla:ḍa. In addition, during 1963 I got the following *percentages* on occupations (Table 10.5) from a sample of the residents in four villages within the study area. These were Hulla:ḍa, O:rana:yi, its Kaṇakka neighbour Ka:ṭe:ri, and the *Gauḍa* part of Ke:ti. These were not self-designated occupations, since the data were given to me by a knowledgeable relative in

Table 10.5
PER CENT OCCUPATIONS OF A SAMPLE IN FOUR VILLAGES, 1963

Occupation	Males				Females			
	Hulla:ḍa	Ka:ṭe:ri	Ke:ti	O:rana:yi	Hulla:ḍa	Ka:ṭe:ri	Ke:ti	O:rana:yi
Farmer	66	38	26	22	74	67	–(*u*)	62
Farm labourer	10				16			
Tea planter		6		14				
Housekeeper						25	54	11
Teacher		8		7				
Businessman/ broker	1	6	6					
Construction worker	13							
Clerk/postman	3	8	10	5				
Cordite factory worker	6		17	13	21			
Transportation	1							
Retired/ unemployed		6	3	5	10			2
College student			3					
Schoolchild	–(*u*)	6 (*u*)	32	20	–(*u*)	6 (*u*)	32	18
Infant	–(*u*)	5 (*u*)	6	5	–(*u*)	2 (*u*)	14	
N =	70	66	31	44	19	51	28	45

every case. I do, however, know that there has been some under-representation (*u*) of children in particular villages of the sample. In Hulla:ḍa the children were not questioned, while in Ke:ti the informant chose not to represent housewives as cultivators too. This was in direct conflict with my own observations, for I often saw women working in their fields there. In defense of the informant it must be admitted, however, that farming was a part-time job for them, and in 1963 there was indeed very little field work for them to do because of the ravages of a potato parasite. Otherwise the table is notable for its sex distinctions: evidently men never do housework, women never work outside the village, and women never retire! Only one youth in the three village samples was a college student, but the nearly identical figures for schoolboys and schoolgirls strongly suggest total attendance of school-age children in these three villages.

Factory Work

Given the present shortage of arable land, it is not surprising that a small minority of the Badagas in my sample villages have gained jobs as factory labourers or clerks, in three local factories. The most important one has been the Government Cordite Factory at Aravanga:ḍu, a central government munitions enterprise opened in 1900. A smaller employer has been the needle industries in the nearby village of Ellena:yi. Founded about 50 years ago, it—like the other factory—was built on the site of a 19th century brewery which probably gave employment to a few Badagas too (Francis 1908: 290, 312). Thus both of these factories have been in existence for a very long time, and are nothing new to the local Badagas. In the past few years the Ponds Company has opened a factory processing mushrooms at a point somewhere between Ki:y Oḍeyaraṭṭi and Hulla:ḍa. In addition, one may find in the neighbourhood several co-operative tea factories which also offer some labouring positions. It must be understood, however, that these latter are essentially drying and packing sheds equipped with machinery that owes its design to the late 19th century. In summary, factory work for these Badagas has mainly meant tedious labouring experience with unchanging types of equipment and work habits. During the course of my study, however, a new factory making raw film was opened on the other side of Ootacamund, the district headquarters. This was Hindustan Photo Films (HPF), another government undertaking which has given employment to several hundred Badagas, including a few from Hulla:ḍa. In contrast to the more traditional factories just mentioned, this one obviously has to use modern equipment and procedures. It tends to employ college graduates, who seem to relish the opportunity of having a government clerical or manufacturing job within the boundaries of their native district. Of these several factories, the Cordite Factory has been the longest employer of the greatest number of villagers. It alone has been helping certain households for over three generations now, by adding the regular income of one or two men to the uncertainties of their cultivated produce.

Migration

Migration is a subject of great importance in demography, for it has a broad impact on other life data, including nuptiality, natality, fertility and mortality. This is easily seen if we observe that the mechanics of population growth in our four villages can be reconstructed according to the following formula:

> 1963 population (886) + incoming brides + other immigrants – outmarrying brides – other emigrants + births – deaths = 1990 population (1,298)

In these villages migration has certainly been occurring over a quarter-century. Yet the Badagas still have a very stable society, and the population has not become subject to major movements in recent decades. It has felt the impact, on the other hand, of the heavy, government-sponsored immigration of Tamilians from Sri Lanka, who have been 'dumped' in the Nilgiris district and who in some localities have caused social problems by becoming squatters on Badaga lands.

With the minor exception of the Hulla:ḍa group who chanced on employment with the railways, any motivation to migrate away from these Badaga villages has been slight. This contrasts with some other parts of India. Dandekar's book, *Men to Bombay, Women at Home* (1986), for example, is about the importance of the economic ties with the city that have attracted many poor migrants from a Maharashtrian village. Charlotte Wiser (Wiser and Wiser 1989: 186–92) has given a detailed account of how in Karimpur, Uttar Pradesh, a number of traditional craftsmen (from the 'service castes') have found their old *jajmani* obligations are no longer being sufficiently honoured to give them an adequate living. People were going instead to the nearby towns for common goods and services which used to be obtained within the village. So the more enterprising craftsmen as a consequence were moving to town themselves to counter the decline in trade. Within the Badaga villages there is no such tendency, as they are not multicaste and they contain few if any service personnel; and previously every family had essentially the same occupation of farming, to which animal husbandry was sometimes attached. Badagas were never dependent on each other for craft services, since these were traditionally provided by the Kotas of Kollimale (Kolmel) and elsewhere; and after about 1930 the towns were already meeting all the service needs of village Badagas through cash transactions.

In my own study, taking the village as my unit of analysis, I have been able to identify five kinds of migration pattern among Badagas themselves.

(1) In-migration of brides, which is balanced against out-migration of other brides, since these are patrilocal and mostly exogamous villages;
(2) Youths going off to the cities for study, or to take up urban professions;
(3) Families moving to land available elsewhere in the Nilgiris: this may be a family-owned plantation somewhere nearby, or it may be farmland that chances to be available in the wife's natal village. In other words, the general rule of virilocal residence is sometimes converted to uxorilocal residence, especially when the wife does not have any brothers to inherit her father's land;
(4) Families moving to other parts of India because of urban employment opportunities or job transfers;
(5) Widows often and divorcees nearly always return to their father's or brother's home. Some bring children with them too.

Study-migration (2, above) may only take a young person away for three or four years, but the other patterns of migration identified here are likely to be fairly permanent. Not listed here because it is not a long-term migration is the frequent visiting of their natal home by married daughters. During the warm and then wet months of May–July, the period of all my censuses, I recorded numerous instances of such women who were on a visit at the time (but have not been included here in my household data). Only one instance was ever recorded, however, of a woman migrating elsewhere without a husband or children (and her life in Bangalore was reportedly quite scandalous). Some widows returned to their natal homes; a few females have left the Nilgiris district altogether in marriage, however, and others are temporarily in other parts of India for advanced education. 'The female population of a village is never constant in size and never composed of the same individuals for more than a few days at a time' (Jacobson 1977: 266).

A measure of how much emigration had occurred in the past for reasons of both employment and higher education is given in the figures from the national Census of India which initiates the period of my study. It cites the number of Badaga speakers throughout India in 1961 as 85,463; and the number of Badaga speakers in the Nilgiris district as 84,823. The difference is thus 640, or 0.7 per cent. These 640 people were mostly living elsewhere in Madras state, and were primarily college students or the permanent inhabitants of a small and ancient Badaga settlement in the Biligiri Rangan Hills of neighbouring Periyar district, to the east. Only 55 males and 37 females were to be found elsewhere, and then only in Kerala or Mysore states. This small number represented a significant increase from the emigrants of 20 years before: in 1941 there were only 270 Badagas living elsewhere, and nearly all of them were in the nearby Biligiri Rangan hamlets (Hockings 1980a: 32). These people then represented only 0.48 per cent of the Badaga total, and cannot be viewed as migrants anyway.

For the period of my study it is possible to tabulate all instances of migration in the four sample villages (Table 10.6).

It will be noticed that many more of the Hulla:ḍa people seem to be mobile than is the case with other villagers. This should be related to the fact that they have good road and rail transport right from their

Table 10.6

INSTANCES OF VILLAGE MIGRATION, 1963–1990

	Ki:y Oḍeyaraṭṭi	O:rana:yi	Hulla:ḍa	Ke:ti Toreke:ri	All sites
Popn., 1963	181	212	415	78	886
Popn., 1990	317	310	573	98	1,298
Increase, %	75	47	38	26	47
Man leaves by himself	4	3	9	–	16
Family moves to other land or job	6	12	4	–	22
Family moves beyond the Nilgiris	–	3	1	1	5
Presumed in-migration of a family	1	–	24	4	29
Presumed out-migration of a family	3	1	26	–	30

village, that it is the largest village, that some found employment with the railways, and that many have factory or office experience and personal connections at the neighbouring village of Aravanga:ḍu or in one of the nearby towns.

NOTES

1. All of the statistics early in this chapter were drawn from the report, *Economic Intelligence Service — Profiles of Districts — November 1993.* (Bombay: Centre for Monitoring Indian Economy.)

Chapter 11

EDUCATION, MASS MEDIA, AND THE FUTURE

It made me gladsome to be getting some education,
it being like a big window opening.
— Mary Webb

Badaga Schooling

Demographic literature in recent years has repeatedly concluded that there is a definite relationship between increasing education (particularly for girls) and declining fertility. John Caldwell and associates found in Karnataka, as I have done amongst these Badagas, that 'the cost of educating successive children over a short period of time' combined with the availability of family planning procedures, does lead to a decline in fertility (Caldwell *et al.* 1988: 161). This is a relationship of great significance for the future of rural India. Its *modus operandi* has been convincingly outlined by Holsinger and Kasarda (1976; summarized in Ghosh 1990: 24–25):

> *Indirect effects*: (*i*) schooling delays age at marriage and thereby the child-bearing span of female life; (*ii*) education helps acquisition of information on contraceptives and their use; (*iii*) education increases exposure to mass media and printed materials on family planning; (*iv*) education increases aspiration for upward mobility and accumulation of wealth and reduces the desirability of large families; (*v*) education increases employment prospects that compete with child-bearing; (*vi*) education reduces the perceived economic utility of children, thus lowering the demand for them; (*vii*) education facilitates communication between husband and wife that is conducive to lower fertility; (*viii*) education affects fertility by reducing in-

fant and child mortality; and (*ix*) education provides a sense of self-efficacy and rationality that induces the use of contraception as a means of controlling one's life and destiny.

Direct effects: Education is supposed to directly affect family size by influencing a broad spectrum of psychological attributes, including freedom from tradition, heightened aspirations, firm views concerning ideal family size, contraceptions, and other modern values.

I did ask questions about education of household members during the survey I conducted in 1963; but funding was unobtainable for a resurvey along exactly the same lines in 1990, with the same population and the same questions and interview conditions, so as to discover what sort of changes had occurred over one generation; (support was refused on the grounds that survey research is no longer 'fashionable').[1] We are thus left to guess at how much attitudes about education may have changed since 1963. Certainly literacy rates have improved nationally over this period, as the Census of India makes clear (Table 11.1), and must have improved amongst Badagas too. But because of Badaga access to schools, particularly in the Ke:ti area, their literacy rates have been much higher than national rates ever since the later 19th century.

True literacy however, like true madness, is no easy thing to define. The criteria by which the threshold of literacy is determined can vary considerably. Thus the Indian census-takers in 1951 considered the ability to read and write a simple letter as their standard of literacy; others have defined literacy as the ability to write at least one's name; I tried to apply the standard of whether one could read a simple story in the newspaper. Whether the Indian census-takers' criteria had changed by 1961 is not certain: 'The test of literacy for the 1961 Census was satisfied if a person above the age of four could with understanding both

Table 11.1

NATIONAL PERCENTAGE OF LITERACY, 1961–1991

Census	Persons literate › 4 yrs.	Lit. males › 4 yrs.	Lit. females › 4 yrs.
1961	28.31%	40.40%	15.34%
1971	34.45%	45.95%	21.97%
1981	41.42%	53.45%	28.46%
1991*	52.11%	63.86%	39.42%

* The 1991 figures relate to percentage aged 7 years and above.

read and write' (India 1962: xxxii). It is nevertheless clear that these various criteria actually refer to widely differing abilities: a man who has learnt to write his name often remains quite illiterate when it comes to anything else; a man who learnt to read and write many years ago at school but has never used either skill much since then may now be a functional illiterate and yet claim literacy; a man asked if he *can* read a newspaper (or can read and write letters) may answer 'no' because he never *does* such a thing. Translation of my question about literacy into the languages used in interviewing probably obscured the difference between the English verbs 'can read' and 'does read'. A more significant pitfall than this, however, also stemmed directly from the translation process: in most south Indian languages the word 'to read' (*paḍikka* in Tamil, for example) also carries the meanings 'to learn, to attend school'. Which of these meanings is the appropriate one in any particular context is usually of no importance to the villager, who simply senses that those who have been to school can read, and those who can read have attended school. For the research worker, on the other hand, the ambiguity here may be obscuring some valuable data, since the villager's generalization is by no means altogether true.

I mention these matters as preface to one of the more important findings of the survey: there was a high standard of literacy, as defined by my criterion of the ability to read a newspaper.[2] In a sample of 101 adults coming from two of the sample villages, 38 per cent claimed to be illiterate in 1963. The sample, however, was asymmetrical, for it included 75 males but only 26 females. It is thus not correct to say that 62 per cent of this population was literate in 1963; but what is fairly certain is that 71 per cent of males were then literate and—from my much smaller female sample—some 35 per cent of adult females were literate. A check was made on this important topic at a later point in the interview, when questions were asked about reading habits. Here an almost identical percentage—70 per cent of males and 37 per cent of females—claimed to be literate, and the difference is probably to be explained by my exclusion of a blind person. Among that part of the sample questioned in O:rana:ẏi, no one admitted to being illiterate.

An interesting and important difference between the four sample villages of this study can be seen from Table 8.2 (p. 175), which totals the number of children of school and college age. It shows us that these children, aged 5–19, have greatly increased in number from 1963 to 1990 in Ki:y Oḍeyaraṭṭi (+81 per cent), and most notably in Ke:ti Toreke:ri (+592 per cent); whereas Hulla:ḍa and O:rana:yi both showed a decline of –8 per cent in the school-age population. The two villages that recorded an increase between 1963 and 1990 had an excess of girls over boys at both these censuses too. One can safely expect that these educated girls will have a shorter reproductive life than their mothers did and that the relative if slight backwardness of the Woḍeya and Toreya villages *vis-à-vis* the other two may well be eliminated during the coming generation.[3]

By 1993 the literacy rate for the whole district was estimated at 63 per cent, including of course its urban population, but no figure is available for the Badaga community, which should be distinctly higher than this. Already at the outset of my study, however, published census figures for 1961 give basic information about the population of Ketty Panchayat, an area roughly coterminous with my study area but including a dozen more hamlets. Its total population then was 15,253; and if we remove from that figure 1,715 people classified as Scheduled Castes or Scheduled Tribes, we are left with 7,036 males and 6,502 females, the great majority of whom—perhaps 6,000 of each sex—were Badagas. (I am thus guessing that about 1,000 non-Badaga males and 500 females were immigrant labourers who belonged to neither of the just mentioned categories.) Excluding the Scheduled Castes and Scheduled Tribes, I have estimated that the dominant Badaga majority, along with these labourers, then had a male literacy rate of 56 per cent and a female one of 30 per cent. A comparable calculation for Ketty Panchayat in 1971 yielded a predominantly Badaga literacy rate of 74 per cent for males and 47 per cent for females. Yet more recent rates are impossible to estimate for lack of data, but have presumably increased further for both sexes. My own survey in 1963, however, yielded a literacy rate of 71 per cent for Badaga men in the sample and 35 per cent for women. Table 11.2 gives the reported educational attainments of the informants in the two sample villages at that time; (this sample is introduced on p. 233).

To the extent that the sample was adult and educated—and 60 per cent had attended school for at least a few years—this experience tended to have occurred during World War II or earlier. It was therefore necessary also to ask these informants about the general pattern of education within their households, as of 1963, to reflect more recent trends. Table 11.3 summarizes those findings.

The school system in this area has recently provided for five years of elementary school, followed by three years of middle school and then

Table 11.2
EDUCATION OF INFORMANTS IN TWO VILLAGES, 1963

Level of education	Men	Women
No schooling, illiterate	21	17
No schooling but literate	2	–
1–3 yrs. primary school	9	1
Completed primary school (5 yrs.)	14	4
1–3 yrs. middle school	20	2
2 yrs. high school (to S.S.L.C.*)	8	2
To Intermediate* (Arts or Science), P.U.C.* or diploma	1	–
	(*N* = 75)	(*N* = 26)

* S.S.L.C. = Secondary School Leaving Certificate; Intermediate = halfway towards a B.A. or B.Sc.; P.U.C. = Pre-University Course

three years of high school. At the end of primary schooling a few students might choose to be examined for a diploma, the Elementary School Leaving Certificate (E.S.L.C.); but the main aim of all diploma-covetous scholars is the Secondary School Leaving Certificate, which can be obtained in the final year of high school and may get one accepted to a college. So prestigious a mark of attainment is it that there are many who will own to being 'S.S.L.C. (failed)'; and I even recorded cases of Ke:ti Valley students who had committed suicide after failing it, and

Table 11.3
LEVELS OF EDUCATION IN SAMPLE HOUSEHOLDS, 1963

No schooling for anyone	17
Only younger males to primary school	21
Males and females to primary school	6
Males to high, females to primary school	10
Younger males to high, older males to primary, females none	15
Males and females to high school	13
Males to college, females to primary or high school	–
Other	3
Not ascertained	2
	(*N* = 87)

whose ghosts later returned to haunt their families (Hockings 1980b: 164–67). In the 1963 survey, I did not distinguish between those who had passed and those who had failed the S.S.L.C.: all matriculates were put in a single category with those who had completed several years of high school. We have already seen (pp. 108–09) how M.N. Thesingh's school years came to an end with the S.S.L.C. because of his family's opposition to higher education.

The educational attainments in Table 11.3 can usefully be compared with those gained in 1963 in four villages of Tumkur district, near the Caldwell–Reddy study area, in an unpublished study by the Menefees (1964; Table 11.4). The percentage attainment in the two Badaga villages I sampled is somewhat less than that in the Tumkur villages, at all levels except middle school.

As to the perceived purpose of education, I again find myself in full agreement with the Caldwells and Reddy (who also worked in Tumkur): 'We find education in rural south India to be favored both as a route to a nonfarming job and as a means of securing literacy and enlightenment. The educated can cope with the modern world and its bureaucrats more easily' (Caldwell *et al.* 1988: 164). This sentiment, which relates primarily to males, was prognosticated very long ago in a Nilgiri resident's comment that, after two schools had been opened in 1821 and 1830, the Badaga pupils already thought they were fitted for something better in life than manual labour (Harkness 1832: 69–70).

Table 11.4
LEVELS OF EDUCATION IN TUMKUR AND NILGIRI VILLAGES, 1963

Education completed	All respondents		Men		Women	
	Tumkur	Nilgiris	Tumkur	Nilgiris	Tumkur	Nilgiris
No schooling	35.4%	39.6	27.1	30.7	48.1	65.4
Primary School	29.2	27.7	31.9	30.7	25.0	19.2
Middle School	19.0	21.8	20.5	26.7	16.7	7.7
High School	16.3	9.9	20.5	10.7	10.2	7.7
College	.0	1.0	.0	1.2	.0	.0
N =	282	101	169	75	113	26

His observation serves to introduce here the exceptional fact that Ke:ti has had an elementary school continuously since a local benefactor, Judge George J. Casamajor, set one up in the year 1845, with 20 boys and two schoolmasters; and indeed, since 1901, the village had a higher elementary and later still a high school. These early schools were within walking distance for pupils from the other three sample villages. Within a year of its founding, the first Ke:ti school came under the administration of the Basel Evangelical Mission, and continued so until those missionaries were expelled from India in 1914 (when the Wesleyans took it over). It may be added that by 1961, on the eve of my study, the Ketty Panchayat area had 16 primary schools, one middle school, one high school, and one (none too impressive) public library.

A brief chronology will summarize the development of education in and around Ke:ti during the 19th century. This list only identifies some of the milestones in what was in fact a quite remarkable development for a rural area anywhere in India. Few American rural communities if not along the East Coast have schools of such antiquity; and in the nine Karnataka villages of the Caldwell–Reddy study, only the largest had had a school for just the past half century.

1846 Missionaries running 'parochial' school at Ke:ti, with 20 boys.
1849 Now a 'vernacular' school, with 77 boys and 6 girls.
1855 From this year on, Ke:ti had 2 schools, one 'parochial' with 10 boys and 4 girls, the other 'vernacular' with 6 boys.
1858 The first Badaga man converted to Christianity. Vernacular school now had 103 boys, while parochial school had only 7 boys and 3 girls.
1859 A teacher-training class in Ke:ti.
1867 Now 3 schools, as in most years down to 1881.
1870 Two day-schools and two night-schools.
1871 Boarding-school and orphanage established, with 5 boys and 3 girls.
1888 Teacher training school with 7 students; total now of 14 schools, with 333 boys and 9 girls.
1890 English-medium school started with 6 boys.
1900 Now 26 schools in the Ke:ti area; also 5 seminaries and 5 training schools. Total pupils under instruction were 95 Christian boys, 30 Christian girls, 555 Hindu boys and 31 Hindu girls, altogether 711 pupils; plus 202 Sunday School students. (In addition to these, the Basel Mission had a further 190 pupils in 6 schools in the Kotagiri area, 16 km ENE of Ke:ti.)

Several features emerge from this listing. One is that although there were ups and downs in the enrolment figures for specific years, in general there was a continuing expansion of the educational network that the Basel Mission was spreading in the villages close to Ke:ti. A second point is that female education was never neglected, even though the great majority of Badaga parents could see no point in sending their daughters to school, and for a while a small monetary inducement had to be offered. Further, for an entire century prior to the conclusion of my study (1890–1990), an English-medium education has been available here without going to town. The system did not rely heavily on European teachers, but from 1859 undertook the training of local Christians (who were not always Badagas) as teachers. By 1900 there were four male and four female missionaries from Europe at Ke:ti; but 42 local Christian catechists and schoolmasters. The parish then contained 401 Protestants, over *10 per cent* of whom were thus employed in education. It is evident that most of the schools were quite small, averaging 27 pupils in 1900. And because they were by then dispersed throughout two dozen Badaga hamlets near Ke:ti, they did succeed in bringing basic education, and no doubt much biblical exposure, to the local people. Early in the 20th century we are told that Badaga schoolboys were 'eager for reading matter of any description' (Stone 1925: 20); the missionaries supplied it.

While the Basel Evangelical Mission, which was rather Lutheran in its orientation, was the first and always the most dominant evangelizing agency in Badaga history, there were actually two other Christian organizations that had a further impact on the Ke:ti area villages. Catharine F. Ling, of the Church of England Zenana Mission, is well-known in local history as the person who, during 1904–1940, formed the Toda Christian community by single-handedly converting 37 Toda tribal people (Walker 1986: 263–71). What is not well known is that she and Winifred Stone, another English colleague, did a certain amount of evangelical work in the Badaga villages near Ka:ṭe:ri too, including O:rana:yi and probably Ki:y Oḍeyaraṭṭi. At the same time Kišker̲ (Kishkar),[4] the first Toda Christian convert, was running a night school in or near Ka:ṭe:ri (Rivers 1906: Table 59; Stone 1925: 18–28). As Miss Stone observed, 'The men of this village are mostly attracted by that coveted goal of Indian ambition, Government service ….' (Stone 1925: 28). Exactly 50 years later a Badaga delegation told the Backward Classes Commission: 'They feel that they are not adequately represented in Government services, in the public sector projects and particularly in the local offices. They attach great importance to Government service' (Backward Classes Commission 1975: 9).

And this was not all. By 1916, the Roman Catholic Church was active in these same villages, thanks to the Missions Étrangères de Paris. The first Catholic baptism of a dying old Badaga near Wellington was recorded in 1873, just 15 years after the first Protestant conversion. But then several later converts apostasized. During the 1890s Fr. M.-L. Robin did some itinerant preaching in O:rana:yi, among other places. It then had 20–25 households, and was already being visited with some regularity by sisters of the Franciscan Missionaries of Mary in Ootacamund, who were much appreciated because they brought medicine and cared for the sick (Tignous 1912: 156). It was only during the period 1916–1922 that a permanent Catholic foothold was established in the study area, at sites right next to the scenes of Basel Evangelical successes, when Fr. E.J.B. Foubert built a new chapel and presbytery in Santu:r, near Ke:ti, baptising about 50 Badagas there before he died. His successor, Fr. H.P.J.A. Tignous, continued this activity and built schools in several of the villages. It was he who got the Franciscan Missionaries of Mary to open St. Michael's Convent there in 1927, at a point midway between Ke:ti and Kereha:ḍa (see Map 2.1); to this convent a dispensary, an elementary school, and a girls' orphanage were attached. In 1924 the Bishop of Coimbatore, Msgr. A. Roy, came and baptised the Ke:ti headman and 38 other converts, thus bringing the Badaga Catholic total to about a hundred. When Tignous died in 1930 the Catholic Church was thus well established in Ke:ti, and with some hyperbole the good father was hailed as 'the Apostle to the Badagas'. The following year a decent-sized church, St. Michael's, was built in place of the former chapel (with French financing) by Fr. E. Périé. The school and other facilities continue in operation to this day (Béchu 1948: 65–69).

In the face of all this evangelical activity the great majority of the Badaga population remained unconverted, yet they absorbed several important lessons over the years from the agenda of these schools, namely: (1) knowledge of Bible stories; (2) some appreciation of Christian morals and the extent to which they were actually exemplified in the behaviour of the missionary families; (3) an association between being a Christian European and having a perceptibly higher standard of living than any Badaga villagers; (4) an understanding of the European work ethic; (5) a firm awareness that those with schooling could get minor clerical jobs, or become catechists, overseers on plantations, and schoolteachers; and (6) some perception of how the German, Swiss and British family relationships differed from those within the Badaga family.

The progressive effects of education and the desire for modernization among ordinary villagers are clearly reflected in the impressions of an English missionary 75 years ago, recorded in words that hark back to M.N. Thesingh's early life (Chapter 4):

> ... the Badagas are a naturally industrious, go-ahead people, often working as rickshaw coolies, builders, road-menders, etc., in order to supplement the scanty income they earn by cultivation of their little fields and the sale of their crops. Many Badaga boys, not content with the education to be had in their own villages, tramp over the hills many miles daily to attend the C.M.S. Higher Elementary or the Municipal High School at Ootacamund, or the Wesleyan [formerly Basel Mission] Higher Elementary School at Kaity. They thus pick up a limited knowledge of English and a less limited knowledge of the newspapers, and so learn of the trend of thought in their own country and beyond. (Stone 1925: 25)

No doubt all of these developments began long ago; but they have continued throughout the entire 20th century, bringing to modern Badagas a non-traditional view of the relations between work, education, and family relationship, even for those who did not actually attend the mission schools themselves. I would suggest that household structure has been modified in this area during the present century in the direction of Western models which have now been present in Ke:ti itself for over a century and a half.

At the mid-point of my study,

> In a memorandum submitted... [to the Backward Classes Commission], it is stated that they have 1,500 graduates, including 50 Engineers, 30 Doctors and 30 Lawyers. For a community of their size this is an impressive achievement. In high schools also their numbers are impressive. A large number of their graduates and under-graduates are employed as teachers in high schools and elementary schools. (Backward Classes Commission 1975: 9)

The implications of these changes are broad and far-reaching. Jack Goody, thinking primarily of modern Africa, recently wrote about this common shift:

> Certainly there was nothing to be ashamed of in being non-literate.
>
> But the position is now changing. The new literacy, associated with predominantly secular teaching at European-type schools, lies at the basis of a dual economy, a dual economy of the spirit as well as of labour. What does the advent of modern literacy do to societies that were previously non-literate? The extent to which new commercial and political activities depend upon literacy hardly needs stressing. The growth of towns, the growth of the economy, the growth of the political system involving mass participation, the growth of the media, all these depend to a greater or lesser extent upon changes in the mode of communication. But eighty per cent of Africa, as of other parts of the developing world [here one could read, India], remains rural. What effect does the growth of literacy in their midst have on this segment of the population?
>
> It gives rise at once to an extending ladder of mobility. It forces the gaze towards considerations of achievement rather than birth .... This new system of achievement carries a new system of rewards leading to a new system of stratification. It takes the successful individual out of the local setting and enables him to operate on a national level .... The new elite, seeking to maintain its own position, encourages its children to pursue the same goals, and the system of education, earlier an open channel to social mobility, now becomes the instrument of status preservation.
>
> But even in the early phase it is not simply a matter of individual achievement; there is also a yawning gap between those who have been to school and those who have not, between haves and have nots....
>
> Under these conditions there is inevitably a sense of inferiority which forces the pace of educational development, thus leading to an over-development of schools. For there are soon too many educated for the available jobs. While people have been educated out of subsistence agriculture (as they see it), there is no alternative occupation. We find the classic dichotomy ... the educated unemployed, the school leaver who refuses to go back on the land, who regards himself as destined for a white-collar job ... many of the literates working in the country will be doing so reluctantly, with their eyes on the town and on its life. (Goody 1987: 139–41)

These processes are quite evident in the lives of modern Badagas, and in the florescence of schools around Ke:ti.

In talking about modernization, I have viewed it as a general process of cultural and economic change which can encompass three more specific processes: these are westernization, urbanization or industrialization. At any given time each can be occurring by itself or in combination with the other two.

The historical impact of Europeans connected with the Basel Mission and of other British residents, railway personnel, and local officials is relevant to an important debate within demography: has it been possible in Third World countries for fertility to decline without westernization occurring more or less simultaneously? Freedman (1979) has developed such an argument. From what I have presented here, however, it should be quite clear that in the four sample villages near Ke:ti the visibility of European family models and of Christian values has been consistently present for the length of two lifetimes, despite the lack of urbanization or industrialization there. One could hardly argue that even though present these alien lifestyles had no impact on Badagas, when it is apparent that quite a few hundred Badagas who were attracted to a Church did adopt the ideal of a nuclear household and even a European style of men's dress and of *décor* in their houses. Whatever the original motives of the missionaries may have been, it would now seem evident that they offered models for modernization in their schools and in their own family relationships.

Sex Differences and Modernization

While formal educational attainments of both males and females are not perhaps exceptionally high (Table 11.4), there is a related area in which everybody excels, namely, multilingualism. Since the Nilgiris is a multilingual region, and Tamil rather than Badaga is the most widespread language today, it is not surprising that people find an ability to speak secondary languages is a necessity (Table 11.5). From this table, based on responses I got from a small sample in two of the four villages, and from other interviews, it was found that in general adult males speak a greater number of languages than females, and that indigenous Nilgiri peoples like the Badagas speak a greater number than the immigrants do. The sexual difference apparent in Table 11.5 is only in part accounted for by educational differences (Table 11.3), for it is also reflected in Table 11.6 which documents the relevant matter of frequency of visits to one of the neighbouring towns, among the same sample. It is clear that men do much of the shopping in town, while women are commonly obliged to stay at home for food preparation or child-minding duties. In addition, the pattern of male occupations (Table 10.5) includes half-a-dozen that are urban and so obviously requiring a man's presence in town.

Table 11.5
NUMBER OF SPEAKERS OF SECONDARY LANGUAGES, 1963

Badagas	Number of other languages spoken					
	None	One	Two	Three	Four	Five
Men (*N* = 75)	1	5	41	9	13	6
Women (*N* = 26)	0	17	8	0	0	1

The important point made earlier (Table 9.5, on p. 204), that it was women rather than men who in 1963 were solidly in favour of modern doctors and hospitals, brings out the significance of sex differences for modernization. These differences are very wide as compared with those in any Western country today. The matter is clearly illustrated by the Tables 11.5 to 11.19, which document responses I got in the 1963 survey. The sex differences appear equally profound in various matters connected with modernization, such as the source of news, knowledge of news items, and film-going habits.

As awareness of news is a crucial aspect of modernization psychology, I attempted to discover the news-gathering habits of men and women in the two sample villages. Although this was in 1963, 20 years before television came to the villages, there were already several distinct sources of news, namely newspapers, radio, friends, relatives at home, or a local official. Since I expected some variations not just in the source of the news items, but in the breadth of their dissemination too, it was necessary to design a series of questions focusing on specific items that had been in both the Tamil and English language press, and

Table 11.6
FREQUENCY OF VISITS TO A TOWN, 1963

Visits made	Men	Women
Has never been to town	0	0
Once a year or less often	1	6
Two to three times a year	2	5
Once in 2–10 weeks	15	10
Once a week or more often	57	5
	(*N* = 75)	(*N* = 26)

on the radio news, within the preceding three weeks or so. The series of questions was presented verbally to each respondent, and then he or she was asked whether he had heard of it, and how initially? Clearly some items were considered more relevant than others, or at least were better remembered, by the same group of respondents. Relevancy must explain why the local news item, which one might have expected to be most widely known about—one that had been reported in the various media—was nevertheless known by relatively few people. It concerned potato-farming, and the consultation of a Scottish agronomist to combat a parasitic disease.

This question was immediately followed with another one about the source of news in each case. Table 11.8 shows the responses for the international news item, which concerned the first Soviet woman's space flight (June 14–19) and was the item most widely known in the villages. The role of newspapers and discussion with friends are obviously crucial in the dissemination of news (Plate 30). Women however, being more restricted to the home, more often hear the news there, or else fail to altogether.

It is quite evident from Table 11.8 that radio was not a major source of news in 1963, despite the best attempts of All India Radio to broadcast it in numerous languages twice daily. However, when they were asked what kinds of radio programme they preferred, the same sample replied as in Table 11.9.

Table 11.7

KNOWLEDGE OF CURRENT NEWS ITEMS, 1963

Scope of news item	Men		Women	
	Heard	Not heard	Heard	Not heard
Local item	41	34	7	18
State item	60	15	19	7
National item	63	11	12	14
(not ascertained)	1	0	0	0
International item	73	2	16	10
Administrative item	65	10	6	20
Technological item	42	33	7	19
	($N = 75$)		($N = 26$)	

Table 11.8

SOURCES OF AN INTERNATIONAL NEWS ITEM, 1963

Sources of news items	Men	Women
From papers	31	1
From radio	3	1
From papers and radio	2	0
From friends and papers	1	0
From friends	34	4
From a relative at home	2	10
From a village official	0	0
Item not heard about	2	10
	(*N* = 75)	(*N* = 26)

When questions were asked about frequency of radio listening, it was found that a majority of people listened every day. This contrasted with the situation in four villages of Tumkur district, studied by the Menefees in 1963, as Table 11.10 makes clear.

Another matter on which the same Badaga sample was questioned concerned reading habits. Here again we encounter (Table 11.11) a big sex gap, the women reading very much more seldom, whether because of inability, lack of interest, or lack of spare time.

Table 11.9

PREFERENCES IN RADIO LISTENING, 1963

Preferences	Men	Women
'Any kind of programme'	2	1
News	49	9
Music (i.e., Radio Ceylon)	36	21
Weather forecasts	1	0
Lectures and dramas	0	0
Voice of America (in Tamil)	0	0
Nothing heard	9	4
	(*N* = 75)*	(*N* = 26)*

* Preferences total more than the count of respondents because some chose more than one category.

Table 11.10
PERCENTAGE FREQUENCY OF RADIO LISTENING, 1963

Frequency	Men		Women	
	Near Tiptur	Badagas	Near Tiptur	Badagas
Listen daily	25.2%	66.7	20.7	42.3
Listen occasionally	57.9	21.3	53.4	42.3
Never listen	16.9	12.0	25.9	15.4
	(*N* = 169)	(*N* = 75)	(*N* = 113)	(*N* = 26)

Film-going is one popular activity that does not require literacy, and hence is potentially open to all. In 1963 I therefore asked my sample a series of questions about film-going activities (Tables 11.12–11.15). The main question inquired what type of film they preferred to see. An *ad hoc* categorization of films thus arose out of the responses informants gave, but they do represent easily recognizable types. Apparently the two most widely appreciated kinds of film are (1) mythological and semi-historical melodramas, which include plenty of singing and dancing, and which I would consider as traditional and escapist; and (2) social dramas, including modern comedies, romances and tragedies, which suggest an engagement with contemporary urban society and its problems. Table 11.12 gives the details. From this it should be apparent that the escapist themes of historical-mythological films, presented by attractive actors and actresses in a panoply of song and dance, are very much more what the Badagas like to see than modern social dramas, whether tragedies or comedies—or, at least, this was the case in 1963.

Table 11.11
BADAGA READING HABITS, 1963

Items read	Men	Women
Newspapers	21	2
Newspapers and magazines	25	1
Magazines	0	0
Read nothing	6	7
Illiterate and/or blind	23	16
	(*N* = 75)	(*N* = 26)

Table 11.12

PREFERRED CATEGORIES OF FILM, 1963

Films viewed	Men	Women
All kinds: no preference	8	6
Historical, mythological, epic, dancing	38	8
Social, comedies, romance, tragedy	23	2
Adventure, sports, detective	3	1
None seen	9	6
Not ascertained	3	3
	(*N* = 75)*	(*N* = 26)*

* Preferences total more than the count of respondents because some chose more than one category.

A subsidiary question about the preferred language of films seen was not especially diagnostic, as it mainly reflected the dominance of the Tamil and Hindi film industries in the local cinemas (Table 11.13). It was noticeable that films in Hindi or English (but probably dubbed in Tamil) were appreciated by half of the men but scarcely any of the women.

A question was also asked about the frequency with which the respondent saw films (Table 11.14). The median falls around once or twice a month for men, once a month or less often for women.

Table 11.13

PREFERRED LANGUAGE OF FILMS, 1963

Film language preferred	Men	Women
Tamil	66	20
English	37	2
Hindi	34	2
Malayalam	2	–
No films seen	9	6
	(*N* = 75)*	(*N* = 26)*

* Preferences total more than the count of respondents because some chose more than one category.

Table 11.14
ESTIMATES OF FILM-GOING FREQUENCY, 1963

Film-going frequency	Men	Women
'Never'	9	6
'Rarely'	18	7
'Once a month'	14	3
'Once a week'	22	2
'More than once weekly'	3	0
Not ascertained, 'can't tell'	9	8
	($N = 75$)	($N = 26$)

As a check on the information given in Table 11.14, they were also asked about the film-going habits of their entire household (Table 11.15), but now the dominant response was that people 'rarely go'.

In a general way, it can be seen that the women's knowledge of and interaction with the outside world is less than men's; yet they definitely have sufficient information at their disposal to make up their own minds about important issues of modernization, and the men would seem not to be highly influential over them since the opinions and preferences of the two sexes are often quite divergent.

Table 11.15
ESTIMATES OF HOUSEHOLD FILM-GOING FREQUENCY, 1963

Family film-viewing	Males and females
All go often	12
Men go often, women rarely	4
Men go sometimes, women never	5
Only younger men and women go	2
Younger men only	3
All go rarely	55
None go	18
Not ascertained	2
	($N = 101$)

Villagers View their Future

Given the amount of their exposure to the mass media, it seemed worth asking whether these people would prefer an urban life. On the question of whether they would rather live in town or in the village, this sample's replies were as given in Table 11.16. While a minority did prefer the urban life (city glamour?), it is clear that most liked their rural life, though for men its relative cheapness was the most important factor. As one villager commented, 'Town is good only for the educated'.

The start of this field study fell in the middle of India's Third Five-Year Plan. The basic aims of that Plan were to sustain a rate of economic growth of over 5 per cent a year; to develop a self-generating economy, with self-sufficiency in the production of grains; to expand industrial capacity until, after a decade, India could in the early 1970s be largely independent of foreign aid for further industrial development; to make maximum use of manpower, and open new areas for employment; and finally to move towards greater equality of income and opportunity for all social groups in the country.

It did not altogether work out that way, of course. Foreign aid has continued to pour into the country for decades; and, as Epstein has shown (1973), the rural rich have been getting richer as the poor get poorer. The Green Revolution did help in the increased production of grains, and there has been much industrial development, however. Overall, this was intended as a programme by which the nation might 'pull itself up by the bootstraps'. For the Nilgiris, in particular, the Plan

Table 11.16
PREFERRED PLACE OF RESIDENCE, 1963

Residence preferred	Men	Women
Town more 'cultured', modern		1
Town has better entertainment	2	
Town better in general	3	
Neutral on question	2	7
Village better, quieter	20	11
Village, because relatives here	5	2
Village is cheaper	38	1
More work in village	5	4
	($N = 75$)	($N = 26$)

meant the start of the raw film factory, the extension of rural co-operative organizations, and above all else the continued construction of a huge Canada-sponsored hydro-electric system (see Map 1.1, on p. 27).

How did centralized planning affect the Badaga residents in 1963? In the 1950s this approach to the future had been a new, vast and crucial concern for the Indian government; and even if the Plan did not seem to have any direct influence on the life of a Badaga villager, it is still worth considering what he thought about the *idea* of planning. Many people had their own views about it. A few of those interviewed, for instance, claimed that the Plan did nothing but construct dams; and dams were not seen as an unequivocal blessing because they destroyed large areas of agricultural or grazing land. I will not concern myself here with the detailed provisions for the economic development of Madras State (as it was then called): these have been published by the Government of India Planning Commission in its *Third Five Year Plan* (Planning Commission 1960) and are also discussed at more length in the *Techno-Economic Survey of Madras* (NCAER 1961).

The villager's opinion, though seldom sought, is an important one to gauge, and for several reasons. Most obviously, the process of governmental planning necessarily has little feedback; many rural Indians are still illiterate or under-educated and so are generally neither interested nor competent to express serious opinions about economic programmes developed by scholarly technocrats in New Delhi. This has not been altogether true, however, of the unusually well-informed Badaga villagers this book deals with. They realize that plans are ultimately directed towards themselves, and their reactions to governmental planning could in fact be most instructive to community development administrators. As the levels of literacy and of public awareness are very high in these particular villages, we have perhaps located a rural population already able in 1963 to state articulately how they think planning affects them. Such a unique contribution to the evaluation of national plans has been lacking, and the machinery of local government seems designed to stifle any feedback of popular opinion. The implications of this are serious, for as the *Fourth Five-Year Plan* admitted, 'No comprehensive surveys were available of the [employment] situation in urban and rural areas at different points of time which would make it possible to check the validity of the estimates made. The estimates carried over from plan to plan appeared less and less firmly based' (Planning Commission 1969: 341). In short, there was no real evaluation of the local impact of the preceding plans anywhere.

If a villager is to feel that such plans have any relevance for his own life — that he should actually take account of them — then we need to understand how his attitude towards planning and saving fits into his entire system of values, and how the habit of adopting plans might operate in traditional terms of social organization.

Until about 1950 no Nilgiri villager had ever considered that plans for one's own future might be made by a government, especially one based 1,200 miles away. The intent of various early pieces of British Indian legislation had generally been viewed as restrictive upon long-established ways of life: witness the agrarian reforms of the 1860s and 1870s which put a stop to shifting cultivation in the Nilgiri forests and led to a methodical assessment of land revenues based on cadastral surveys (e.g., Figure 7.3; Hockings 1980a: 151–52, 184–87). There were actually 100-year plans for the forests, but nobody knew about them except those few reading Forestry Department reports.

Reforms can usually be misconstrued as favours for certain interest-groups; and in India the interest-group most widely suspected of benefitting from reforms was the government itself. Independence brought no fundamental change in this time-honoured belief. At the root of this unfortunate attitude there lies a widespread and long-standing mistrust of officials and of the means by which they gain their objectives. In 1963, a certain ambivalence was noticeable on this point among Nilgiri residents who were not above damning a corrupt or incompetent officialdom in one breath, but in the next urging their sons to become officials too! Even with such a background, only a tiny minority of the respondents in my survey of 1963 spoke of the Five-Year Plan as a programme for wasteful official spending, and only a small minority of the villagers became officials.

Most of those interviewed had heard of the Plan (Table 11.17) either through newspaper articles or else through informal explanations of why the dozen great dams were being built. Only 20 per cent of the Badaga men admitted that they did not know whether or not the Plan was succeeding, although twice as many in the sample did not know the most general goals of the Plan, so that it was difficult for me to see how such a high percentage could offer confident opinions about its success (Table 11.17). These seemingly firm responses become more questionable when one takes into account the answers given in Table 11.18, evaluations of the Plan by the same sample. Since the Plan is a multi-purpose economic programme it no doubt may succeed in one

Table 11.17
OPINIONS ABOUT THE AIMS OF THE FIVE-YEAR PLAN, 1963

Aims of Five-Year Plan	Men	Women
'General improvement' of nation	35	7
Industrialization, produce cheaply	4	0
Create social equality, socialism	6	1
Peace, happiness, non-alignment	17	0
Do not know	13	18
	($N = 75$)	($N = 26$)

sector but not in another; or succeed over a short period but fail in the long term. So, because of the diversity of its parts, no one can really give an accurate assessment of its overall success, and very few can present an adequate listing of its aims in one or two sentences; certainly not the Planning Commission! For this reason the questions asked about the Plan were altogether too simplistic to produce meaningful answers for planners: the responses given must be viewed for what they are, a measure of the villagers' faith in the Plan rather than a careful evaluation of its effects. In short, they were believing what they chose to believe about something that was really too complex to size up.

A similar question about India's need to industrialize brought a strong, almost unbelievable sexual difference in the results (Table 11. 19) from this rural sample, small as it was. One might argue that in general the question was also too complex to handle adequately, yet the fact remains that men and women replied quite differently, the women

Table 11.18
EVALUATIONS OF THE FIVE-YEAR PLAN, 1963

Success of the Plan	Men	Women
It is succeeding	32	4
Succeeding partially	5	1
Not succeeding at all	23	9
Do not know	15	12
	($N = 75$)	($N = 26$)

Table 11.19
OPINIONS ABOUT THE NEED TO INDUSTRIALIZE, 1963

Preferred aims of the Plan	Men	Women
India should industrialize	12	22
Should remain solely agricultural	54	3
Stress both industry and agriculture	8	0
Do not know	1	1
	($N = 75$)	($N = 26$)

opting heavily for industrialization and the men feeling almost as strongly that India should remain agricultural. This unexpected finding harks back to my earlier one (Table 9.5, on p. 204) that, while women are mostly in favour of modern medical care, the men are not. Both findings are important because they break with received opinion about the innovative role of *males* in modernization.

NOTES

1. This is no unique case, for other anthropologists have also complained informally that the NSF in recent years has hardly been allocating any funds for replication studies or for re-evaluations of earlier work. Its administrators should understand that such a procedure is essential if *any* science is to progress.
2. Writing was not made a criterion because many people who can read a paper, and thereby participate in mass communications, never have occasion to write a word.
3. People would not send married girls to school because of the likelihood that they would discuss with their virginal classmates what their husbands have done to them.
4. He is referred to in a Toda song; Emeneau notes (1971: 813, Song 210, Vs. 6): 'He taught Christian doctrine, as a catechist. He was the first Christian convert ..., son of three brothers ....' It is tantalizing to speculate that this son of three brothers may in all likelihood have been teaching about the Son of a virgin mother to Badaga audiences that included the sons of two or even three mothers! The communication would have been intriguing.

Chapter 12

SOME CONCLUSIONS

Whoso neglects learning in his youth,
loses the past and is dead for the future.
— Euripides

The Modernization Process

This book has been concerned very broadly with the recent development of Badaga society and of household life, and it thus continues a story that was first set down in an earlier work, *Ancient Hindu Refugees: Badaga Social History 1550–1975* (Hockings 1980a). I am aware that the term *modernization* 'slips and slides, alludes and obtrudes' throughout this book (Apthorpe 1989: 532), but without definition.

The term is often applied by development economists to government policy; but while modernization has certainly been the gist of India's Planning Commission activities for some 50 years, my use of the term here has been more cultural. I have viewed modernization as a communication process wherein traditional peasant populations acquire and use more education and more information about the nation-state in which they live. As a result their orientations towards the outside world change, and their attitudes towards urban Indian culture raise new possibilities in their minds. Modern sports and 20th century forms of entertainment, pre-eminently television, cinema, and film music, have become very attractive. The films not only offer a mental escape, but suggest new fashions in dressing, behaving, travel, housing, being employed, and relating to the opposite sex. A result of this exposure is urbanization, a change in values which favours the employment, shopping, social life and general ambience associated with cities. Its practical effect has been a move to the towns by some of the most educated, most progressive, most employable and competent young and middle-aged people. The relative wealth of this new elite or 'new middle class', if I may so designate it, has been invested in houses in town, equipment for those houses, private English-medium schooling for their children, cars and motorcycles, and modern styles of clothing and furniture. The change is certainly an irreversible process. This is not to say that everyone who wants to get modernized must move to a town; but they will adopt many of the urban-centred values just referred to, even if still living in a village out of preference or necessity.

The modernization of these people has been different from that of the Western world, and indeed of other parts of India, for it has not been dependent on industrialization so much as on the commercialization of agriculture and plantations. Only a small minority of male Badagas in the sample villages have been working in factories. Clearly modernization means more than just getting a steady job in industry. It is participation in the mass media of the nation — viewing films frequently, reading newspapers and magazines, listening to radio or watching television. It is attaining a sufficient level of education to obtain 'white collar' urban (and preferably government) employment and, in the case of young women, to attract a well-employed groom. And it is shopping in town or visiting, even studying in, modern cities.

These aspects of modernization turn the eyes of the youth away from farm-work, which is easily seen today as dirty, tedious, unrewarding and low-status. Tea is at least a better prospect than traditional agriculture, if a family owns some land, and it can then produce green leaf with the labour of cheaply hired pluckers rather than family members. Whether tea or vegetables are grown, the demonstrably shrinking landholdings do not require the numbers of family workers that they employed in previous generations. This fact, when combined with the shortage of good urban jobs, the high costs of bringing up children, and the receding need to produce extra sons to replace those who might die in childhood, goes a long way towards explaining the reduced fertility over the past generation among the Badagas. All of these factors were certainly understood by the Badaga womenfolk, whether educated or not.

Long-available school education, and recent participatory use of several mass media, have combined to propel the Badaga community towards modernization. While men tend to have more education, more urban contacts, and greater multilingualism—as is true throughout most of Asia — it is the slightly schooled body of Badaga women who in

1963 saw India's future lying in industrialization; who have opted for modern medical practices; and who, by agreeing to sterilization after one or two children, have over the past two decades begun to take control of their fertility and hence play a more central role in the future of their families. Any development worker or public health official who thinks that in a patrilineal society it is the males who will always be 'in control' of attitudes and developments should take note of this finding.

The effects of this recent change have been widespread in Badaga society. The child–woman ratio has dropped appreciably, and with lower fertility and lower infant mortality the toll on women's health has lessened and their life expectancy increased. A switch from potatoes and other farm crops to tea has also had a similar effect, by much reducing the number of days that Badaga women would be labouring in their fields. With fewer children per family, college education has become more accessible to teenagers, especially as several undergraduate colleges were opened in the Nilgiris during the course of this study. The employment, lifestyle, and longevity prospects of the younger generation thus look brighter than they ever did before.

Population Decline

How can we generalize from the Badaga case presented here? Following from Leibenstein's work (1957, 1975), an economic theory of population decline has been developed which is generally called the cost-benefit approach. Its central assumption is that parents recognize that they derive some utility from their children (as a kind of consumer goods, as producers, and as old-age insurance); but also that they incur costs for the children. A principle thus emerges which balances the benefits, which generally decrease with economic improvement, against the costs which regularly increase. This principle qualifies the desired number of children.

Bahnisikha Ghosh has usefully summarized a household economics approach to the family that was proposed by an American economist:

> T.W. Schultz (1974) has noted four interrelated developments: (*i*) investment in human capital that treats children as a form of capital in which parents make investments and derive future satisfactions; (*ii*) allocation of human time in decisions with respect to market and non-market activities

where bearing and caring for a child are highly labour-intensive activities for the mother; (*iii*) the household production function that treats market goods and household time as inputs in the production of the true object of utility within the family; and (*iv*) treatment of the family as the decision-making unit with regard to both consumption and household production of goods and services including children. The dominant characteristic of this approach is the treatment of time of the members of the family as a scarce resource, the implicit value of which ultimately determines the point of equilibrium for the family's decision-making process. (Ghosh 1990: 20)

If the central concern of economics is the allocation of scarce resources among competing ends so as to maximize utility, then the household with which the present study grapples is an economic microcosm in the sense that it is the locus of decision-making over generations, concerning forms of investment of time and income and the production and rearing of children. Even the organization of the funeral is changing (p. 119) in response to the economic exigencies and time constrictions of the modern household and its employment pattern. So far as declining fertility is concerned,

> The new home economics has been successfully used to explain the phenomenon of demographic transition. A decline in infant mortality would have inverse repercussions on desired family size since parents would be expected to derive greater satisfaction the longer a child survives, thus generating greater demand for children.
>
> However, at the same time, a decline in child mortality, raises the costs of 'child quantity' relative to 'child quality'. The net effect not only depends on the production conditions within the household but also on the perceived importance of child quantity relative to child quality, and as such needs to be diagnosed through empirical applications of the new home economics. (Ghosh 1990: 21)

Is this the mechanism by which Badagas have recently been shifting from a *Gemeinschaft* to a *Gesellschaft* type of society (Tönnies 1957: 248-49)? We can see in the Table 12.1 the beginnings of the demographic transition among the Badagas, but should use caution in reading that table.

> It would be tempting to explain these changes as a demographic sequence whereby one demographic change compelled another. It is probably true that

Table 12.1
FACTORS LEADING TO A DEMOGRAPHIC TRANSITION

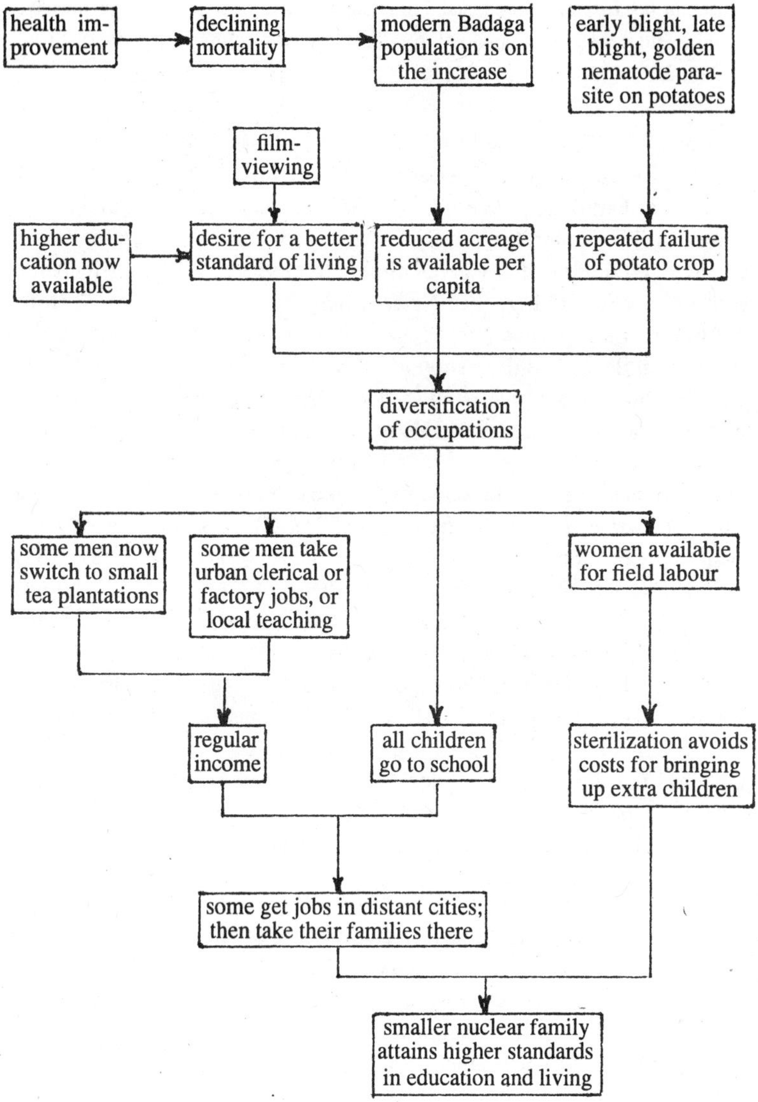

> declining mortality has to a considerable extent allowed fertility decline and to a lesser extent the rise in the age at female marriage, but in neither case has it been the cause. The truth seems to be that a range of demographic changes occurred at much the same time neither because of close interrelation nor because of coincidence, but because they are all products of massive social and economic changes during the last half-century. (Caldwell *et al.* 1988: 255)

Caldwell (1982) rejected the universality of the demographic transition, but focused on the differential value of children. On the basis of research he had done in West Africa, he postulated that an examination of wealth flow within the family is critical for understanding the value accorded to children at any given time. He observed African tribesmen to prefer more children in their families since benefits flowed from children to their parents, especially the elderly. Thus, so long as the labour of children and their support of the parents remains possible, the value of sons remains high and so does fertility. Badaga proverbs were quite clear about the traditional demographic situation: 'If a girl is born she's useless; if a boy is born he's an asset' (Hockings 1988: 148, Item no. 154a). But one was not enough: 'Is one eye an eye? Is a single son a son?' (Hockings 1988: 149, Item no. 157a). Also, 'Girls are a disappointment, but the eldest son [is like a] hearth' (Hockings 1988: 151, Item no. 162). Some proverbs extolled the joint family; e.g., 'Who has been spoilt by living in a joint [family]? Who has flourished after partition [of the family property]?' (Hockings 1988: 340, Item no. 656a). No doubt all peasant societies cherished such attitudes: an ancient Chinese writer, for example, advised, 'Raise sons for old age, pile up grain for times of famine'. With the Badagas, such attitudes are now past; and the direction of vertical flow of care and services within the household has recently reversed itself, from upwards to downwards.

Namboodiri systematized Caldwell's ideas about wealth flow in a series of hypotheses (1986):

> (1) it is only if the family becomes nucleated that fertility will decline;
> (2) industrialization is *not* a necessary precondition for fertility decline;
> (3) fertility decline starts with the reversal of direction of the inter-generational wealth flow, which in all traditional peasant societies has been from the younger to the older generation.

All three features have been found true of recent Badaga household life, now that their hallowed attitudes about the family have altered. Many sons were called for when there was high infant mortality, and everyone worked on the land; but no longer. (One Indian study concluded ominously that in order to achieve a 95 per cent probability of having one son survive to adulthood, a couple would need to produce six children; May and Heer 1968.)

The village economies have not been industrialized, in part, because local farming does not lend itself to mechanization in the way that it had to in vast tracts of Australia, the U.S.A., Canada, the Ukraine, Russia and Argentina that fed the newly developing countries of the West. There will be no great growth of machinery sales and repair shops in an area of small landholdings like the Nilgiris. Even tea, the main plantation crop, which is now harvested by machine on flat land in Japan, will continue for long to be plucked by human labour on the Nilgiri Hills (just as it is in China and Assam). It makes no economic sense to bring in costly machinery when labour remains so readily and cheaply available, and wholesale tea prices so depressed. But one can use cheap cooly (non-Badaga) labour, without involving one's wife and sons in the tedious fieldwork of a small tea plantation.

A change in values about household organization and size is not just a response to changing economic conditions, but is an acknowledgement that the quality of life today is different. Thus, generalizing from his African study (done just prior to the Karnataka one), Caldwell wrote:

> From the demographic viewpoint, the most important social exports (from Western Europe) have been the concept of the predominance of the nuclear family with its strong conjugal tie and the concept of concentrating concern and expenditure on one's children. The latter does not automatically follow from the former, although it is likely to follow continuing westernisation; but the latter must be preceded by the former. (Caldwell 1976: 356)

In this regard, following from the discussion of schooling in the previous chapter, one must ponder whether the example of the German, Swiss, British and westernized Indian (missionary and schoolteacher) families in the Ke:ti Valley area in the last century already suggested an alternative approach to child raising for local Badagas; it was certainly very visible. I conclude that these people became a significant reference group and avenue for modernization, though without prompting mass conversions: barely 4 per cent of Badagas are Christian today.

Differential Development in Badaga Villages

My original purpose in choosing four sample villages located within a tiny, confined historico-geographical zone yet containing four different phratries was to hold environmental factors constant and find out what cultural effects were manifested in the vital data. An answer should now be sought. One way of doing so might be to rank the four villages in terms of their response to certain salient features of modernization; from most traditional (*1*) to most modernizing (*4*) in Table 12.2.

This is without question a somewhat impressionistic way of evaluating degrees of modernization. The items listed on the left of the table are not independent variables, but to a considerable extent entail each other and are reflections of the same things, population growth and modernization. Nonetheless, several significant conclusions may be drawn from this rank ordering, even though it does not permit of sophisticated statistical analysis.

(1) Ranking is different for five of the six 'communication' factors tabulated, suggesting there is no strong correlation between accessibility of schooling, accessibility of a town, number of villages with which there are marriage ties, amount of village exogamy, whether there are telephones, and the possibility of television viewing.
(2) Certain rankings are correlated; thus number of viewers per television set correlates with mean size of household and number of years the village has had a school: the lower the increase in the village population, the larger the mean household size, and the greater the number of people per television set.
(3) The greater the percentage increase in the number of households in a village (1963–1990), the greater is the percentage reduction in the child-woman ratio.
(4) The masculinity ratio, which should be lower where female children have better survival rates, is inversely correlated with the percentage of nuclear households in a village: the higher the percentage of nuclear households, the lower the masculinity ratio.
(5) On questions of fertility reduction, we find that the lower the child–woman ratio, the lower the number of fertile years of the younger women (born since 1930), the greater the reduction in those fertile years as compared with the older women (born before that date), and the greater the number of villages with which they have marital ties.

Table 12.2

RANKING OF FOUR VILLAGES ON CERTAIN CRITERIA ASSOCIATED WITH MODERNIZATION

	Ki:y Oḍeyaraṭṭi	O:rana:yi	Hulla:ḍa	Ke:ti Toreke:ri
Communication factors (1990)				
Distance from town by road	2	1	4	3
No. of years with village school	1	2	3	4
No. of viewers per television set	1 (159)*	2 (104)	3 (57)	4 (49)
No. of telephone lines in village	0	0	1 (3)	2 (14)
No. of villages with marriage ties	2 (17)	3 (19)	4 (47)	1 (11)
Village-exogamous marriages	1 (57.1%)	4 (99.2%)	4 (97.9%)	4 (98.0%)
Population size (1990)				
No. of households	3 (65)	3 (65)	4 (127)	1 (26)
Mean size of household	1 (4.88)	2 (4.77)	3 (4.51)	4 (3.77)
Percentage of nuclear households	3 (82%)	1 (66%)	3 (82%)	4 (88%)
Increase in no. of households	4 (132%)	1 (38%)	3 (74%)	2 (63%)
Greatest longevity	4	3	1	1
Increase in absolute population	4 (75%)	3 (46%)	2 (38%)	1 (26%)
Fertility				
Masculinity ratio (1990)	3 (0.8)	1 (1.1)	2 (0.9)	4 (0.7)
Child–woman ratio (1990)	4 (204)	1 (407)	4 (204)	2 (355)
Reduction of the child–woman ratio	4 (66%)	1 (20%)	3 (60%)	2 (36%)
Generation length (1963–1990)	2 (26.0)	3 (26.7)	1 (24.5)	4 (27.4)
No. of fertile yrs., younger women	1 (11.5)	3 (8.2)	4 (7.9)	2 (9.4)
Yrs. reduction, from older women	1 (2.0)	3 (6.9)	4 (8.3)	2 (2.7)
No. of items of rank *4*	5	1	7	7
No. of items of rank *3*	3	7	6	1
No. of items of rank *2*	3	3	2	6
No. of items of rank *1*	6	6	3	4
Ranking score (*r*)	41	37	53	47

* Rank order is given first, then particular values are in parentheses.[1]

(6) Overall—and rather impressionistically—I conclude that O:rana:yi is perhaps the most conservative or traditional of the villages; yet it is no less modernized than Ki:y Oḍeyaraṭṭi, the other Lingayat village. Both lacked telephone service and had fewer television sets in 1990. To some extent the degree of modernization of each village is in inverse proportion to its traditional social ranking. One can score the rankings on these modernization factors (in Table 12.2, bottom line; $r = \Sigma 4a_4 + 3a_3 + 2a_2 + a_1$ where $a_{1...4}$ is the number of rankings at each of the four degrees of modernization). The result is that the large Gauḍa village scores highest, while the 'minority groups' all score lower, and the two Lingayat villages—highest in social status—rank lowest of all. The Toreya village, traditionally considered as lowest, ranked quite high on the scale. If one considers only the factors headed 'Fertility', the ranking is the same. This implies that modernization entails a process of social levelling.

A View of the Future

We have been examining economic and demographic variables here for the most part. I cannot say that religion is an important factor in the conduct of daily household affairs; but (not being a religious person myself) I have possibly overlooked its influence in this study. Religion no doubt does enter the household on occasions other than life-cycle rituals. The householder may, and traditionally should, begin every day with at least a prayer, if only a repetition of the names of God. Some men will spend the period before their breakfast in meditation, or in offering *puja* to images of deities that belong in the house. Later in the day the housewife too may say prayers or make offerings to images or holy lithographs in the house. But the extent of such daily observations is not clear, and it is difficult to argue that religion (apart from Christianity) has provided any moral support for the process of modernization. It seems to be the case that the many hundreds of Badaga proverbs I examined (Hockings 1988), which are definitely guides to everyday tasks and to accepted ethical behaviour, almost never mention the name of any Hindu divinity: there is morality without theological sanction.

What we do not find in this corner of India is any definite religious *opposition* to sterilization, education for girls, divorce, widow remarriage, or adult marriage for girls, as is still commonly encountered elsewhere in Hindu and Muslim societies. Badaga Saivism, never having been a scriptural religion, is not a rigorously prescriptive one either. More than one villager attending a funeral confided to me that he had no real conviction there was any life after death. Funerals themselves are often curtailed or reorganized for the convenience of family members. I would estimate that these lightly held religious views have made it easier for the Badagas to modernize. The fact that they have so rapidly reduced their fertility is perhaps related to this: women, who in other peasant societies tend to be poorly educated and conservative, here showed me as early as 1963 that even if poorly educated they were much more likely to turn to scientific medicine for resolving health problems than were their menfolk; and a decade later they turned to sterilization too.

What of the future? Can a social scientist tell the Badagas anything that may be a guide to the coming generations? The act is a risky one, even if social activists might wish for it, since no one can predict the aberrant rise of a dictator like Napoleon or his contemporary Tipu Sultan, nor can one suggest what natural calamities may occur, what extremist 'godmen' may arise, or what yet-unformed political philosophies may mobilize this part of India in the 21st century.

With diffidence, therefore, I will say that the future is not a bright one for the Nilgiris. Already many people there are complaining quite justifiably about overcrowding in the towns, saturation tourism, unchecked immigration from the plains and Sri Lanka, lack of adequate sanitary facilities, the menace of diesel fumes, rapid deforestation, the rising cost of living, and the shortages of potable and irrigation water, of housing and fuel. At the time of writing this (1995), the only cause for hope over any of these issues lies in the fact that they are being discussed locally and in the south Indian press; in this the local Save Nilgiris Campaign has been showing commendable leadership.

Meanwhile the Badagas are still strongly maintaining their ethnic identity by rigorous rules of community endogamy and by speaking their own language; but how useful will this psychological strength be to them now that the Government of India, through its census, has begun to disregard the separate identity of Badagas and treat them, since 1971, as Canarese speakers? Even if they succeed in capping their population, in keeping with a recognition that their lands will not expand and there are limits as to how much fertilizer can be put into a field and how much money can be spent on children, they will still face economic and political pressure from other immigrant communities with ever-expanding populations. Badagas have never been numerically dominant in the district during the 20th century, having throughout been less than a third of the total population. Already during the 1980s the Tamil Nadu government, with its own priorities and with its capital on the opposite side of the state, was relocating Tamil refugees from Sri Lanka in the Nilgiris district on the assumption that they might find employment there in the tea industry and not cause political trouble in Madras. These generally unskilled people have made themselves deeply unpopular with local inhabitants by their encroachment on Badaga and other farmland, squatting in Badaga villages, aggressive politicizing, and evident liaisons with and protection by Tamil government officials in the district (Heidemann 1996).

It is not entirely unrealistic to suppose that some such large sector of the population in the future, supported by narrowly ethnic politicians, might well be able to force the cession of Badaga lands and houses to other communities on the grounds of greater need occasioned by their overpopulation. Since this style of ethnic politics is already a well-established reality in India, the Badagas may then find themselves with no powerful friend to turn to for succour. Should the law no longer protect them either, one option that is likely to grow in popularity is that of emigration to cities in other parts of India and in the United States where their education will serve them well. (Already, in 1994, there were about 200 Badaga households in the latter country.) One trusts that armed rebellion will not arise (as it has in northeast India), as there is little precedent for it in this part of the country. But the coherence of a community who only inhabit the Nilgiri Hills could be seriously compromised.

NOTES

1. Some of these valuations perhaps call for an explanation, lest they be dismissed as arbitrary:
Distance from town: Much Indian research has indicated that the closer to town a rural settlement is, the more access it has to modern facilities.
Age of village school: The older a school is, the larger the total number of villagers who have been directly affected by it.
Number of viewers per television set: The greater the mean number of viewers, the more difficult or unlikely is it that they will all see news or modernizing programmes with regularity.
Number of villages with marriage ties: Evidence suggests that the more villages one particular village has marital ties with, the better will be the chances

of its members to secure personal loans when necessary. For the same reason the greater the incidence of *village-exogamous marriage*, the better the chances of getting loans from others less adversely affected by a local crop failure.
Number and mean size of households, increase in number of houses and of *absolute population*, and *size of village*: These variables are all linked with the political importance of a given village, since the larger its vote pool is perceived to be, the more interest will local, usually Badaga, politicians show in it and its needs. *Greater longevity* is closely associated demographically with a growing population.
When *masculinity ratio, child–woman ratio*, and *generation length* decrease, these are indications that the health and treatment of women are improving.
As the *child–woman ratio* and the *number of a woman's fertile years* decrease, fertility of the population will tend to decline and so reduce the pressure on resources.

Appendix I

GAZETTEER OF THE KE:TI NEIGHBOURHOOD

The following entries are abstracted from *A Badaga–English Dictionary* (Hockings and Pilot-Raichoor 1992, with some corrections). Names are spelt phonetically, but conventional spellings appearing on the local maps are also given in parentheses. *GEN* indicates genitive case. The numbers of households in each hamlet are estimates.

Accanakal (Acchinakal, Achinikallu), a hamlet 3.5 km SSE of Ootacamund, belonging to Ke:ti commune; it has three parts: **a**. Accanakal Ki:yaṭṭi (also called *Kaḍehaṭṭi*); **b**. Manepaṭṭu (q.v.); **c**. Accanakal Me:laṭṭi (Kasturi, Maduve/Haṭṭara, and Ma:ri *kulas*; 200 Gauḍa houses in 1994; ‹ *ajja+na+kal,* 'ancestor+GEN+stone')

Aṇehaṭṭi (Anehatti, Anaihatti, Anuihutty, Anihutty, Aneihatti, Anihatti), a part of Kereha:ḍa, a hamlet 4 km SSE of Ootacamund, belonging to Ke:ti commune (Kasturi and Ma:ri *kulas*; in existence prior to 1809; 68 Gauḍa, 3 Haruva, and 4 Christian houses altogether in 1970; Macleane 1893: 583; ‹ *aṇe+haṭṭi,* 'ridge+hamlet')

Aravanga:ḍu (Aravankadu, Arvencaud, Arvenghat, Aravungaad, Aruvankad, Aruvankadu, Aravankad, Aravankods, Arvenkod, Arvan Ghaut, Glen Owen, Glen Arven), name of a valley (not the Ke:ti Valley) and a village of mixed population (including many Badaga factory workers settled over the past thirty years) on the main road from Ootacamund to Coonoor, 9 km ESE of Ootacamund, 4 km NW of Coonoor. (Head village of Aravankadu Panchayat, with a 1991 population of 5,562; Honeywell's brewery was built here in 1859, but since 1900 it has been noted only for its cordite factory; it marks one of the limits of Poranga:ḍu division; Macleane 1893:43; Francis 1908: 312–15; Eagan 1916: 80–81; ‹ *are+(v)e:ṇu+ka:ḍu,* 'flat rock+edge+forest')

Arehaṭṭi, an early name for Poro:raṭṭi (q.v.)

Ba:ruhaṇe (Lovedale), former name of a locality 3.5 km S of Ootacamund (former name no longer in use; cf. *Lavde:l* for recent history; site of the Lovedale railway station, near Lawrence School; ‹ *ba:ru+haṇe*, 'verdure+meadow')

Ba:vaṭṭi (Bahatty), former name for a part of Ellena:yi hamlet, 5.5 km SE of Ootacamund, belonging to Ke:ti commune (only shown on the 1822 map, which does not name Ellena:yi; probably destroyed in subsequent road building; ? ‹ *ba:va+haṭṭi*, 'brothers-in-law+hamlet', i.e., an affinal section of the hamlet)

Beḷḷimoraha:ḍa, the site of the present Laidlaw Memorial School & Junior College, formerly known as St. George's Homes, adjoining Hulla:ḍa and 6 km SE of Ootacamund. A former village, *Beḷḷimorahaṭṭi*, was the original home of the Aççanakal clan (‹ *beḷḷi+mora+ha:ḍa*, 'silvery+trees+flat ground', reference to a large stand of eucalyptus)

Cakkaḷaṭṭi/Sakkaḷaṭṭi (Chukal-hatti, Sakkalatti, Jackalatti), a hamlet 8.5 km SSE of Ootacamund, formerly belonging to Ke:ti but now to So:gatore commune (from which it is said to have been settled originally; had *ca.* 20 Adikari, 15 Gauḍa houses in 1970; Thurston and Rangachari 1909: 101–02; ‹ *jakkaḷu+haṭṭi*, 'Nilgiri barberry+hamlet', or *cakkaḷa+haṭṭi*, 'skin+hamlet')

Daḍahaṭṭi (Tadahatti), a part of the hamlet of Kereha:ḍa (q.v.), 4 km SSE of Ootacamund, belonging to Ke:ti commune (*ca.* 10 Ha:ruva houses in 1994; Kasturi kula; ? ‹ *daḍḍa+haṭṭi*, 'fine+hamlet')

De:nale (Denalai, Denalle, Thenalai), name of a hamlet 6 km W of Coonoor, belonging to Ke:ti commune (Maduve/Haṭṭara and Ma:ri kulas; *ca.* 160 Gauḍa houses in 1991; ‹ *de:+na:yi*, 'Kuṟumba's cry+neck of land')

Doḍḍaṇṇi (Doddani, Thoddanni, Thud-hatti), a hamlet 7 km SSE of Ootacamund, formerly belonging to Ke:ti but now to So:gatore commune (Kasturi or Ko:ye:ru/Ko:vu:r/Ko:ve:ri *kula*; *ca.* 14 Adikari houses in 1970; cf. *Jo:ṇuhaṭṭi, Sa:lemu:r*; ‹ *doḍḍa+haṇṇi*, 'big+swamp', a reference to the Pa:la:ḍa valley below)

Doḍḍa Beṭṭa (Dodabetta, Doddabetta Mountain, Do-Do-Bet, Dodatetta), the highest mountain in Tamil Nadu, 2637 m in elevation, 3.5 km ESE of Ootacamund (location of Doddabetta Panchayat, with 1981 population of 8,991; lookout point and the site of a meteorological station since 1847; junction of the indigenous boundaries between Todana:ḍu, Poranga:ḍu and Me:kuna:ḍu; previously called *Ko:ḍabeṭṭa*; Burton 1851: 276–77; Macleane 1893:279; Francis 1908: 4, 243, 251; ‹ *doḍḍa+beṭṭa*, 'great+mountain')

Doḍḍa Beṭṭu (Thodda-bettu, Thodabetta), a mountain *ca.* 2260 m in elevation, 4.5 km SSE of Ootacamund; ‹ Kota *doḍḍu*+Bad. *beṭṭu*, 'wild buffalo+

mountain' or < *doḍḍa+beṭṭu,* 'great+mountain')

Eḍehaṭṭi (Yedaihatti, Yeduhatti), is 8 km SSE of Ootacamund, belonging to Ka:ṭaru/Ka:ṭe:ri/Ka:ṭe:ru commune (Beḷḷi *kula*; 3 Kaggusi houses in 1970; < *eḍe+haṭṭi,* 'middle+hamlet')

Ellena:yi (Yellanhalli, Yellanully, Yellunhally, Yellanhully, Yelanhalli, Yellanhulli, Yellanalli, Hully), name of a hamlet, now of mixed population (including non-Badaga tradesmen and labourers), on the road from Coonoor to Ootacamund, 5.5 km SE of the latter, belonging to Ke:ti commune (Kasturi *kula*; in existence prior to 1809; site of one of the earliest travellers' bungalows, and of the former Rose & Crown brewery, established in 1895; 35 Gauḍa houses in 1970; a part was formerly called *Ba:vaṭṭi,* q.v.; cf. *Osaṭṭi/Hosaṭṭi/Hosahaṭṭi*; Macleane 1893: 584; < *elle+na:yi,* 'boundary+neck of land', i.e., at the boundary between Me:kuna:ḍu, Todana:ḍu and Porangana:ḍu)

Ha:la:ḍa (Hallada, Ha:la:ḍa, Allada, Alhada), a part of Kereha:ḍa (q.v.), 4 km S of Ootacamund, belonging to Ke:ti commune (Bra:ma and Maduve/Haṭṭara *kulas*; in existence prior to 1812; 15 Haruva, 3 Adikari houses in 1970; < *ha:lu+ha:ḍa,* 'milk+flat place')

Ha:laṭṭi/Ha:luke:ri, former name of a hamlet, now part of *Ka:ṭaru/Ka:ṭe:ri/Ka:ṭe:ru,* q.v.

Hotege (Ootacamund, Ooty, Udhagamandalam), large town and Nilgiri district headquarters 428 km WSW of Madras and 55 km NNW of Coimbatore, and to the W of the Ke:ti Valley; founded in 1821 by John Sullivan (population in 1991, 81,763; common Badaga name today for the town, which they formerly called *Oṭṭikalmandu,* and which was formerly spelt Hottegemund, Oatacamund, Utakamand, Otacamund, Oatakamund, Ootakumund, Whatakaimand, Whotakamund, Whotakaymund, Whotokaymund, Wootaycamund, Wotay, Wotaycamund, Wotokymand, Wuttacamund, Otacamund, and now Udhagamandalam; 'Whotakay' on the map of 1822; Ward 1821: lxii; Burton 1851: 277–313, 353–55; Metz 1864: 6–7; Macleane 1893: 620–21; Francis 1908: 357–63; Price 1908: passim; Eagan 1916: 29–46; Emeneau 1963: passim; Hockings 1989b: passim)

Hulla:ḍa (Hullada, Oolauda, Vullada, Ulanda), a hamlet 4.5 km SE of Ootacamund, beside Ketti railway station, belonging to Ke:ti commune (one of our four sample hamlets; Bra:ma and Kasturi *kulas*; in existence prior to 1812; 1 Haruva, 127 Gauḍa houses in 1990; cf. Figures 7.5 and 7.6; cf. *Ko:ḍa to:*; < *hullu+ha:ḍa,* 'grass+level ground')

Je:naṭṭu, a high slope 4.5 km SSE of Ootacamund, near Kammandu (q.v.; < *je:nu+aṭṭu,* 'honey+cliff')

Jo:ṇuhaṭṭi (Jonihatti), an abandoned Badaga hamlet 7 km SSE of Ootacamund, formerly Kereha:ḍa (q.v.; now given over to vegetable and eucalyptus cultivation; ‹ *jo:ṇu+haṭṭi,* 'waterlogged land+hamlet')

Kaḍehaṭṭi (Kadehatti), former name for Accanakal Ki:yaṭṭi, a Gauḍa hamlet 3.5 km SSE of Ootacamund, adjoining Accanakal (q.v.) and belonging to Ke:ti commune (‹ *kaḍe+haṭṭi,* 'last+hamlet')

Kalla:ḍa Beṭṭu (Kalada bettu), a hill 2422 m in elevation, on the southern flanks of Doḍḍabeṭṭa (q.v.), 4.5 km SE of Ootacamund (‹ *kallu+ha:ḍa+beṭṭu,* 'stone+flat ground+mountain')

Kammandu (Kammandu, Kamandu, Kammand, Kummund, Camanth), a hamlet 6.5 km SSE of Ootacamund, belonging to Ke:ti commune (Kasturi and Ma:ri *kulas*; 39 Gauḍa, 2 Haruva houses in 1970; in existence before 1812, and built on a former Toda site Kemeṇ, at which its priest allegedly violated so many ritual prescriptions that the clan died out; Harkness 1832: 105; 'the only extinct clan of which I have a record is a Teivali clan, the Kemenol, which is said to have become extinct about a hundred years ago…' — Rivers 1906: 692; cf. *Je:naṭṭu, Ne:rikambe*; ‹ Toda *Kemeṇ* +Bad. *mandu,* '[name of extinct clan]+Toda hamlet')

Kaṇṇaraluha:ḍa/Kaṇṇaṭṭa:ḍa, old name for the site where Sa:ntu:r hamlet now stands (q.v.; so named because herdsmen used to gather there to play the game of *kaṇṇaralu*; ‹ *kaṇṇu+haralu+ha:ḍa,* 'eye+bean+flat ground')

Ka:ṭaru/Ka:ṭe:ri/Ka:ṭe:ru (Kateri, Kaultray, Katteri, Katary, Kautari, Kartairy, Cartairy, Cautairy, Kartari, Kartery, Karteri), name of a hamlet located 8 km SSE of Ootacamund, near the source of the small Kateri R. and the well-known Kateri Falls (*Kengo:ḍu Uli,* q.v., where India's first hydroelectric power station was opened in 1904); head village of Ka:ṭaru/Ka:ṭe:ri/Ka:ṭe:ru commune (with only two other hamlets; Ma:ṇikka kula; in existence prior to 1812, one of the original nine villages of Me:kuna:ḍu; site originally called *Ha:laṭṭi* or *Ha:luke:ri*; 205 Kaṇakka houses in 1970; Harkness 1832: 112; Macleane 1893: 405; Francis 1908: 330; Hockings 1980a: 282, etc.; cf. Kota *ka·ṭ+e·r,* 'scene+river')

Ka:ṭe:ru Beṭṭu (Karteri bettu), a hill 2006 m in elevation, 5.5 km W of Coonoor (‹ *Ka:ṭe:ru+beṭṭu,* '[name]+hill')

Ka:ṭe:ru Haḷḷa (Karteri Halla), name of a stream that flows S from Ke:ti village to plunge over the Kateri Fall 6 km W of Coonoor (above the falls known as *Muḷḷisopputore Haḷḷa,* q.v.; cf. *Kengo:ḍu Uli*; Eagan 1916: 57–58, 95; ‹ *Ka:ṭe:ru+haḷḷa,* '[name]+stream')

Kekkaṭṭi (Kekkatti, Kek-hatti, Kelihalli, Cakutty), a hamlet 6 km SE of Ootacamund, belonging to Ke:ti commune (Kasturi *kula*; in existence prior to 1812; 52 Gauḍa and Adikari houses in 1970; cf. *Kera:ḍakambe, Ke:titore/Ke:tore,* and *Mokkaṭṭi,* all parts of Kekkaṭṭi; ‹ *kekke+haṭṭi,* 'uncultivable soil+hamlet')

Kengo:ḍu Uli (Kateri Falls, Karteri Fall, Khaity Falls), a waterfall *ca.* 55 m high, 9 km SSE of Ootacamund on the Ka:ṭe:ru Haḷḷa (q.v.; Burton 1851: 269–70; Francis 1908: 8, 313; Eagan 1916: 57–58, 95; ‹ *keng+ko:ḍu+uli,* 'red+ridge+waterfall')

Kengunde/Kengundu (Kengunde, Kengundu), part of Kereha:ḍa, 4 km SSE of Ootacamund, belonging to Ke:ti commune (Kasturi *kula*; 19 Gauḍa houses in 1970; ‹ *keng+kuṇḍe,* 'red+dell')

Kera:ḍakambe (Keradakambai), a hamlet now part of Kekkaṭṭi (q.v.), 6 km SE of Ootacamund, belonging to Ke:ti commune (Kasturi *kula*; 25 Gauḍa and Adikari houses in 1970; cf. *Ke:rkaṇḍi*; ‹ *kere+ha:ḍa+kambe,* 'pond+flat place+ridge')

Kereha:ḍa (Kerehada, Kerayada, Kerehauda, Kerihada, Kerihadu, Kariada, Caryada, Cariauda), name of a hamlet 4 km SSE of Ootacamund, belonging to Ke:ti commune (Kasturi and Ma:ri *kulas*; in existence prior to 1809; 68 Gauḍa, 3 Haruva, and 4 Christian houses in 1970; cf. *Aṇehaṭṭi, Kengundu/Kengunde, Ti:ḍehaṭṭi, Daḍahaṭṭi, So:reguṇḍu, Ha:la:ḍa,* all parts of this hamlet; Macleane 1893: 83; ‹ *kere+ha:ḍa,* 'pond+level ground', i.e., a small pond used to form in a depression there after rains)

Ke:rkaṇḍi (Kerkandi), a part of *Kera:ḍakambe* 6.5 km SE of Ootacamund, belonging to Ke:ti commune (Kasturi kula; ‹ *ke:ru+kaṇḍi,* 'pond+small tableland')

Ke:ti (Keti, Ketti, Ketty, Kaety, Kaity, Kaiti, Kaitia, Käti, Kaythee, Kaytee, Khaity, Kittoo), a hamlet and the surrounding Ketti Valley, 4.5 km SE of Ootacamund; head village of Ke:ti commune (and of Ketty Panchayat, with 1981 population of 21,336); site of a former experimental farm, later a prison-farm for Boer prisoners, and now the Primary Health Centre, (cf. *Ko:ṇagaṭṭi*); also of 'Mission Bungalow', a house used by Lord Elphinstone and the Governor of Pondicherry; this subsequently became the local headquarters (1849–1914) of the Basel Evangelical Mission. (Hamlet in existence before 1809, one of the nine communes that originally made up Me:kuna:ḍu, and said to have been settled from Kongahaḷḷi near the Karnataka border; Kasturi, Bra:ma and Ma:ri *kulas*; 78 Gauḍa, 26 Toreya, 3 Haruva, 4 Christian houses in 1994; Burton 1851: 269; Macleane 1893: 403; Francis 1908: 331–32; Thurston and Rangachari 1909: 123; Noble 1968: 122–28, 136–39; Hockings 1980a: 61, 282, etc.; cf. Kota *ke· kaṭy,* '[place of] clinkers', ref. to where smelting once occurred. *Tuduru devvu* was an evil spirit who 'was supposed to reside in the small wood facing the Mission house at Kaity … the Missionaries put a stop to the sacrifices which used to be offered there ….' — Metz 1864: 69; ‹ *tudu:ru+devvu,* 'tip-toeing+being')

Ke:ti Toreke:ri, the section of lower Ke:ti (q.v.) village inhabited by 26

Toreya households in 1990 (one of our four sample hamlets); cf. Figure 7.4; cf. Kota *ke· kaṭy*+Bad. *tore+ke:ri,* '[place of] clinkers+Toreya+sector'

Ke:tore (Kettithorai, Ketithore, Katore), part of Kekkaṭṭi 8 km SSE of Ootacamund, belonging to Ke:ti commune (Kasturi *kula* ; ‹ *ke:i+tore,* 'Nilgiri tahr+dale')

Ki:y Oḍeyaraṭṭi (Kilodaiyaratti, Kil Oder-hatti), a hamlet 6 km WNW of Coonoor, belonging to Ke:ti commune (one of our four sample hamlets; *Kolekambe* was given as an alternative name on the 1871 map; 65 Wodeya houses in 1990; cf. Figure 7.1; ‹ *ki:e +(y)oḍeya(r)+haṭṭi,* 'lower+Wodeya+hamlet')

Ko:ḍato:, a cattle pen which used to stand where Ketti railway station now is, above Hulḷa:ḍa (‹ *ko:ḍu+to:,* 'border+kraal')

Kollimale (Kollimale, Kollimalai Kottagiri, Kalamae Kotagiri, Kollimalei, Colimullay, Collimuttay, Cotacarah, Kolmel), a Kota village 7 km S of Ootacamund (in existence prior to 1809, one of the nine communes that originally made up Me:kuna:ḍu; *ca.* 50 houses in 1970; it is an *u:r* with no other hamlets; in Kota, *Kolme·l*; Breeks 1873: 41; Mandelbaum 1960; ‹ *kolla+male,* 'iron-smelting site+mountain')

Ko:ṇagaṭṭi, a location near Ke:ti hamlet, 4 km SE of Ootacamund, where a buffalo sacrifice used to occur (site of the old Boer prison camp, from 1970 the Primary Health Centre; ‹ *ko:ṇa+kaṭṭu,* 'buffalo+tie')

Kunnu:r (Coonoor; formerly Cunoor, Kunur, Koonoor or Kooner), name of a large town 14 km SE of Ootacamund and 425 km WSW of Madras, lying to the E of the Ke:ti Valley; originally a Badaga hamlet of the same name (or *Kunnu:r Haṇe*), in existence prior to 1812, with a Toda hamlet (Pem, Päm, belonging to İṇkity clan) at the site of the Coonoor Club; taluk headquarters on the main road from Ootacamund to Coimbatore, at the head of the Coonoor Ghat road (road completed in 1833; population in 1991, 48,003; Burton 1851: 264–65; Macleane 1893: 216; Francis 1908: 317–24; Eagan 1916: 59–70; ‹ *kunnu+o:re,* 'escarpment+slope', ref. to their position on the edge of the plateau in each item; but for alternative etymologies, cf. Zvelebil 1982: 54)

Lavde:l (Lovedale), a locality 3.5 km S of Ootacamund (name first recorded in 1854; formerly called *Ba:ruhaṇe,* q.v.; site of the Lawrence School, a railway station, and an artificial lake originally called St Lawrence's Lake; cf. *Lovedale,* the name of the house where Napoleon stayed on St Helena; also a South African mission station 142 km NW of East London, Cape Province; Francis 1908: 11–12, 41, 262; Eagan 1916: 81)

Manepaṭṭu (Manepattu), a part of Accanakal, 3.5 km SSE of Ootacamund, belonging to Ke:ti commune (21 Gauḍa houses in 1970; ‹ *mane +paṭṭu,* 'house+plot of land')

Me:l Oḍeyaraṭṭi (Melodayaratti, Meloderhatti, Mel Oderhatti), a hamlet 5.5 km S of Ootacamund, belonging to Ke:ti commune (67 Wodeya houses in 1970; ‹ *me:l+oḍeya+haṭṭi,* 'upper+Wodeya+hamlet')

Modaḷikambe, a locality between Ke:ti and Accanakal hamlets, 4 km SE of Ootacamund (‹ *modaḷi+kambe,* 'Kuṟumba headman+ridge')

Mokkaṭṭi (Mokkatti, Mock-hatti, Mocutty, Mokkeyatti, Mockahatti), part of Kekkaṭṭi hamlet 6.5 km SE of Ootacamund, belonging to Ke:ti commune (Kasturi and Maduve/Haṭṭara *kulas*; in existence before 1812; 14 Gauḍa houses in 1970; ‹ *mokke+haṭṭi,* 'gravelly land+hamlet')

Muḷḷisopputore Haḷḷa (Mullichoppu thore halla), name for the upper reaches of the Ka:ṭe:ru Haḷḷa (q.v.), which flows S from Ke:ti to plunge over the Kateri Fall 6 km W of Coonoor (‹ *muḷḷi+soppu+tore+haḷḷa,* 'bramble+greens+ dale+stream')

Naḍuhaṭṭi (Naduhatti, Nadhuhatty, Nuddoovutty, Nadduhutty), a hamlet 8 km SSE of Ootacamund, formerly belonging to Adigaraṭṭi but now to Ka:ṭaru/ Ka:ṭe:ri/Ka:ṭe:ru commune (Ma:ṇikka kula; 25 Kaṇakka houses in 1970; ‹ *naḍu+haṭṭi,* 'middle+hamlet')

Ne:rikambe (Nerikambai, Nerekambe, Nerikambe, Nerkambe, Nercambe, Nercambai, Nircumbey, Nercamby, Nirkambai, Nirkambe, Nerikomoe), a former Adikari hamlet 5 km W of Coonoor, belonging to So:gatore commune (4 Christian houses in 1970; site of a chapel built for the Badagas by the Basel Mission, consecrated on Sept. 8, 1864; Macleane 1893: 583; previous to Badaga settlement it had been the Toda funeral site for the extinct Kemeṇ clan of Todas; cf. Kammandu; ‹ Toda *nö·ṟ*+Bad. *kambe,* 'sun+ridge')

O:rana:yi/Ho:rana:yi (Horanalli, Hornatti, Oranali, Voranhalli), a hamlet 7 km S of Ootacamund, formerly belonging to So:gatore commune (one of our four sample hamlets; Kasturi *kula*; not in existence prior to 1812; 65 Adikari houses in 1990; cf. Figures 7.2 and 7.3; ‹ *o:ra+na:yi,* 'sloping+neck of land')

Osaṭṭi/Hosaṭṭi/Hosahaṭṭi (Hosatti, Hosahatti, Osatti, Osahutty, Osa-hatti, Osayatti), a part of Ellena:yi, a Gauḍa hamlet 5.5 km SE of Ootacamund, belonging to Ke:ti commune (Kasturi *kula*; there are 15 other hamlets of the same name; ‹ *osa+haṭṭi,* 'new+hamlet')

Pa:la:ḍa, a valley and a modern village of mixed population, near Doḍḍaṇṇi (q.v.), 7 km SSE of Ootacamund (‹ *pa:la+ha:ḍa,* 'shared territory+valley')

Po:ro:raṭṭi (Pororatti, Boruvare Hatti), a hamlet 4.5 km SSE of Ootacamund, belonging to Ke:ti commune (Kasturi *kula*; 19 Gauḍa houses in 1970; formerly called *Arehaṭṭi*; name given after the railway cutting was made, at the beginning of the 20th century; ‹ *po:re+o:re+haṭṭi,* 'earth-cutting+slope+hamlet')

Saḷḷitore, a dale S of Ellena:yi, recently the site of the Pond's factory

Sa:lemu:r, a part of Doḍḍaṇṇi, an Adikari hamlet 7 km SSE of Ootacamund, formerly belonging to Ke:ti but now to So:gatore commune (population nearly all Christian, hence the change in name; ‹ *Sa:lem+u:r*, '[Jerusalem]+village')

Sa:ntu:r (Shantur, Shantoor), a Badaga Christian hamlet adjoining Kereha:ḍa 4.5 km SSE of Ootacamund (in existence before 1862; site formerly called *Kaṇṇaraluha:ḍa* ; Sa:ntayya was the name of the Haruva man who built the first house in Sa:ntu:r during the 1860s: an early Christian convert, originally from Maṇuhaṭṭi, q.v., he first moved to Ne:rikambe before settling here; cf. *Kaṇṇaraluha:ḍa, Toreja:ḍu*; ‹ *Sa:ntayya+u:r*, '[name]+head village')

So:gatore/So:gaṭṭi (Sogathorai, Sogathore, Sogathoray), a hamlet 8 km SSE of Ootacamund, formerly belonging to Ke:ti commune but now head village of So:gatore commune (Kasturi or Ko:ye:ru/Ko:vu:r/Ko:ve:ri *kula*; in existence before 1812 and said to have been settled from nearby Adigaraṭṭi; 96 Adikari houses in 1970; ‹ *so:ge+tore*, 'stink tree+embankment', or *so:ge+haṭṭi*, 'stink tree+hamlet')

So:regunḍu (Soregundu), a Gauḍa part of Kereha:ḍa (q.v.) hamlet 4 km SSE of Ootacamund, belonging to Ke:ti commune (Kasturi *kula*; ‹ *so:re+gunḍu*, 'dove+big boulder')

Talehaṭṭi/Taleyaṭṭi, newer upper part of Accanakal Me:laṭṭi, in Accanakal hamlet, 3.5 km SSE of Ootacamund, belonging to Ke:ti commune (‹ *tale+haṭṭi*, 'upper+hamlet')

Tere (Thire), a location 3.5 km S of Ootacamund and 200 m S of a cutting for the Nilgiri Railway; it adjoins Poro:raṭṭi (q.v.; ‹ *tere*, 'cutting in a hillside')

Ti:ḍehaṭṭi (Tidehatti), a Gauḍa part of Kereha:ḍa hamlet, 4 km SSE of Ootacamund, belonging to Ke:ti commune (Kasturi and Ma:ri *kulas*; ‹ *ti:ḍe+haṭṭi*, 'mist+hamlet')

Ti:riyeremandu, a former Toda *ti:* dairy once located SE of Ootacamund, near Ke:ti (adjoining Welbeck Estate; 8.1 ha land in 1893, but abandoned before then; there were at least 11 other dairies of the same name; ‹ *ti:ri+(y)ere+mandu*, 'dairy-temple+temporary shed+Toda hamlet')

Toreja:ḍu, name of the Roman Catholic settlement within Kereha:ḍa hamlet (q.v.; ‹ *tore+ja:ḍu*, 'river-bank+jump across', as it is across the stream from the Protestant settlement in Sa:ntu:r; but the name predates that settlement)

Toreke:ri, a part of Ke:ti hamlet, 4.5 km SSE of Ootacamund, belonging to Ke:ti commune (here specifically Lower Ke:ti, one of our four sample hamlets; 25 houses in 1990; ‹ *tore+ke:ri*, 'dale+sector')

Tu:raṭṭi (Thud-hatti, Turatti), a hamlet 8.5 km SSE of Ootacamund, belonging to Ka:ṭaru/Ka:ṭe:ri/Ka:ṭe:ru commune (Kasturi *kula*; 57 Kaṇakka houses in 1970; ‹ *tu:ru+haṭṭi*, 'cattle pen+hamlet')

Appendix II

SOME COMPARABLE LONGITUDINAL STUDIES

Although several longitudinal studies have been mentioned in this book, there have been a number of others done in India which, even if not actually cited, have still informed my analysis in one way or another. As a guide to the main studies examined, Table AII.1 will offer a succinct summary. While this table does not in fact carry very much information, it does bring out the uniqueness of the present study, for it is the only longitudinal study done in India with single-community villages; and it is one of only five that were carried through from start to finish by the same personnel. It is furthermore one of only three studies that showed a decline in household size — though such broad averages are involved that the extent of intra-village variation in household size is quite lost sight of. The Caldwell–Reddy study has been included in the table for comparative purposes, although strictly speaking it was not a longitudinal study. A previous study had been done in *one* of their nine villages by the Mysore Population Study in 1951–1952, but this the Caldwell team have made little use of except as background information. Further suggestive longitudinal studies carried out in India and Bangladesh, with roughly one generation of time depth, may be found in Breman, Kloos and Saith's recent book (1997).

It has not proved possible in a book of this length to compare systematically a range of social variables for each of these studies and the four Badaga villages: I felt that dissipating my energies in this type of work might not prove especially fruitful, in view of the basic incomparability of multicaste villages and of 'unitary' ones such as those of the Badagas —and no other study in Table AII.1—have.

A unique historical study done in central India, and one with which the present Badaga study can hardly compare, was initiated in 1819 in the Maharashtrian village of Lonikand by Surgeon Thomas Coats. It was continued by the sociologist G.S. Ghurye in 1958, and completed

Table A II.1. SUMMARY OF LONGITUDINAL VILLAGE STUDIES IN INDIA, 1819–1990

Village(s) & Authors	Dravidian Area	Multicaste Villages	Varying research Persons	Depth › 1 genern.	Population range	Mean household size	Years of Study
Vilyatpur (Punjab) Kessinger	–	+	+	+	565-1197	4.6–7.2	1848–1968
Shanti Nagar (Delhi) Freed & Freed	–	+	–	–	799-1324	7.3–10.5	1958–1978
Karimpur (U.P.), Wiser & Wiser, Wadley	–	+	+	+	754-2048	4.7–6.3	1925–1984
Palanpur (U.P.) Ansari, Bliss & Stern, Drèze	–	+	+	+	528-1133	—	1957–1993
Parhil (U.P.) Saith & Tankha	–	+	–	–	1106-1516	5.98–6.06	1970–1987
Radhvanaj (Gujarat), Shah	–	+	+	+	716-1305	4.5–4.6	1825–1955
Sugao (Maharashtra) Dandekar	–	+	+	–	1621-2583	5.0–5.2	1942–1977

Lonikand (Maharashtra) Coats, Ghurye, Kolenda	–	+	+	+	565-1734	5.3–6.6	1819–1967
Nine *Tumkur* vills. (Karnataka) Caldwell, Caldwell & Reddy	+	+	–	–	4773	6.1	1979–1984
Two *Mysore* vills. (Karnataka), Epstein, Suryanarayana & Thimmegowda	+	+	–	–	1665-2675	4.8–4.7	1954–1994
22 (5) *Madras Pres.* vills. (T.N., A.P., & Kerala), Slater, Thomas & Ramakrishnan, Haswell	+	+	+	+	…	…	1916–1961
Two *Tanjore* vills. (T.N.), Gough	+	+	–	–	1626-1991	5.4–4.2	1952–1976
Four *Badaga* vills. (T.N.), Hockings	+	–	–	–	886-1298	5.4–4.6	1963–1990

(for the present, anyway) by Pauline Kolenda in 1967. Such an unusual time depth regrettably cannot be paralleled for any village of the Nilgiri Hills, whether Badaga or other; although it has been possible in this study to make some quantitative and qualitative statements about the 19th century Badagas of the small area that is roughly bounded by our four sample villages, known then in Christian circles as Ketti Parish.

Coats' study of Lonikand (which is 19 km from Pune) is valuable to us not just for its great antiquity but also because he showed serious demographic interest in his description; telling us for instance that the place contained 107 houses, 130 married men (including 11 or 12 with two wives), and 203 children. There were further tabular breakdowns of these figures, as well as data on 16 castes. Mean household size was then 5.3. The population of 565 which Coats had enumerated in 1819 had become 1,404 by 1958, and 1,734 by 1967 (Kolenda 1987: 166, 175). One important conclusion to be gleaned from this study is that even if we go back to the very beginning of modern times in India, in 1819, the joint family was by no means the norm. Lonikand had either 19.5 or 29.0 per cent joint families in 1819 (depending on definition); the others were various sorts of nuclear family. By 1958 this proportion had *risen* to 50 fl joint (Kolenda 1987: 168). The same point is made by Wadley and Derr (in a study to be mentioned in the following pages), when they say that 'the joint family was not as prevalent as is traditionally assumed. One source of confusion is that most studies of preindustrial societies have focused on native ideology, rather than on social reality. While the ideal may have been a joint family, demographic and economic realities often precluded its existence' (Wadley and Derr 1988: 119).

A modern study done in the same region as Lonikand, at the Maharashtrian village of Sugao, spans the period 1942–1982. The initial, unpublished survey was carried out in 1942–43 by staff from the Gokhale Institute of Politics and Economics, at Pune, and was repeated by them in 1957–58. Then a follow-up study was completed and reported on by Hemalata Dandekar after fieldwork in 1976–77 and 1979–82, not only in Sugao but also with its villagers working in Bombay. A major thrust of her book (1986), as its title suggests, is the impact of labouring opportunities in the city of Bombay, which is over 150 miles from Sugao. 'The village provides not only cheap labour to the city's industries but also an expanding market for the city's exports, receiving in return remittances of cash and kind that allow the village population, which has outgrown the bearing capacity of its land, to survive. This comes at considerable personal cost, however' (Dandekar 1986: 259).

Highly comparable to the Lonikand study was another also done in a single village of western India, in this case Radhvanaj in Gujarat. It was first examined in a quantitative way by British officials in 1825, and then again 130 years later by A.M. Shah and associates. As with all of the longitudinal studies, this is a multicaste village, home to 25 castes in 1825 (with a population of 716); the mean size of the 159 households was then 4.5. Much later Shah, Shroff and Shah were able to use the long time depth, and local records, to examine the lineage structure of the village. The precise history of local lineages during the intervening years could be reconstructed by them thanks to books of genealogical records that had been faithfully maintained by a caste of bards, the Vahivancha Barots. By 1955 the population had nearly doubled to 1305, but the mean size of households, i.e., 4.6, had hardly changed at all. By that time too 7 of the 25 former caste groups were no longer present, while three 'new' castes had appeared there (Shah, Shroff and Shah 1963; Shah 1973, 1977).

Among the most extensive ethnographies of any one Indian village is that of Shanti Nagar by Stanley and Ruth Freed. Between 1976 and 1993 they published a series of nine short monographs detailing their analysis of this small community some 11 miles northwest of Delhi. The village contains 13 castes and, althrough primarily agricultural, the population included 37 people with jobs in Delhi at the time of the Freeds' 1958/59 census. That census enumerated a total of 799 people; and in 1977/78 the authors were able to produce a second census totalling 1,324. This enabled them to publish a demographic study (1985) with a time depth of 19.5 years, which gives considerable detail on population growth, fertility and sterilization.

Yet another very long study in northwestern India, this one in the Punjab, was the subject of Tom Kessinger's book, *Vilyatpur 1848–1968* (1974). With all of the longitudinal studies discussed in this Appendix (unlike my own), the dates which define the temporal limits seem to be fortuitous. So too in the case of Kessinger's study of the village Vilyatpur: the early date of 1848 happened to be when the earliest British records of the village were made, while 1968 was the year of Kessinger's fieldwork. Like the Lonikand and Radhvanaj studies, this one spans something like two lifetimes; not in itself a structurally significant feature, beyond the unarguable fact that 1848 data can be called 'premodern or traditional', whereas 1968 is definitely 'modern'.

The author relies on basic demographic data and land records that on the face of things appear comparable for the two periods. Again we are looking at a multicaste village, this one having 16 castes in 1848, with a total population of 565—exactly the same as Lonikand in 1819—living in 123 houses. Yet again we find a mean household size of 4.6 (though varying across castes), exactly as in Radhvanaj (Kessinger 1974: 50). The population had doubled, to 1197, in 1961 when there were only 12 castes. The number of households in 1961 was 165, whereas the 1951 Census had enumerated 248: therefore in recent years the size of household has been fluctuating considerably, probably an effect of the return of some migrants from West Punjab after Partition. Kessinger states (1974: 195) that 'the joint family has remained the statistical norm', and has explained that he determined this 'only after eliminating all property groups which on the basis of land owning records and the "legal" genealogies showed no living male relatives in or outside the village with whom a joint structure could be formed. Put another way, the joint family was the norm among those property groups who had a choice' (letter, Aug. 7, 1995). In 1848, the castes with mean household size somewhat greater than five people were for the most part lower-ranking service castes rather than dominant landholding ones.

A fruitful study that is of special interest as it is located in the southernmost parts of India was begun during World War I by a group of economics students under the direction of Gilbert Slater, then a professor at Madras University (1916–1921) but afterwards head of the London School of Economics. A sampling system was hit upon that was haphazard though hardly random: 'Each student chose his own village, it might be his native village, or some other village where he had friends ....' (Slater 1918: 21). The resultant volume published accounts of variable length on 22 villages, none of them in the Nilgiris district (ibid.). One of the students followed up this experience with a book-length study of a Cochin village (Subbarama Aiyar 1925). Then 20 years after the original fieldwork another of Slater's students, P.J. Thomas, conducted a resurvey of eight of the original villages in 1936 (Thomas and Ramakrishnan 1940). These several field studies had reached across Madras Presidency into regions today included in Kerala, Tamil Nadu, Karnataka and Andhra Pradesh. Finally, the British economist Margaret Haswell picked five of the same villages that were within Tamil Nadu and conducted a further restudy, again with the help of a local student, in 1961. This study (1967) reached out in another direction, however, for it also embraced five villages in Orissa, one of which had previously been reported on in detail by F.G. Bailey (Bailey 1958). All of these studies were heavily concerned with rural economic questions, as one would expect, but they still contain much valuable ethnographic detail, and elucidate the nature of socio-economic change in South Asia.

The subject of yet another longitudinal study was Karimpur, a well-known village in western Uttar Pradesh. This study was initiated by two long-resident, well educated American missionaries, William and Charlotte Wiser, in 1925, who together wrote *Behind Mud Walls* (1930, 1960, 1989 edns.); but it was continued by the anthropologists Susan Wadley and Bruce Derr in 1968, 1975 and 1984. This study thus spanned something like two generations. Perhaps its main conclusion was that 'joint families were much less common than thought and have increased over time .... Modernization has worked to increase the number of joint families ....' (Wadley and Derr 1988: 120). A valuable overview to the Karimpur study was provided by Wadley, too (1994).

The comparison between Karimpur and the four Badaga sample villages cannot be pushed too far because, like Lonikand, Shanti Nagar and the other Indian communities that have been the subjects of longitudinal studies, Karimpur is a multicaste village. It has *jatis* of every status from wealthy landowning Brahmins to landless, often under-employed, Harijans. This contrasts with the relatively more egalitarian distribution of resources, and unity of social status, within any one Badaga village. But there is one point in Wadley and Derr's study that bears reflecting on: in 1911–1920, following a period of several epidemics, life expectancy was as low as 20.1 years in the Karimpur area. Hence few married couples could count on having both of the husband's parents still living with them. The joint or stem family was generally an impossibility under such conditions.

Another longitudinal study by an economic anthropologist, Scarlett Epstein, in southern Karnataka has yielded even richer material. She initially studied two villages, Wangala and Dalena, one with irrigated cultivation and the other dry, in 1954–56 (Epstein 1962). Then, 15 years after her first visit, she was able to return to the same villages for a thorough restudy, with the help of four local assistants (Epstein 1973), to understand the nature of modernization there. And finally, a review of 'forty years of rural transformation' has just been published (Epstein, Suryanarayana and Thimmegowda 1998).

Another useful longitudinal study was conducted by Gough in two multicaste villages of Thanjavur district, Tamil Nadu, and published in

1989. Her book was the culmination of a long interest in the political economy of the villages, for which she gives various kinds of social and economic data collected in 1952 and 1976. The latter set of observations coincides in time with the mid-point in my own study; but close similarities to the Badaga situation cannot be pressed, for again her villages were both multicaste, with Brahmin landowners dominating, and moreover they were engaged in the cultivation of irrigated rice. Gough analyses the interplay of socio-economic 'classes' within each village, something that is not a prominent feature within a Badaga village.

One other longitudinal study with similar time parameters to Gough's (1956–1978) was published by Aiyappan and Mahadevan (1988). However, since it deals with Mangadu, a multicaste small town near the east coast, scarcely 16 miles from Madras, I have not considered its findings for comparative purposes. Urbanization is too large a factor in the life of Mangadu.

Another interesting longitudinal study that I was regrettably unable to make use of because of its design was a quite remarkable one done by Arvind Das (1987). This spanned three centuries of life in Changel, a village of northern Bihar, but it lacked the necessary statistical data.

With the exception of the restudies by Epstein and her associates, by Gough, by Saith and Tankha, and by the Freeds, none was done by the same people responsible for the original study. It should be evident that, even if unavoidable, this has been a methodological weakness of longitudinal studies in India; for different investigators, even if coming from the same discipline, inevitably have different agendas, different research interests, different experiences, and hence ask different questions or develop different sorts of conclusion. To some extent the very terms of the comparison are non-comparable.

I can hardly refrain from noting that a study with almost the same 27-year timeframe as mine was carried out in Mexico, on the other side of the world, by Frank Cancian and others, and reported on in his book, *The Decline of Community in Zinacantan; Economy, Public Life, and Social Stratification, 1960–1987* (1992). Since Zinacantán is in a hilly area of Chiapas far from the national capital and at an elevation of about 7400 feet, the book certainly invites a comparison with my own study, at least from a geographical viewpoint.

As commonly happens, however, when one does attempt to compare disparate ethnographic accounts, the terms of the comparison easily become lost in diverging particularisms and 'localisms'. Cancian's study devotes much of its space to economic and political change in what is clearly a volatile society. My own study, by focusing on the household structure of the Badagas, deals less with economic factors and has little to say about political change in what is perhaps a politically more stable society. In particular, a substantial part of the Zinacantecan study is concerned with changes in the cargo system, a hierarchically organized system for redistributing surpluses in a religious mode (Cancian 1992: 97–100). In modern times there has been nothing very like this institution in the Nilgiri Hills, and even when the redistributional system linking Badagas with Kotas, Todas and other groups was still in full operation, it did not have the religious dimension which is central to this Roman Catholic example.

Appendix III

FORM USED TO SUMMARIZE HOUSEHOLD CENSUSES

SURVEY OF FOUR BADAGA VILLAGES, 1963-1990

Village: Hulla:ḍa		No.	Lineage:
W is from:	(1)	(2)	(3)
SW is from:	(1)	(2)	(3)
	(4)	(5)	(6)
Ds married:	(1)	(2)	(3)
	(4)	(5)	(6)

Estimated age in:	1963	1972	1981	1990	W's age at: 1st live birth	W's age at: Last live birth
Head of family						

References

Aiyappan, Ayinipalli, and **K. Mahadevan,** 1988. *Population and Social Change in an Indian Village (Quarter Century of Development in Managadu Village, Tamil Nadu).* Delhi: Mittal Publications.

Ansari, Nasim, 1964. *Palanpur: A Study of its Economic Resources and Economic Activities.* Delhi: Agricultural Economics Research Centre, University of Delhi; [Continuous Village Survey, no. 41].

Apthorpe, Raymond, 1989. 'Modernization'. In *The Social Science Encyclopedia,* (Adam and Jessica Kuper, eds.); 532–33. London and New York: Routledge.

Arputhanathan, J.I., 1953. *1951 Census Handbook: The Nilgiris District.* Madras: Government Press.

Backward Classes Commission, Tamil Nadu State, 1975. 'Badagas'. In their *Report of the Backward Classes Commission Tamil Nadu,* 1: 7–9. Madras: Government of Tamil Nadu; mimeograph.

Bailey, Frederick G., 1958. *Caste and the Economic Frontier: A Village in Highland Orissa.* Manchester: Manchester University Press; Bombay: Oxford University Press.

Béchu, Léon-Auguste, 1948. *History of the Coimbatore Mission (South India).* Bangalore: Bangalore Press.

Belli Gowder, M.K., 1923–41. 'A Historical Research on the Hill Tribes of the Nilgiris'. Ketti, Nilgiris District; unpublished manuscript.

——, 1938–41. 'Origin of the Badagas'. [In Tamil and English]. Ketti, Nilgiris District; unpublished manuscript.

Benson, Ralph Sillery, 1884. *Descriptive Memoir...[and] Survey and Settlement Register of the Village of Sholur in the Toda-nad Division of the Nilgiri District.* Ootacamund: Revenue Settlement Office.

Birch, Edward A., 1902. *The Management and Medical Treatment of Children in India.* 4th edition. Calcutta: Thacker, Spink & Co.; London: W. Thacker.

Bliss, Christopher, and **Nicholas Stern,** 1982. *Palanpur: The Economy of an Indian Village.* Oxford: Oxford University Press.

Bloch, Maurice, and Jonathan Parry, 1982. 'Introduction: Death and the Regeneration of Life'. In their *Death and the Regeneration of Life*; 1–44. Cambridge: Cambridge University Press.

Breeks, James Wilkinson, 1873. *An Account of the Primitive Tribes and Monuments of the Nīlagiris,* (Susan Maria Breeks, ed.). London: India Museum.

Burton, Richard Francis, 1851. *Goa, and the Blue Mountains; or, Six Months of Sick Leave.* London: Richard Bentley. [New edition, 1991. Berkeley and Los Angeles: University of California Press.]

Caldwell, John C., 1976. 'Toward a Restatement of Demographic Transition Theory.' *Population and Development Review,* 2: 321–66.

—— 1982. *Theory of Fertility Decline.* New York: Academic Press.

Caldwell, John C., Allan G. Hill, and **Valerie J. Hull** (eds.), 1988. *Micro Approaches to Demographic Research.* London: Kegan Paul International.

Caldwell, John C., Palli Hanumantha Reddy, and **Pat Caldwell,** 1988. *The Causes of Demographic Change: Experimental Research in South India.* Madison: University of Wisconsin Press.

Cancian, Frank, 1992. *The Decline of Community in Zinacantan; Economy, Public Life, and Social Stratification, 1960–1987.* Stanford: Stanford University Press.

Centre for Monitoring Indian Economy, 1993. *Economic Intelligence Service — Profiles of Districts — November 1993.* Bombay: Centre for Monitoring Indian Economy.

Chakravartti, R., and **Y. Renuka,** 1970. 'The Trend of Age at Menarche in India'. *Journal of Social Research,* 13 (2): 82–94.

Coats, Thomas, 1823. 'Account of the Present State of the Township of Lony'. *Transactions of the Literary Society of Bombay,* 3: 172–264.

Dandekar, Hemalata C., 1986. *Men to Bombay, Women at Home: Urban Influence on Sugao Village, Deccan Maharashtra, India, 1942–1982.* Ann Arbor: University of Michigan; [Michigan Papers on South and Southeast Asia, Center for South and Southeast Asia Studies].

Das, Arvind N., 1987. 'Changel: Three Centuries of an Indian Village'. *Journal of Peasant Studies,* 15: 3–60.

Drèze, Jean, 1997. 'Palanpur 1957-93: Occupational Change, Land Ownership and Social Inequality.' In *The Village in Asia Revisited,* (Jan Breman, Peter Kloos, and Ashwani Saith, eds.); 126-74. Delhi: Oxford University Press.

Driver, Edwin D., 1963. *Differential Fertility in Central India.* Princeton: Princeton University Press.

Eagan, John Samuel Chiswell, 1916. *The Nilgiri Guide and Directory, a Handbook of General Information upon the Nilgiris for Visitors and Residents.* [Second edition.] Madras: S.P.C.K. Press.

Elmore, Wilber Theodore, 1915. *Dravidian Gods in Modern Hinduism.* Lincoln: University of Nebraska; [*University Studies,* 15(1)].

Emeneau, Murray Barnson, 1939. 'The Vowels of the Badaga Language'. *Language,* 15: 43–47.

—— 1944–46. *Kota Texts.* Vol. IV. Berkeley and Los Angeles: University of California Press; [University of California Publications in Linguistics, 3(2)].

—— 1963. Ootacamund in the Nilgiris: Some Notes. *Journal of the American Oriental Society,* 83: 188–93.

—— 1971. *Toda Songs.* Oxford: Clarendon Press.

Epstein, T. Scarlett, 1962. *Economic Development and Social Change in South India.* Manchester: Manchester University Press; Bombay: Oxford University Press.

—— 1973. *South India: Yesterday, Today and Tomorrow; Mysore Villages Revisited.* London and Basingstoke: Macmillan.

Epstein, T. Scarlett, A.P. Suryanarayana, and **T. Thimmegowda,** 1998. *Village Voices: Forty Years of Rural Transformation in South India.* New Delhi, London, and Newbury Park: Sage Publications.

Finicio, Jacome, 1603. [Two manuscripts on the mission of Todamalâ.] Trans. by A. de Alberti, in Rivers (1906: 719–30).

Fortes, Meyer, 1949. *The Web of Kinship among the Tallensi.* London: Oxford University Press.

—— 1970. 'The Structure of Unilineal Descent Groups'. In his *Time and Social Structure and Other Essays*; 67–95. New York: Humanities Press; London: Athlone Press; [London School of Economics Monographs on Anthropology, 40; originally in *American Anthropologist* 55 (1)]

Fox, Robin, 1983. *Kinship and Marriage: An Anthropological Perspective.* Cambridge: Cambridge University Press.

Francis, Walter (ed), 1908. *Madras District Gazetteers. The Nilgiris.* [Vol. 1.] Madras: Superintendent, Government Press.

Frazer, James George, 1918. *Folk-lore in the Old Testament: Studies in Comparative Religion, Legend and Law.* London: Macmillan & Co.

Freed, Stanley A., and **Ruth Freed,** 1985. 'Fertility, Sterilization, and Population Growth in Shanti Nagar, India: a Longitudinal Ethnographic Approach'. *Anthropological Papers of the American Museum of Natural History,* 60 (3): 230–86.

Freedman, Ronald, 1979. 'Theories of Fertility Decline: a Reappraisal'. *Social Forces,* 58 (1): 1–17.

Ghosh, Bahnisikha, 1990. *The Indian Population Problem: A Household Economics Approach.* New Delhi: Sage Publications.

Ghurye, Govind Sadashiv, 1960. *After a Century and a Quarter.* Bombay: Popular Book Company.

Goodenough, Ward H., 1957. 'Cultural Anthropology and Linguistics'. In *Report of the Seventh Annual Round Table Meeting on Linguistics and Language Study,* (Paul L. Garvin, ed.); 167–73. Washington: Georgetown University; [Monograph Series on Languages and Linguistics, 9].

—— 1963. *Cooperation in Change.* New York: Russell Sage.

Goody, Jack, 1987. *The Interface between the Written and the Oral.* Cambridge: Cambridge University Press.

Gough, Kathleen M., 1989. *Rural Change in Southeast India 1950s to 1980s.* Delhi: Oxford University Press.

Gray, John N., and **David J. Mearns,** 1989. 'Household and Domestic Group—Society from the Inside Out'. In their *Society from the Inside Out: Anthropological Perspectives on the South Asian Household*; 13–34. New Delhi: Sage Publications.

Grigg, Henry Bidewell (ed.), 1880. *A Manual of the Nílagiri District in the Madras Presidency.* Madras: E. Keys, Government Press.

Guilmoto, Christophe, 1992. 'Looking through the Census Eye: Tamilnadu's Demographic Sources, 1871–1981'. In *Themes in Development Economics: Essays in Honour of Malcolm Adeseshiah,* (S. Subramanian, ed.); 12–77. Delhi: Oxford University Press.

Handwerker, W. Penn, 1990. 'Demography'. In *Medical Anthropology: Contemporary Theory and Method,* (Thomas M. Johnson and Carolyn F. Sargent, eds.); 319–47. New York and London: Praeger Publishers.

Harkness, Henry, 1832. *A Description of a Singular Aboriginal Race Inhabiting the Summit of the Neilgherry Hills, or Blue Mountains of Coimbatoor, in the Southern Peninsula of India.* London: Smith, Elder, and Co.

Haswell, Margaret R., 1967. *Economics of Development in Village India.* London: Routledge & Kegan Paul; New York: Humanities Press.

Heidemann, Frank M., 1996. 'Immigrant Labourers and Local Networks in the Nilgiris'. In *Blue Mountains Revisited: Cultural Studies on the Nilgiri Hills,* (Paul Hockings, ed.); 148–63. New Delhi and New York: Oxford University Press.

Hertz, Robert, 1960. *Death and the Right Hand.* (Rodney and Claudia Needham, trans.) London: Cohen & West.

Hirschman, Albert O., 1958. *The Strategy of Economic Development.* New Haven: Yale University Press.

Hockings, Paul, 1977. 'Communication Networks'. In *Dimensions of Social Change in India,* (M.N. Srinivas, S. Seshaiah, and V.S. Parthasarathy, eds.); 475–86. Bombay: Allied Publishers Private Limited.

—— 1980a. *Ancient Hindu Refugees: Badaga Social History 1550–1975.* The Hague and New York: Mouton Publishers; New Delhi: Vikas Publishing

House.

—— 1980b. *Sex and Disease in a Mountain Community*. New Delhi: Vikas Publishing House; Columbia, Mo.: South Asia Books.

—— 1982. 'Badaga Kinship Rules in Their Socio-Economic Context'. *Anthropos*, 77: 851–74.

—— 1988. *Counsel from the Ancients, a Study of Badaga Proverbs, Prayers, Omens and Curses*. Berlin and New York: Mouton de Gruyter.

—— 1989a. 'The Badagas'. In *Blue Mountains: The Ethnography and Biogeography of a South Indian Region*, (Paul Hockings, ed.); 206–31. New Delhi, Oxford and New York: Oxford University Press.

—— 1989b. British Society in the Company, Crown and Congress Eras. In *Blue Mountains: The Ethnography and Biogeography of a South Indian Region*, (Paul Hockings, ed.); 334–59. New Delhi, Oxford and New York: Oxford University Press.

—— 1996. *Bibliographie générale sur les monts Nilgiri de l'Inde du sud, 1603–1996 / A Comprehensive Bibliography for the Nilgiri Hills of Southern India, 1603–1996 / Ein umfassende Bibligraphie der Nilgiri-Berge Südindiens, 1603–1996*. Bordeaux: Université Michel de Montaigne; [Espaces tropicales, 14].

—— 1997. 'Badaga Epic Poetry'. In *Blue Mountains Revisited: Cultural Studies on the Nilgiri Hills*, (Paul Hockings, ed.); 293–315. New Delhi and New York: Oxford University Press.

—— 1999. *Mortuary Ritual of the Badagas of Southern India*. Chicago: Field Museum of Natural History; [Fieldiana: Anthropology Series, i.p.].

Hockings, Paul, and **Christiane Pilot-Raichoor,** 1992. *A Badaga–English Dictionary*. Berlin and New York: Mouton de Gruyter.

Holsinger, D.B., and **J.D. Kasarda,** 1976. 'Education and Human Fertility: Sociological Perspectives'. In *Population and Development: The Search for Selective Interventions*, (Ronald G. Ridker, ed.); 154–81. Baltimore and London: Johns Hopkins University Press.

India, Government of, 1962. *Census of India. Paper No. 1 of 1962. 1961 Census, Final Population Totals*. Delhi: Government of India Press.

Jacobson, Doranne, 1977. 'Flexibility in Central Indian Kinship and Residence'. In *The New Wind: Changing Identities in South Asia*, (Kenneth David, ed.); 263–83. The Hague and Paris: Mouton Publishers.

Jagor, Andreas Fedor, 1914. *Aus Fedor Jagor's Nachlass mit Unterstützung der Jagor-Stiftung...*, (Albert Grünwedel, ed.). Berlin: Dietrich Reimer (Ernst Vohsen).

Jogi Gowder, B.S., 1934. *Malaivācikaḷin ācāra tiruttam* [Change of the Hill People's Traditions; in Tamil]. Ootacamund: Joti Press.

Kessinger, Tom G., 1974. *Vilyatpur 1848–1968: Social and Economic Change in a North Indian Village.* Berkeley and Los Angeles: University of California Press.

Keys, William, 1812. 'A Topographical Description of the Neelaghery Mountains'. Reprinted *in* Grigg (1880: xlviii–li).

Khan, M.E., and **Raj Behari Gupta**, 1985. *Determinants of High Family Planning Practices: A Case Study of Nilgiris.* Bombay: Himalaya Publishing House.

Kolenda, Pauline M., 1967. 'Regional Differences in Indian Family Structure'. In *Regions and Regionalism in South Asian Studies,: an Exploratory Study* (Robert I. Crane, ed.); 147-226. Durham, NC: Duke University Program in Comparative Studies on Southern Asia, Monograph No. 5.

—— 1987. *Regional Differences in Family Structure in India.* Jaipur: Rawat Publications.

Kopytoff, Igor, 1987. 'The Internal African Frontier: The Making of African Political Culture'. In *The African Frontier: The Reproduction of Traditional African Societies,* (Kopytoff, Igor, ed.); 3–84. Bloomington: Indiana University Press.

Leibenstein, Harvey, 1957. *Economic Backwardness and Economic Growth: Studies in the Theory of Economic Development.* New York: Wiley.

—— 1975. 'The Economic Theory of Fertility Decline'. *Quarterly Journal of Economics,* 89 (1): 1–31.

McIver, Lewis, and **Gabriel Stokes,** 1883. *Imperial Census of 1881. Operations and Results in the Presidency of Madras.* Madras: E. Keys, Government Press. (5 vols.).

Macleane, Charles Donald, 1893. *Manual of the Administration of the Madras Presidency, in Illustration of the Records of Government & the Yearly Administration Reports. In Three Volumes. Vol. III.—Glossary, Containing a Classification of Terminology, a Gazetteer and Economic Dictionary of the Province, and Other Information, the Whole Arranged Alphabetically and Indexed.* Madras: Superintendent, Government Press.

MacNamara, Thomas F., 1912. 'Some Ceremonies of South Indian Hill Tribes'. *Irish Ecclesiastical Record,* (ser. 4) 31: 141–55.

Madras, Government of, 1928. *Madras District Gazetteers. Statistical Appendix for the Nilgiri District. [The Nilgiris, Volume II.]* Madras: Superintendent, Government Press.

Mahadevan, Krishnan, 1979. *Sociology of Fertility; Determinants of Fertility Differentials in South India.* New Delhi: Sterling Publishers Pvt. Ltd.

Mandelbaum, David Goodman, 1960. 'A Reformer of His People'. In *In the Company of Man,* (Joseph Casagrande, ed.); 273–308. New York: Harper and Bros.

May, David A., and **David M. Heer,** 1968. 'Son Survivorship Motivation and Family Size in India: A Computer Simulation'. *Population Studies, a Journal of Demography,* 22: 199–210.

Menefee, Selden, and **Audrey Menefee,** 1964. *Communications in Village India: A Social Experiment.* Tiptur: Kalpataru College [mimeo].

Metz, Johann Friedrich, 1864. *The Tribes Inhabiting the Neilgherry Hills: Their Social Customs and Religious Rites.* 2nd edition. Mangalore: Basel Mission Press.

Morris, Brian, 1992. 'Hill Pandaram'. In *Encyclopedia of World Cultures,* (Paul Hockings, ed.); 3: 98–101. Boston: G.K. Hall.

Mudaliar, N. Murugesa, 1957. 'Change Comes to the Ketty Valley'. *Indian Farming,* 6 (10): 17–18.

Murdock, George Peter, 1949. *Social Structure.* New York: Macmillan Company.

Murthy, M.S.R., 1993. *Sex Awareness among Rural Girls.* Delhi: B.R. Publishing Corporation.

Nagaraj, K., 1992. 'Infant Mortality in Tamilnadu'. In *Themes in Development Economics: Essays in Honour of Malcolm Adisheshiah,* (S. Subramaniam, ed.); 98–150. New Delhi: Oxford University Press.

Namboodiri, N. Krishnan, 1986. 'Social Development and Population Change: A Reappraisal of Selected Theories'. In *Fertility and Mortality: Theory, Methodology, and Empirical Issues,* (K. Mahadevan, ed.). New Delhi: Sage Publications.

Nanjundayya, H.V., and **L. Krishna Ananthakrishna Iyer,** 1930. *The Mysore Tribes and Castes. Volume III.* Mysore: Mysore University.

Natesa Sastri, Sangendi Mahalinga, 1892. 'The Baḍagas of the Nîlagiri District'. *Madras Christian College Magazine,* 9: 753–64, 830–43.

National Council of Applied Economic Research (NCAER), 1961. *Techno-Economic Survey of Madras. Economic Report.* Madras: Department of Industries, Labour and Co-operation.

Noble, William Allister, 1968. *Cultural Contrasts and Similarities among Five Ethnic Groups in the Nilgiri District, Madras State, India 1800–1963.* Baton Rouge: Louisiana State University; Ph.D. dissertation in Geography and Anthropology.

—— 1976. Nilgiri Dolmens (South India). *Anthropos,* 71: 90–128.

Noble, William Allister, and **Louisa Booth Noble,** 1965. 'Badaga Funeral Customs'. *Anthropos,* 60: 262–72.

Nyerges, A. Endre, 1993. 'The Ecology of Wealth-in-People: Agriculture, Settlement, and Society on the Perpetual Frontier'. *American Anthropolo-*

gist, 94 (4): 860–881.

Pandian, Jacob, 1985. *Anthropology and the Western Tradition: Toward an Authentic Anthropology*. Prospect Heights: Waveland Press, Inc.

Parry, Jonathan, 1982. 'Sacrificial Death and the Necrophagous Ascetic'. In *Death and the Regeneration of Life*, (Maurice Bloch and Jonathan Parry, eds.); 74–110. Cambridge: Cambridge University Press.

Planning Commission, 1960. *Third Five Year Plan*. New Delhi: Planning Commission, Government of India.

—— 1969. *Fourth Five Year Plan*. New Delhi: Planning Commission, Government of India.

Price, John Frederick, 1908. *Ootacamund. A History. Compiled for the Government of Madras*. Madras: Superintendent, Government Press.

Rivers, William Halse Rivers, 1906. *The Todas*. London: Macmillan & Company Limited.

Rostow, Walter W., 1960. *The Stages of Economic Growth: A Non-Communist Manifesto*. Cambridge: Cambridge University Press.

Saith, Ashwani, and **Ajay Tankha,** 1997. 'Longitudinal Analysis of Structural Change in a North Indian Village, 1970-87.' In *The Village in Asia Revisited,* (Jan Breman, Peter Kloos, and Ashwani Saith, eds.); 79-125. Delhi: Oxford University Press.

Saxena, G.B., 1965. *A Study of Fertility & Family Planning in Three Villages of Uttar Pradesh*. Delhi: Institute of Economic Growth; mimeograph.

Schultz, Theodore W., 1974. 'Fertility and Economic Values'. In his *Economics of the Family: Marriage, Children and Human Capital*. Chicago: University of Chicago Press.

Shah, Arvind M., 1973. *The Household Dimension of the Family in India: A Field Study in a Gujarat Village and a Review of Other Studies*. Delhi: Orient Longman.

—— 1977. 'Lineage Structure and Change in a Gujarat Village.' In *Dimensions of Social Change in India,* (M.N. Srinivas, S. Seshaiah, and V.S. Parthasarathy, eds.); 339-67. Bombay: Allied Publishers Private Limited.

Shah, Arvind M., R.G. Shroff, and **A.R. Shah,** 1963. 'Early Nineteenth Century Records in Gujarat'. In *Contributions to Indian Economic History II,* (Tapan Raychaudhuri, ed.); 89–100. Calcutta: Firma K.L. Mukhopadhyay.

Shariff, Abusaleh, 1989. *Fertility Transition in Rural South India*. New Delhi: Gian Publishing House.

Slater, Gilbert (ed.), 1918. *Economic Studies. Volume I. Some South Indian Villages*. Madras: University of Madras.

Stevenson, Margaret (Mrs. Sinclair Stevenson), 1920. *The Rites of the Twice-Born.* London: Oxford University Press.

Stokes, William, 1882. 'Mission Work amongst the Badagas and Other Hill-Tribes on the Nilgiris'. *Harvest Field,* 3: 169–79.

Stone, Winifred M., 1925. *Ups and Downs on the Nilgiris.* London: Church of England Zenana Missionary Society.

Subbarama Aiyar, S., 1925. *Economic Life in a Malabar Village.* Bangalore: The Bangalore Printing & Publishing Co., Ltd.

Subrahmanyam, C.V., 1962. Socio Economic Survey, with Special Reference to the Assessment of the Effects of Plan Projects and Savings Patterns. Ootacamund: Government Arts College; mimeographed ms.

Thomas, P.J., and **K.C. Ramakrishnan,** 1940. *Some South Indian Villages: A Re-Survey.* Madras: University of Madras.

Thurston, Edgar, and **Kadamki Rangachari,** 1909. 'Badaga'. In their *Castes and Tribes of Southern India,* I: 63–124. Madras: Superintendent, Government Press.

Tignous, Henri-Pierre-Joseph-Arthur, 1912. 'In the Nilgherries' [pt. 3]. *Illustrated Catholic Missions,* 26: 154–57.

Tönnies, Ferdinand, 1957. *Community and Society — Gemeinschaft und Gesellschaft.* (Second edn., trans. and supp. by Charles P. Loomis.) East Lansing: Michigan State University Press.

United Nations, 1961. *The Mysore Population Study.* (Population Studies, no. 34) New York: United Nations, Dept. of Economic and Social Affairs.

—— 1994. *United Nations State of the World Population Report, 1994.* New York: United Nations.

Wadley, Susan Snow, 1994. *Struggling with Destiny in Karimpur, 1925–1984.* Berkeley and Los Angeles: University of California Press.

Wadley, Susan Snow, and **Bruce W. Derr,** 1988. 'Karimpur Families over Sixty Years'. *South Asian Anthropologist,* 9: 119–32.

Walker, Anthony R., 1986. *The Toda of South India: A New Look.* Delhi: Hindustan Publishing Corporation.

Ward, Benjamin Swain, 1821. 'Geographical and Statistical Memoir of a Survey of the Neelgherry Mountains in the Province of Coimbatore Made in 1821 under the Superintendence of Captain B.S. Ward, Deputy Surveyor-General'. *In* Grigg (1880: lx–lxxviii).

Weigt, Ernst, 1970. 'Beobachtungen in den Nilgiris mit besonderer Berücksichtigung der Dörfer Nanjanad und Srimadurai'. *Tübinger geographische Studien,* 34: 325–43. [Wirtschafts- und sozialgeographische Studien in Südindien V.]

Wiser, William, and **Charlotte Wiser,** 1989. *Behind Mud Walls 1930–1960, with a sequel: The Village in 1970, and a New Chapter by Susan S. Wadley: The Village in 1984*. Berkeley and Los Angeles: University of California Press.

Yeatts, William Walter Murray, 1932. *Census of India, 1931. Volume XIV. Madras. Part II: Imperial and Provincial Tables.* Calcutta: Government of India Central Publication Branch.

Zagarell, Allen, 1996. 'The Megalithic Graves of the Nilgiri Hills and the Moyar Ditch'. In *Blue Mountains Revisited: Cultural Studies on the Nilgiri Hills,* (Paul Hockings, ed.); 23–73. New Delhi and New York: Oxford University Press.

Zvelebil, Kamil Veith, 1982. *The Irula (Ḗṟla) Language. Part III Irula Lore, Texts and Translations.* Wiesbaden: Otto Harrassowitz; [Neuindiche Studien, 9].

INDEX

About the Author

Paul Hockings is a Professor of Anthropology in the University of Illinois at Chicago, and an Adjunct Curator at the Field Museum, Chicago. Although primarily a cultural anthropologist and linguist, he has done archaeological and bibliographic work, and has also made anthropological films. Among those films is *The Village*, made in Ireland with Mark McCarty.

Professor Hockings has studied at the Universities of Sydney, Toronto, Chicago and Stanford, and holds a Ph.D. in Anthropology from the University of California, Berkeley. He has written or edited 13 books and dozens of articles, many of them dealing with the Badagas and related south Indian peoples. His most recent books are *Blue Mountains Revisited: Cultural Studies on the Nilgiri Hills* (1997, written with several collaborators), and *A Badaga–English Dictionary* (1992, with Christiane Pilot-Raichoor). He is editor of the South Asia section of the forthcoming *Encyclopedia of Asia*, as well as of the journal, *Visual Anthropology*; a Fellow of the Royal Anthropological Institute of Great Britain and Ireland; and a life member of the American Anthropological Association.